Schoolhouse Politics

Schoolhouse Politics

Lessons from the Sputnik Era

Peter B. Dow

HARVARD UNIVERSITY PRESS
Cambridge, Massachusetts
London, England
1991

This book is printed on acid-free paper, and its binding materials have been chosen for strength and durability.

Library of Congress Cataloging-in-Publication Data

Dow, Peter B.
    Schoolhouse politics: lessons from the Sputnik era / Peter B. Dow.
        p.   cm.
    Includes bibliographical references (p.) and index.
    ISBN 0-674-79240-8 (alk. paper)
    1. Politics and education—United States—Case studies.
    2. Education and state—United States—Case studies.
    3. Anthropology—Study and teaching (Elementary)—United States—Case
studies.   I. Title.
LC89.D68   1991   91-9031
372.83—dc20   CIP

For Mimi

whose love made this possible

Acknowledgments

Writing this book has been a collaborative enterprise. I am grateful to the National Science Foundation for supporting the initial research that made the book possible. I am also indebted to Education Development Center (EDC), which released the Man: A Course of Study (MACOS) archives, and to the Harvard Graduate School of Education, which helped to organize the archives for research purposes. In particular, Malcolm Hamilton of the Monroe C. Gutman Library gave generously of his time and provided research assistance during the project's early phases.

I am also thankful for the insights of the fifty or so friends and colleagues whose lives were touched by the Man: A Course of Study project and who willingly shared their experiences in the interviews that have provided much of the firsthand information in this account. Their perceptions about what we were trying to achieve have greatly enriched my understanding of the MACOS effort and have drawn my attention to the broader issues and the insights that contemporary educational reformers can derive from a study of the *Sputnik*-inspired science curriculum reform movement.

An earlier incarnation of this book, prepared as a doctoral dissertation, was greatly aided by my thesis advisor, Joseph Featherstone, who was a participant in the early deliberations from which MACOS evolved and who first set me thinking about the historical significance of the scholar-led curriculum reforms of the 1960s. Both Fletcher Watson and Lawrence Kohlberg of the Harvard Graduate School of Education were also helpful, as was Patricia Albjerg Graham, who provided detailed suggestions on the manuscript. I would like to thank Lawrence Fuchs of Brandeis University, my boss and colleague at EDC, who inspired me to undertake this project and provided warm words of encouragement along the way. I am also grateful to Elting Morison, founding chairman of EDC's

Social Studies Program, whose insights about schooling and whose vision of social studies reform provided many hours of stimulating discussion that have never subsequently been matched in my professional life.

Jerome Bruner's influence on my thinking will be obvious throughout. The inspiration of his fertile mind and the warmth of his friendship have shaped my thinking about education, and his passion for the improvement of schooling has made me want to share with others what we learned in trying to translate his heady ideas into a workable course of study. The effort to recapture this story has reminded me once again how pervasive Bruner's impact was on all who worked with him. While the final course reflected the thinking of many individuals, Bruner's influence was present in the contributions of each, whether it was a scholar designing the structure of an individual unit, a teacher devising lessons for the classroom, a writer preparing a manuscript, a designer seeking to invent the most engaging means of presentation, or a filmmaker working at his editing table.

I am thankful for the special contributions of Irven DeVore and Asen Balikci, who, in many discussions, shared with me the meaning of MACOS in their own lives. I was intrigued that these two young scholars, at the beginning of their careers, were willing to take time from their demanding academic responsibilities to join in the design and development of an elementary school course. Their willingness to place school matters ahead of professional advancement exemplified the attitude of many of those who joined the curriculum reform movement. As I observed their daily participation in the curriculum-making process—from conceptual design, to the teaching of experimental classes, to the preparation of children's materials, to the development of teacher-training programs, to participation in workshops and professional meetings—I came to believe that university research scholars had a fundamental role to play in helping teachers rethink the process of schooling.

This idea, which is central to the book, was the brainchild of M.I.T. physicist Jerrold Zacharias. In 1956, Zacharias, the father of the Physical Sciences Study Committee at M.I.T., conceived the notion of reforming education by bypassing the professional education establishment and bringing university research professors together with teachers to create new school programs. As the founder of Educational Services Incorporated (ESI, later Educational Development Center), he created an organization that provided the resources to design, test, revise, and implement these programs. He was the driving intellectual force behind ESI for twenty years and proved the value of his approach through the creation of hundreds of innovative projects both here and abroad. In fact, the ESI model was so successful it became the prototype for a new type of educational research organization, the Regional Educational Laboratory, established by the Elementary and Secondary Education Act of 1965. The privilege of knowing and working with Zacharias profoundly influenced my thinking about the eduational reform process.

I am also thankful for the interest of Richard Atkinson, president of the University of California at San Diego and former director of the National Science Foundation, who read the original text and suggested the addition of Chapter 6, which examines the demise of the educational program at the NSF under pressure from congressional conservatives and, ultimately, the Reagan administration. Atkinson provided me with valuable insights about the inner workings of the NSF, shared his own experience with the critics of MACOS, and helped to educate me about the political dimensions of educational reform. Indeed, my discussions with Atkinson finally convinced me, if I had any remaining doubts, that education in America is politics.

Barbara Herzstein was a true partner in the preparation of the first manuscript. As a member of the MACOS team, she brought her personal knowledge of the course as a writer, editor, and editorial director to my effort to bring order to a complex story. She aided the project immeasurably by organizing the archives, providing unflagging encouragement, and rescuing early drafts from innumerable lapses into incoherence with her deft editorial pen. For work on later drafts I am particularly grateful to Michael Aronson and Maria Ascher of Harvard University Press, whose tough-minded critiques coupled with patient encouragement saw me through many hours of seemingly endless revision at a time when the demands of a family business left me little energy to complete the work. The final text was prepared under the editorial supervision of Linda Howe. I am deeply grateful for her professional help in seeing the project to completion.

Most of all, I am thankful for the support and forbearance of my wife, Mimi, who knows in her bones more about what makes for good teaching than I ever will. To her this book is lovingly dedicated.

Contents

You can't change the world, but you can make people think.

—*Jack Nicholson*

Introduction

The ascent of *Sputnik* on 4 October 1957 has come to symbolize a turning point in American education. The Soviet space triumph, the launching of a one hundred and eighty-four pound communications satellite into Earth orbit before the United States could claim any comparable feat, convinced many Americans that the USSR had achieved scientific superiority over the United States. This conviction was reaffirmed a month later when the Soviets compounded their technological and public relations coup by orbiting a half-ton rocket carrying a live dog. Although the United States soon replied by placing our first *Vanguard* satellite in space the following March, it was a mere grapefruit-sized, twenty-one pound weakling by comparison, and the achievement did little to reassure a public fearful of losing technological superiority to the Communist World. The USSR's demonstrated scientific and engineering prowess sent a chill through the spines of a citizenry already frightened by the Cold War and the spy investigations of the McCarthy era.

Long before *Sputnik*, postwar criticism of American schooling had been gaining momentum both within and outside the education profession. Now the public demanded to know why our space scientists had failed to keep pace with the Soviets, and many critics were quick to place the blame on inferior schooling. In the mid-1950s the popular press teemed with articles extolling Soviet educational practices and questioning our own. In March 1956 *Life* magazine published a story about Soviet science education that praised the "golden youth of communism," and Senator William Benton, following a trip to the USSR in the same year, described the Soviet *Tekhnikum* in the pages of *Coronet* as an "ominous threat to the West." *Scholastic* magazine termed the competition with Russia a "classroom cold war," and the president of M.I.T., James Killian, in a speech before the White House Conference on Educa-

1

tion in 1955, called for a "bold strategy" to address our scientific manpower shortage. Killian linked science education with national security and warned that our scarcity of science teachers, scientists, and engineers was "a clear and present danger to the nation." Killian's "bold strategy" included spending government funds.

But public support for federal involvement in education had never been strong in the United States. During the early 1950s numerous education bills had been introduced by a handful of education-minded congressmen like John Lesinski, the chair of the House Labor and Education Committee, but none of this legislation was able to attract enough votes to reach the president's desk. Historically, Americans have distrusted centralized educational planning as a characteristic of totalitarian systems and looked to the autonomy of the neighborhood school board as the bastion of democracy and the protector of community values. Only a sense of deepening crisis, dramatized by the technological achievements of a formidable foreign adversary, could bring the American people to abandon their historic commitment to a decentralized educational system. For the first time since the Smith-Hughes legislation of 1917, the federal government was spurred by *Sputnik* into giving serious attention to school reform.

In 1958, under pressure from an anxious public, President Eisenhower signed into law the National Defense Education Act, the most comprehensive educational reform bill the nation had ever seen. The name alone reflected the extent of the national concern. For the next dozen years, through this and related legislation, federal dollars flowed as never before to support innovation in all areas of the elementary and secondary school curriculum, from mathematics and the sciences to foreign languages and the creative arts. Stimulated by this influx of federal money and driven by the heightened public demand for educational change, scholars and teachers across the nation joined forces in an unprecedented collaboration to improve the quality of schooling, and for a time it appeared that a full-scale instructional revolution might be underway. Never before had school improvement been such a focus of national concern.

A major participant in this federal effort to stimulate curriculum reform was the National Science Foundation (NSF). Founded following World War II primarily to promote scientific research, the NSF now began to invest a sizable percentage of its budget in the reform of science education at the precollege level. During the next two decades this federal agency, through its Education Directorate, spent more than $500 million on educational materials development, teacher training, and dissemination of new educational ideas. These programs were designed to promote scientific literacy, to encourage young people to enter scientific and engineering careers, and to make the substance and method of science more central to the process of schooling. The scope of the reforms, which began with mathematics and the "hard" sciences, eventually expanded to encompass most of the curriculum, including geography, anthropology, sociology, psychology, and political science.

As a young teacher just beginning my career at the time, I vividly remember the impact of these innovative programs on the classroom. I first learned about the NSF's efforts when physics students in my school began building ripple tanks to examine wave motion and swinging pendulums from the rafters of the gymnasium to study the rotation of the Earth. This was very different from the textbook-based learning I had encountered in my own education. These students were taking part in the early trial classrooms of Jerrold Zacharias's NSF-funded PSSC Physics, a program created under the supervision of the Physical Sciences Study Committee at M.I.T. The new materials and approaches generated enormous enthusiasm among students, who were learning to do science by creating their own apparatus from simple materials and by getting directly involved in solving problems of their own design.

Watching students work with the PSSC materials started me thinking. Would similar approaches work in history classrooms? Did we really need to stick to the text, I wondered, or could we follow the lead of the scientists and introduce students directly to the raw materials of historical scholarship, the original sources, and let them begin to reconstruct history for themselves? When I joined the history department at the Germantown Friends School in Philadelphia in 1962, a group of teachers from the Quaker schools formed the Friends Educational Research Committee and began meeting with local history professors to create courses that drew directly on the scholar's field of research. Soon we were developing a study of thirteenth-century English village life for junior high school students based on the work of a medievalist at the University of Pennsylvania and reconstructing a fifth-century Greek town with fourth graders using materials from a dig in the Peloponnisos that was being directed by a professor in Penn's archaeology department. Original scholarship, we learned, turned out to be as captivating for these budding historians as it did for the physics students.

In the midst of this work I met the Harvard psychologist Jerome Bruner, who came to Philadelphia to describe his NSF-funded project to create an anthropology course for ten-year-olds called Man: A Course of Study, a program that he was putting together with a team of scholars and curriculum designers at Educational Services Incorporated (ESI) in Cambridge, Massachusetts. Hearing Bruner describe his ideas about teaching social science to ten-year-olds deepened my conviction that a collaboration between scholars and teachers could improve the process of schooling, and in 1965 I took a leave of absence to join him at ESI to learn more about how to implement this partnership. When Bruner returned to his research, I stayed on to complete the project and to work with him and other scholars at Harvard and M.I.T. to create a number of other social science courses at ESI and its successor, Education Development Center. That experience, which spanned ten years, taught me a good deal about both the promise and the problems of university-based curriculum reform.

The account that follows examines the development, implementation, and public reaction to Man: A Course of Study. It traces, in particular, the evolution of Bruner's course from its origins and development at ESI, through its widespread national distribution and general recognition as one of the best social science curriculum projects of the period, to its demise in 1975 at the hands of a group of conservatives led by Congressman John B. Conlan of Arizona. As a case study of one of the *Sputnik*-inspired innovations, Man: A Course of Study illuminates many of the issues the reformers of the period faced in trying to relate the heady ideas of academics to the practical reality of the everyday classroom. In an attempt to close the gap between the "frontier of research" and the schoolhouse, the science curriculum innovators had to reconsider the relationship between scholarship and teaching, examine the nature of the learning process, and consider what happens in a classroom when the conventional textbook is replaced by hands-on materials, original sources, and a wide variety of media. They learned about how to organize student-directed learning, devised new strategies for stimulating inquiry, and invented innumerable nondidactic approaches to instruction. And along the way they got an education in the politics of educational reform. By challenging many of the conventional assumptions about both the content and methodology of instruction, they threatened teachers, alienated publishers, and confused parents. And when the Soviet space threat receded following the *Apollo* moon walk in July of 1969, they were eventually driven from the schools by those who did not share their student-centered educational values.

Together with Jerrold Zacharias, who started ESI, Jerome Bruner was one of the leading proponents of the style of learning that characterized the curriculum projects of the period. Bruner was cofounder and the first director of Harvard's Center for Cognitive Studies, and he had written extensively on cognitive development in young children. He was fascinated by Zacharias's effort to close the gap between the university and the schools, and he believed that the findings of his research on early learning supported Zacharias's assumptions about how instruction should be organized in the classroom. A close observer of the early science and mathematics projects, he published *The Process of Education* in 1961, which set forth the educational goals of the movement as they had taken shape in these curriculum reform efforts. Hypothesizing that "any subject can be taught effectively in some intellectually honest form to any child at any stage of development," he spoke for most of the reformers of the period who believed that there was no limit to what young children could be taught if the material was presented in a way that captured the curiosity of the student and respected their age-specific intellectual needs. At the same time Bruner approached the work with as many questions as answers. Taking on the development of an anthropology course for ten-year-olds was as much an opportunity to learn more about the cognitive development of the young within the school as it was an effort to apply pedagogical theory to classroom practice.

When I first began to collect materials for this book, my aim was to tell the story of a bold national experiment in pedagogical innovation. The book was hardly begun, however, when I was called to Washington to explain the origin of Man: A Course of Study to some troubled members of Congress during a congressional investigation of the course in the spring and summer of 1975. From that experience I quickly learned that decisions about educational reform are driven far more by political considerations, such as the prevailing public mood, than they are by any systematic effort to improve instruction. Just as fear of Soviet science supremacy had spawned a decade of curriculum reform led by some of our most creative research scientists during the late 1950s and 1960s, so now a new wave of political conservatism and religious fundamentalism in the early 1970s began to call into question the intrusion of university academics into the schools. In this context, serious study of other cultures by the young was now seen by some as a threat to traditional American values. The controversy over MACOS, as the course came to be known, soon escalated to a floor fight in the House of Representatives in which members on both sides of the aisle vented their views on the government's role in instructional innovation and the appropriateness of teaching anthropology to children. Exposure to this debate caused me to recast the account to give more attention to educational politics. No discussion of school reform, it seems, can be separated from our vision of the society that the schools serve.

The Soviet space achievement briefly disrupted the traditional provincialism of American education. For the first time Americans began to examine their educational system in relationship to the wider world. If the Soviets could challenge us in space, what was to prevent them from confronting our supremacy in other areas as well? To prepare students to cope with a world of shrinking distances and increasingly sophisticated technology the new reformers called for changes in every area of the curriculum, including improved language training, better writing and speaking skills, internationally competitive mathematics and science training, a deeper appreciation of other cultures, and a more fundamental understanding of human nature. Many regarded the traditional anti-intellectualism of the schools as a threat to our national security, and they supported a major federal effort to close what was perceived as an "education gap" between the United States and other countries. Some of the new reformers thought the problem was too critical to be left in the hands of "professional educators," whom they believed had been responsible for allowing the schools to decline to their disastrously low levels of performance. Fixing the schools, they argued, demanded the participation of the best brains in the country.

The involvement of research scientists in the design of school curricula was an entirely novel idea. Never before had large groups of academics, with little or no knowledge of public education, left their laboratories and libraries to take part in the creation of course materials for the "new math," the "new science," and the "new social studies." An approach to educational reform that employed scholars from the academic disciplines to define elementary and secondary school teaching in those fields, that depended heavily on federal funding to accomplish its objectives, and that paid little attention to the educational establishment, was a new chapter in the history of American education. And as long as the USSR appeared to be outpacing us in the development of scientific and technological talent, this scholar-dominated movement enjoyed strong popular support. But the American space achievements of the late 1960s changed the public mood. Once the United States had won the moon race, the so-called "education gap" seemed as ephemeral as the "missile gap," and federal support for curriculum reform began to wane. Before long the professors were retreating to their ivory towers, and curriculum matters once again became the province of professional educators and commercial publishers.

After a decade of declining school performance, Americans in the early 1980s began to worry about the schools again. Once more, as in the 1950s, the national media was awash with articles criticizing elementary and secondary education and contrasting our system of schooling not only to that of our adversaries but that of our allies as well. The new critics deplored years of erosion in achievement scores and decried the poor quality of teaching and the lowering of standards for high school graduation. Politicians appointed blue-ribbon panels to study the problem, and parents wrung their hands over reports that described "a nation at risk" and the "rising tide of mediocrity" in our schools. Yet today, despite many promising initiatives, our schools remain remarkably impervious to change. We continue to compare our educational performance unfavorably to any number of Western countries, most particularly our formidable economic competitor, Japan. We condemn declining levels of student performance as a national disgrace. And we look for quick solutions such as a longer school year and higher teacher salaries in the hope that investing more time and money will somehow solve the problem.

But are we really interested in making the massive changes that it will take to fix our schools? Are we prepared to mobilize not only the tax dollars but the intellectual capital that will be required if we are to have a significant impact on the deplorable condition of our educational system? As problem solvers, we have no peers. Our inventive and organizational genius, and our capacity to bring about orderly social change, are the envy of the world. We possess the brains, resources, and technology to bring off a revolution in instruction, but for some reason we are still unwilling to dedicate the resources it will take to bring about significant educational change. As the late Lawrence Cremin pointed out in his Inglis and Burton Lectures at Harvard in 1989, so long as the Department of Defense has a research budget that is 12 percent of its total budget while the Office of Education only has a research budget that is 2 percent of its total budget, "it is sheer nonsense to talk about excellence in American education."

Perhaps we still harbor a deep current of anti-intellectualism in our society. The *Sputnik*-inspired educational reform movement, with its focus on training the mind and on applying the latest findings of developmental psychology to the design of instruction, was a curious departure from traditional American practice. Historically we have been more concerned about promoting democratic values, transmitting universally accepted skills like the three R's, and socializing the young into useful lives within their local communities than about cultivating the intellect. Too much education, many Americans still think, tends to set people apart from the crowd, makes them leave home, gives them an inflated view of their capabilities, weakens family ties, and destroys religion. Our provincialism and our belief in equality make us uncertain about how much learning we really want to have take place in our schools. Unlike most other nations, we remain suspicious of intellectuals and continue to revere nonacademic routes to success and power. After all, some of our most celebrated national heroes have made it without formal education. Somewhere deep in the American consciousness we probably still shelter a profound distrust of too much schooling.

Given this ambivalence about school it may be helpful to reexamine what happened for a brief period following the *Sputnik* crisis when educational reform was a major national priority, and when some of the brightest minds in the country turned their attention to the improvement of instruction. Although much that was done was imperfectly conceived and executed, knowledge of that prodigious effort can provide some useful building blocks from which future attempts to enhance the learning performance of our children could be constructed. The value of such an investigation lies not so much in an examination of what was actually produced, although the materials remain impressive despite their accumulation of dust on the storeroom shelves of their publishers and in the archives of their developers. What is especially noteworthy, however, is what was learned about how young minds grow, and the knowledge about how that growth can be stimulated through the use of new methods and materials that was generated in dozens of project centers and thousands of faculty rooms in the school systems across the country that participated in these reforms. That experience is still vivid in the minds of those who took part.

The *Sputnik* reforms also reveal something about the perils of curriculum innovation. The story of how MACOS came to be, the response of teachers and students, the problems of publication and implementation, and the debate that it stirred at the highest levels of government shed light on the hazards of introducing intellectually exciting materials in the schools. The developers of this program brought to the precollege classroom the latest findings of scientific research and the methodology of the scientist in an effort to stimulate the thinking processes of the young. In doing so they raised national consciousness about the relationship of scholarship and schooling, and the potential of scholar-led school reform. But a public that first welcomed the participation of research scientists in the schools later questioned that participation because it upset established patterns of teaching, demanded new instructional resources, and challenged some deeply held community values.

In a society that treasures the autonomy of the local school district, is the American public any more ready today than it was a generation ago to allow the teachings of science and the practice of the scientific method to infiltrate teaching at the precollege level? Do we really want to teach our children how to think independently and how to explore the human condition in an open-ended way? Are we prepared, in short, to push the limits of what Bruner called "the perfectability of intellect"? Or are we more comfortable with the transmission of facts and the promotion of accepted values, where the learning outcomes are more predictable? In considering these matters the new advocates of educational reform would do well to reflect upon the experience of the *Sputnik*-driven innovators and look more closely at the politics of schooling.

· 1 ·

Historical Perspectives

The launching of *Sputnik* was not the only catalyst that ignited the school reform movement of the 1950s and 1960s. Public concern about the inadequacy of the schools to meet the challenges of the postwar world was widespread following World War II. Few new school buildings had been built since 1941, rampant inflation had depressed salaries, and in the decade after the war teachers deserted the schools in droves for higher paying jobs in a burgeoning postwar economy. By 1950, as school performance continued to decline, scholars and laypeople alike began taking up their pens to demand a searching reappraisal of public education. The torrent of books and articles that appeared in those early postwar years precipitated what Lawrence Cremin has called "the deepest educational crisis in the nation's history."[1] At the center of the controversy was John Dewey's philosophy of "progressive education," together with its stepchild, the Life-Adjustment Movement.

Lay criticism led the attack. In a little book entitled *And Madly Teach* published in 1949, Mortimer Smith, a retired businessman turned educational critic, accused Dewey and the Progressives of allowing the schools to pursue programs of practical training while failing to specify the intellectual and moral ends of education. Dewey's pragmatism, wrote Smith, which made no value judgments about what should be taught, had brought American education to the brink of chaos. "Instrumentalism," as he called progressive teaching, "reduces education to a vast bubbling confusion, in which . . . hairdressing and embalming are just as important, if not a little more so, . . . [as] history and philosophy."[2] Smith, like others of his era, sought to restore education to its historic role of providing moral and intellectual guidance to the young. The best way to preserve freedom, he argued, is to cultivate the mental and moral capacities of the individual to the highest possible state, not just to

10

train students for specific occupations. He called for a revival of the spirit of Horace Mann and the Common School advocates of the nineteenth century, who aspired through education to produce the "good individual." Smith proposed a return to the teaching of Platonic ideals and suggested that the development of a moral sense in the young was a more important goal than specific skill training. Create the good individual, he said, and good individuals, taken together, will create the good society.

A second assault on Dewey and his followers came from the academic community. In a book entitled *Crisis in Education,* which also appeared in 1949, Bernard Iddings Bell added the weight of academic sanction to the growing criticism. Bell, a former college president and a scholar of distinguished reputation, complained that the schools had become dangerously skewed toward occupational concerns at the expense of developing the outstanding students needed for the intellectual challenges of the postwar years. "If our civilization is to . . . survive," he wrote, "it will be saved . . . by leaders of trained intelligence."[3] He proposed a sweeping series of reforms that included the total reorganization of the teaching profession, the restructuring of the school calendar, the extension of educational benefits to adults, and the provision of religious teaching within the schools. He feared that the increasing democratization of our educational system would reduce American society to "a cage of contending beasts," and he proposed the establishment of special leadership training for the most intellectually gifted students to ensure the development of their superior "diacritical powers." "It is from this chosen group," he said, "that the interpreters and directors of a sane common life must come."[4]

The forays of Smith and Bell were but the opening salvos of what soon became a full-scale war on the practice of schooling in the 1950s. The writings of John Dewey, the apostles of "life-adjustment education," the proponents of "child-centered" learning, and the daily classroom activities of teachers came under increasingly close scrutiny by academics, journalists, and the lay public. By 1953 a flood of articles and books had appeared, including Albert Lynd's *Quackery in the Public Schools,* Paul Woodring's *Let's Talk Sense about Our Schools,* and Arthur Bestor's *Educational Wastelands.*[5] In 1952, the dean of Columbia's Teachers College, Hollis Caswell, argued in his Steinmetz Memorial Lecture before the American Institute of Electrical Engineers that a profound reexamination of the historic role of the American public school was under way. Caswell pointed out that much of the current criticism was directed at the very features of the American school system that had made it historically unique. The attack, he said, went far beyond criticism of the pedagogical theories of the progressive educators and the shoddiness of some of their practices. It called into question something much more fundamental: the populist, egalitarian, nonsectarian philosophy upon which public education in America had been built for a hundred years.[6]

Underlying many of the criticisms leveled at the schools of the era was a challenging new vision for American education. Many of the critics seemed to be suggesting that American schools, in order to meet the rigorous demands of the postwar world, should abandon their historic commitment to a common education for all, and, in the style of European schools, adopt an elitist approach to the cultivation of talent and move the most gifted students ahead as rapidly as possible. This attack on Progressivism coincided with the rise of conservatism in politics and the view that the tough problems facing America abroad could only be met with vigorous, selective, academic training at home. Our schools, said the critics, must respond to the needs of a changing society facing increasing foreign competition, and to do so we must discard our system of equal educational opportunity for all students in favor of a differentiated approach that offered special training to the academically talented.[7]

Dewey and the Progressives

What was it in Dewey's thinking that the critics found so objectionable? A philosophy professor at Columbia for most of his academic career, Dewey fathered the Progressive Education movement. In his central work, *Democracy and Education,* published in 1916, he argued that our system of schooling must be redesigned to respond to the profound changes occurring in American society in the transition from an agrarian to an industrial economy. He believed that the modern school must prepare children to cope with the challenges of a rapidly changing society and provide them with skills that were not easily learned on the farm. Just as a rural upbringing prepared one for an agrarian life, said Dewey, children growing up in the city must learn to cope with an urbanized world that demanded increased scientific and technical training. A knowledge of the evolution of Western civilization, an understanding of the Industrial Revolution, and the ability to reason scientifically, he said, were essential tools for mastering the complexities of contemporary American life.

Dewey was no ivory tower theorist. In 1896, as a fledgling professor at the University of Chicago, he founded a laboratory school to test his ideas. He believed that children learned best through direct experience, through being allowed to cultivate their natural curiosity, and through taking responsibility for their own learning. He maintained that the essentials of creative thinking were embodied in the processes of science and that intellectual activity was much the same, whether in the kindergarten or in the scientific laboratory. Learning to think scientifically, he said, was the primary goal of good teaching, and he suggested that all instruction could be unified through the cultivation of disciplined habits of mind. By this he meant that children must learn how to reflect upon concrete experience in a systematic way. He proposed that the material chosen for examination should be intrinsically interesting to the child, that it should be organized around a problem that stimulates thought, that all the necessary information and observations needed for solving the problem should be available to the child, that the child should be responsible for developing orderly solutions, and that the child should have an opportunity to test and apply those solutions to clarify their meaning and determine their validity.[8]

At the core of Dewey's pedagogy was what he called "the progressive organization of knowledge," the ordering of experience in a way that will lead the learner to seek out new information and ask new questions. New discoveries on the part of children, he said, generate new problems that captivate their interest. In this way, learning unfolds in a continuous spiral. Starting with a simple lever or a jar of pond water, for example, students can pursue a progression of thought-provoking problems that will lead to an early grasp of the organizing conjectures and concepts of physics or biology. Similarly, the same empirical approach can guide the learner from everyday social experiences, such as playground games, to an understanding of the laws that govern society. The key to this pedagogical strategy, said Dewey, is the use of the scientific method. Experimentation, the formation and testing of hypotheses, the recording of the significant features of experience, and reflection upon the information thus discovered were the means by which true learning should take place. The scientific method, he said, "is the only authentic means at our command for getting at the significance of our everyday experiences of the world in which we live,"[9] and he warned that educational practices that departed from the discipline of science might well lead to a "return to intellectual and moral authoritarianism."[10]

Dewey believed that schooling should socialize students into the democratic way of life. He saw democracy as the enemy of privilege, class, race, and special interests of any kind. Democratic education, therefore, must offer the opportunity for personal fulfillment to every individual, and each individual must learn to support the interests of others while learning to adapt to a changing, dynamic environment. In a society that thrives on a belief in growth and progress, he said, children must develop a capacity for personal initiative and adaptability. They must take responsibility for governing themselves and learn to deal constructively and responsively with the forces of social and economic change. Indeed, Dewey regarded the capacity to cope constructively with the processes of change as one of the most important skills to cultivate in the citizenry of a democratic society.

Unfortunately, few of the school systems that set out to implement these ideas were able to sustain his intellectual and pedagogical vision. In time, Dewey himself became disillusioned with Progressive Education as he observed it in a variety of classrooms. Many middle-class communities, he found, interpreted Progressivism as a justification for tailoring teaching to the individual interests of students, while in a number of blue-collar communities he saw progressive methods used to prepare students for specific jobs in industry. For some teachers tailoring education to the curiosity of the child apparently meant "anything goes." The traditional curriculum was often replaced with subjects of trivial significance. In *Experience and Education,* published in 1938, Dewey complained that the deification of "direct experience" in education had degenerated into a formless curriculum in which any experience was seen as having significant educational value. "Just because traditional education was a matter of routine in which the plans and programs were handed down from the past," he wrote, "it does not follow that progressive education is a matter of planless 'improvisation.'"[11] As an old man Dewey repudiated much of the educational practice his writing had inspired.

The Life-Adjustment Movement

Following World War II the Progressives abandoned their dream of an educational system that would prepare students for active participation in a changing society and turned their attention instead to what they called "life-adjustment" education. As the term suggests, the leaders of this new movement had lost the spirit of innovation that had dominated the early years of the Progressive Movement and had replaced Dewey's emphasis on critical thinking with a new concern for the development of practical skills. This change sprang from a belief that large numbers of American schoolchildren were receiving an education that bore little relationship to their everyday needs, and that intellectual training should be replaced by vocationally oriented instruction. Preparation for college gave way to a growing emphasis on career guidance, and courses intended to assist the process of "social adjustment" began to infiltrate the curriculum as this new group of educators looked for ways to reach children whom they deemed mentally unfit for the more intellectually rigorous schooling proposed by the Progressives.

What was "life-adjustment" education? A coherent definition is difficult to find. In 1947, Columbia's Teachers College published a book entitled *Developing a Curriculum for Modern Living* in which the authors described life-adjustment education as learning about "real-life problems." "Fundamentally," they wrote, "this concept of curriculum development is one in which the basic problems and situations of everyday living in our democracy, which are central to life itself, also become central to the education of learners."[12] In 1950, the Illinois Life-Adjustment Curriculum Program published a bulletin that set out to define the "problems of high school youth." The document listed a hodgepodge of undifferentiated "basic problems" ranging from the trivial to the profound, including, among other things, "the problem of improving one's personal appearance; the problem of selecting the 'family dentist'; the problem of developing 'tinkering hobbies'; the problem of developing and maintaining wholesome boy-girl relationships; the problem of acquiring the ability to distinguish right from wrong and to guide one's actions accordingly; the problem of acquiring the ability to study and help solve economic, social, and political problems; and the problem of making oneself a well-informed and sensitive 'citizen of the world.'"[13]

The Life-Adjustment Movement was a far cry from Dewey's original vision of education as a continuous restructuring of experience. Unlike Dewey, the apostles of life-adjustment education refused to articulate a rationale for their proposed reforms, stubbornly arguing that there already existed a "wealth of sound theory." But "problems" alone soon proved to be a shaky foundation on which to build a new curriculum, for the life-adjustment advocates failed to provide a basis for selecting the significant problems to be examined. The "problem approach" turned out to have little value as a focus for educational inquiry because the problems were not selected with a particular learning objective in mind. What has intellectual staying power, Dewey had tried to point out, is not so much the problems themselves as a disciplined method of approaching problems. Lacking a clearly thought-out intellectual framework, the life-adjustment movement was a perversion of Dewey's ideas, and it brought discredit to the Progressive reform movement.

Arthur Bestor

Of all the critics of public education during the postwar period, by far the most vocal and provocative was Arthur Bestor, a professor of American history at the University of Illinois, who had taught for several years at Teachers College, Columbia. Bestor was appalled by the concept of "life-adjustment education" and attacked the movement in a series of articles in publications like the *American Scholar* and the *New Republic*. In 1953, he published a devastating book-length critique of American education entitled *Educational Wastelands: A Retreat from Learning in Our Public Schools.* In *Wastelands,* Bestor charged that American schools were failing because they had given up on the primary goal of a liberal education, to teach people how to think. Rigorous intellectual training, he said, was the first requisite of a liberated individual and the most important protection for a free society. "If we take education seriously," he wrote, "we can no more afford to gamble our safety upon inferior intellectual training in our schools than upon inferior weapons in our armory."[14] We must no longer measure ourselves by the outmoded standards of the past, said Bestor; we must strive to make our educational system the best in the world. To achieve this he set about mobilizing the academic community into action and launching a movement for reform of the public schools that would engage the talents of the best academic minds in the country.

Unlike many of his fellow critics, Bestor was no elitist. With new and more effective methods of teaching, he believed that sound intellectual training could be extended to the overwhelming majority of American youth. He rejected the view that rigorous mental training was functional only in an aristocracy and argued that such training was even more appropriate in a democracy. Every member of the race has the same desire to cultivate his highest powers, he said, and pointed out that in a free society, where social position and income depend on education, learning is even more critical than in other societies. For this reason there should be even greater motivation for achievement. Quoting Horace Mann, who had made a similar case for democratic education a century earlier, Bestor saw a liberal education as "the great equalizer of the conditions of men."[15]

Bestor was shocked by the claim of the Life-Adjustment educators that the majority of American schoolchildren were intellectually incapable of profiting from an academically rigorous education. He placed the blame for this lowering of educational sights on the many teachers and scholars in schools and universities who had never themselves learned what a liberal education was. A liberal education, he said, is "the communication of intellectual power," and such power, he maintained, can only be communicated by someone who possesses it. Teachers who are not also scholars cannot do it, nor can scholars who focus too much on what they know and too little on how they came to know it transmit it either. "To know a few episodes in the past is not to know history," he said. "The essential thing is to comprehend the forces that are at work through a long sequence of events, and to incorporate the perspective of time into one's day-to-day judgements."[16] Then and only then, he argued, has history been properly taught.

According to Bestor, a sound education required rigorous training in the disciplines. Learning, he said, should draw upon the structures of thought provided by the academic fields, and vocational training should be combined with, not separated from, the rigors of scholarship. He wrote passionately about the liberating power of the disciplined mind and claimed that the proper measure of an educational program is the extent to which it trains the student to think, and to "think painstakingly." He contended that the qualities of imagination and discipline, of originality and rigor, must be "welded together" in a liberal education, and that the true test of intellectual ability comes in the production of an original piece of scholarly work, such as the Ph.D. dissertation. He argued that this ideal should guide instruction at every level and that the intellectual discipline resulting from such work would sustain people throughout their lives far more than anything vocational training could possibly achieve. Only a student so trained, said Bestor, is truly liberated. "His is a disciplined mind. And because his mind is disciplined, he himself is free."[17]

Bestor's vision for an intellectually rigorous education for all American youth articulated the faith of the new curriculum reformers who were shortly to burst upon the educational scene. His efforts were more than just a blistering critique of the Life-Adjustment movement. He set about replacing the "problem-centered" curriculum materials that were currently fashionable with a full-blown academic curriculum that was dedicated to the training of the intellect. The profusion of articles and books he turned out in a few short years constituted a scholarly call to arms that challenged his university colleagues to assume responsibility for the restoration of learning in the public schools. He chastised his peers for having failed in their duty to maintain the quality of elementary and secondary education, and he charged that they were "reaping today the whirlwind which their indifference helped to sow."[18] This impassioned appeal must have struck a responsive chord, for it was soon to be followed by the most extensive commitment of university scholarship to educational reform in modern history. Within a few years, in an unprecedented exodus from the ivory tower, hundreds of scholars became deeply engaged in trying to fix the schools.

But how were Bestor's professors supposed to proceed? What did academics know about how to grapple with the massive system of American public education? The main obstacle to educational change, said Bestor, was the "interlocking directorate of professional educationists," a network of education professors, school administrators, and government bureaucrats who monopolized the administration of the public schools and created an "iron curtain" separating the schools from the scholarly community. To establish contact between the universities and the schools, he called for the creation of an alliance between the serious teacher in the secondary school and the scholar in the same discipline on the college or university faculty. In this way he hoped to bypass the educational establishment and forge a partnership between scholars and teachers dedicated to the restoration of liberal education from kindergarten through graduate school. He proposed to return teacher training to the schools of arts and sciences and to transform the schools of education on university campuses into departments of pedagogy equivalent to other academic fields. By thus reducing the power of the professional educator and extending the role of the university research professor to include responsibility for the quality of education at all levels, he sought to restructure the way schooling was defined and bring about an infusion of new intellectual energy into the bloodstream of the public schools.

Bestor's call for rigorous academic training coincided with rising public concern about national security and a growing fear about technological vulnerability because of the poor quality of instruction in the schools. If our ability to establish and maintain a strong system of national defense was dependent upon continuing scientific and technological innovation, the schools must be able to produce graduates capable of meeting increasingly rigorous intellectual demands. Many Americans believed that the challenge posed by the expanding scientific and military power of the USSR could only be met in the long run through the development of more effective scientific training. Mental flabbiness had become equated in the public mind with moral weakness, and Bestor captured the national mood when he said, "Let our totalitarian enemies fear the free, critical, well-trained mind; they have good reason to fear it. Precisely because *they* fear it, *we* must be careful to foster it. Let us not be timid in our avowal of our faith: 'And ye shall know the truth, and the truth shall make you free.'"[19]

The New Reformers

Pronouncements by professors on matters of public concern were rare in the years before the war. Even less frequent was the participation of the university community in programs of social change. Philosophers might speculate about the future of the republic and Franklin Roosevelt employ a "brain trust" to help formulate the New Deal, but with the exception of Dewey and the Progressives, prior to World War II few university scholars aspired to significant influence over the body politic. Most academics were content in their tenured professorships to court the illusive nymph of knowledge with scant concern for society's needs; society, in turn, saw little relationship between academic matters and the day-to-day business of living. Useful knowledge was available from the industrial research laboratories and the engineering schools, but pure scholarship was thought to have very little to do with the problems of the ordinary citizen. Even the word *professor* suggested to many a person inept at coping with everyday life.

World War II changed all that. Following the war came the belief, perhaps stimulated by the success of the Manhattan Project and other war-related research activities, that formal knowledge could make a significant contribution to the conduct of human affairs. The stereotype of the absentminded, long-haired university professor in baggy tweeds gradually gave way to the image of the white-coated scientist, who was highly respected for his technical expertise. As the social value of formal knowledge began to rise, academics were soon selling their services as professional consultants to industry and government in a growing number of fields. The burgeoning defense industry, the development of computers and xerography, and the expanding field of electronics were among the many postwar challenges that called for the participation of the best academic brains in the country. With this growing respect for the social value of trained intelligence came an interest in school reform among university research scientists whose expertise lay outside the field of education.

Among the first such academics to take part in improving instruction at the secondary level was a group of mathematicians at the University of Illinois. In 1952, under the leadership of Max Beberman, faculty members from the Colleges of Education, Engineering, and Liberal Arts and Sciences formed the University of Illinois Committee on School Mathematics. From the beginning the committee was conceived as a collaboration between schoolteachers and university professors. It undertook the development of new materials and approaches to mathematics teaching that would expose high school students to the methods of academic mathematicians. Beberman, who taught mathematics at the Illinois Laboratory School, described the program as an effort to "bring to the mind of the adolescent some of the ideas and modes of thinking which are basic in the work of the contemporary mathematician."[20] Beberman boldly proposed to close the gap between how math was being taught in the university and what was happening in the schools.

"Illinois Math," as the project came to be called, set the pattern for much of the scholar-led curriculum innovation that took place in the 1950s and 1960s. Funded by the Carnegie Corporation of New York, a pioneer among private foundations supporting curriculum innovation during the postwar years, Beberman and his colleagues invented a new way of creating instructional materials and thus influencing what went on in secondary school classrooms. Bypassing the mathematics education establishment and working directly with schoolteachers, they purposely disregarded traditional assumptions about what children could and should learn. Their primary aim was to bring about a collaboration between the university research laboratory and the classroom, to see how far they could succeed in pushing young children to think like professional mathematicians. Drawing on the generous support of a number of foundations, they were able to experiment with ideas without having to prove their value in the commercial marketplace.

Perhaps the most interesting feature of Beberman's work is contained in the phrase, "bring to the mind of the adolescent some of the ideas and modes of thinking which are basic in the work of the contemporary mathematician." Here was a fresh idea. It is hard to imagine the Progressive reformers suggesting that it was important to teach adolescents how to think like mathematics professors. In Dewey's day such knowledge was hardly seen as having much practical value for the average citizen. But in Beberman's view, knowing one's multiplication tables was less important in a world of electronic calculating machines than learning to think in a mathematical way. This meant placing less emphasis on the teaching of computational skills and spending more time examining the conceptual structure of mathematics. Beberman wanted children to understand the difference between "number" and "numeral," for example, and to comprehend the theory of sets. He believed that children must learn to "think mathematically" if they are to function effectively in an increasingly quantitative and computer-driven world.

The Illinois Math project emphasized inductive approaches to learning. Materials and exercises were designed to encourage students to "discover" underlying mathematical principles such as algorithms, equivalence rules, and theorems. Delayed verbalization was considered very important, since it allowed the student time to figure out a mathematical idea before giving it abstract expression. Beberman justified this time-consuming approach by asserting that it led to long-range memory and a greater depth of understanding, rather than merely success on tests or in solving immediate problems. He sought to instill in students an affection for mathematics not just as a useful skill but as a way of using one's mind. "The discovery method of teaching," he wrote, "is practiced by those who believe that mathematics is more than a tool to be used in solving the 'real-life' problems of mankind . . . [it] develops interest in mathematics, and power in mathematical thinking."[21]

Not long after Beberman's mathematics work began to get under way at the University of Illinois, physicist Jerrold Zacharias formed the Physical Sciences Study Committee at M.I.T. Zacharias, who would devote the rest of his life to the improvement of science education, became the single most important force in the science curriculum reform movement. "Zach," as he was known to his friends, was appalled at the outdated content of high school physics texts, and, like Beberman, he wanted to bring to the high school classroom the world of contemporary physics as it was practiced in the university. In March of 1956 he sent a memorandum to James Killian, the president of M.I.T., suggesting the development of "a large number of moving picture shorts" for the improvement of physics teaching in the high schools. Zacharias envisioned ninety films, each about twenty minutes long, accompanied by texts, problem books, question and answer cards, and other teaching apparatus.[22] Killian was enthusiastic about the idea and urged Zacharias to bring together a group of distinguished scientists to plan the project. He shared Zacharias's view that first-rate scholars should be involved in preparing materials for teaching elementary physics because they knew the field best and could replace the "superficial and sometimes erroneous material that appeared in physics textbooks."[23]

Zacharias assembled an impressive collection of scientists, industrialists, and public figures of national reputation in science to form a steering committee for the project. Among the members were Nobel laureates I. I. Rabi and Edward Purcell, inventor Edwin Land, Mervin Kelly of the Bell Laboratories, Morris Meister of the Bronx High School of Science, and the chairman of the M.I.T. corporation, Vannevar Bush. At the first meeting the committee issued a statement of purpose setting forth the view that the teaching of physical science was as significant and important for society as the teaching of the humanities or social sciences. The committee envisioned a course that would provide all students with a deeper understanding of the physical world, attract some to possible careers in science, and provide better preparation for advanced students.[24]

With funding from the National Science Foundation, Zacharias began planning his new physics course with the assistance of his departmental colleague, Francis Friedman. They formed a nonprofit corporation to house the project, converted an abandoned movie theater into a film studio, hired a film director away from CBS, and began production. In five years PSSC produced fifty-six films, published a textbook, developed a series of easily reproduced laboratory experiments that employed inexpensive apparatus, and became the best-selling physics program in educational publishing history. Zacharias's physics project set an example for later reforms in the other sciences, particularly in chemistry and biology, and ultimately for curriculum programs in the social sciences as well. PSSC was a collaboration between research scholars, media specialists, scientific writers and editors, and high school physics teachers. As with Illinois Math, the professional education establishment was largely ignored.

The Struggle for Federal Support

A prevailing myth about the school reform movement of the 1950s is that it developed in response to the launching of *Sputnik*. In fact, as we have seen, postwar concern for improving the schools predated the Soviet achievement by at least a decade, and a number of curriculum improvement initiatives were under way by the mid-1950s. The Cold War had deepened the anxiety of many Americans about the adequacy of the schools, and there was a growing public demand for educational reform. At a White House Conference on Education in 1955, Vice President Richard M. Nixon declared that "our national security has a tremendous stake in our educational system," and Neil H. McElroy, who later became Secretary of Defense, asserted that in our technical age "education has become as much a part of our system of defense as the Army, the Navy or the Air Force." "We must have good schools," he said, "not only because of our ideals, but for survival."[25] M.I.T.'s James Killian also addressed the conference, emphasizing the critical national shortage of scientists and science teachers, but he was careful to point out that the idea of the federal government shaping education to its own ends was a tactic characteristic only of totalitarian societies.

Killian's cautions reflected the prevailing sentiment in public policy. For years Congress had debated the wisdom of spending federal dollars to fix the schools. In 1950 a major education bill died in the House Education and Labor Committee, despite prior passage in the Senate and strong support from President Truman, because of congressional fears that federal funding could lead to federal control over local school districts. In explaining the action, Committee chair John Lesinski said that he and most members of the committee supported federal aid, but, after careful study, they had reluctantly come to the conclusion that "no acceptable bill preventing federal domination of local schools can be drawn."[26] For this reason they failed to report the bill.

For most of the decade there was little change in the congressional stance toward federal support for education. Despite mounting public discussion of the "school crisis" and increasing pressure from educators for federal aid, Congress continued to resist passage of a school bill on the grounds that federal investment meant federal control. Following the *Brown v. Board of Education* decision in 1954, the school aid debate became further complicated by its link to the issue of civil rights. How far, and by what authority, could the federal government legally intrude upon the autonomy of the local school? By 1956 the demand for better science and mathematics instruction was reaching a crescendo in some quarters, stimulated by the fear that we were falling behind the Russians. In that year several popular magazines, including *Life* and *Newsweek,* ran articles featuring Soviet educational achievements. But in a rare refusal to yield to public pressure, Congress remained adamant in its opposition to a federal investment in school reform.

But the orbiting of *Sputnik I* in October of 1957 broke the congressional logjam. Whatever their former positions, legislators on both sides of the aisle now abandoned their scruples and rushed to prepare the nation's first comprehensive education bill. On 2 September 1958, President Eisenhower signed Public Law 85-864, the National Defense Education Act, creating the most sweeping federal education legislation in the nation's history. The bill authorized expenditures of more than $1 billion for a wide range of reforms, including new school construction, vast expansion of language instruction, experimentation with audio-visual materials, fellowships and loans to encourage promising students to seek higher education, and new initiatives in vocational education to meet the critical manpower shortages in the defense industry. Admiral Hyman Rickover, the outspoken director of the Navy's nuclear submarine project, expressed what most Americans felt: "We are engaged in a grim duel. We are beginning to recognize the threat to American technical supremacy which could materialize if Russia succeeds in her ambitious program of achieving world scientific and engineering supremacy by turning out vast numbers of well-trained scientists and engineers. Democracies move slower than totalitarian dictatorships. We have let our educational problem grow much too big for comfort and safety. We are beginning to see now that we must solve it without delay."[27]

The National Science Foundation had already acted. Since its founding in 1950, the NSF education effort had been confined to promoting science fairs and science clubs and funding summer institutes for teachers. In 1955 the NSF annual report expressed a growing worry about the shortage of high school students entering scientific careers and noted a national survey conducted by the Educational Testing Service, which indicated that 200,000 highability high school seniors were not planning to attend college. In 1956 the Foundation had cautiously provided preliminary funding to the Physical Science Study Committee at M.I.T. to support planning for Jerrold Zacharias's new high school physics program. In doing so the NSF took care to ensure that project supervision was national in scope and that steps would be taken to minimize competition with the educational publishing industry. In a memorandum prepared in December 1956, the steering group stated that the federal government should not be asked to support the writing of textbooks that would be distributed in competition with private enterprise and recommended that the completed work be placed in the public domain.[28]

Following *Sputnik* the NSF increased its curriculum support activities at a rapid pace. In 1958 the Foundation funded the School Mathematics Study Group under the direction of Edward Begle at Yale and in the fall of the same year gave support to a major new program in biology, the Biological Sciences Curriculum Study, a project sponsored by the American Institute of Biological Sciences. During the next two years the Foundation provided the funding for two new programs in high school chemistry, the Chemical Bond Approach Project and the Chemical Education Materials Study, the latter an outgrowth of an earlier effort undertaken by the American Chemical Society. All of these programs were organized much like the PSSC physics project. Their steering committees included major figures in the scientific community but almost no professional educators, although the projects relied heavily on the participation of experienced teachers.

These reforms at the high school level quickly led to a reexamination of science teaching in the lower grades. By the early 1960s, with backing from the NSF and the American Association for the Advancement of Science (AAAS), several new programs had begun at the elementary level, including the AAAS program "Science: A Process Approach" and the Elementary Science Study at Educational Services, Incorporated (ESI), Zacharias's nonprofit corporation, which had produced PSSC Physics.[29] Scholars who had been successful in developing new curricula for adolescents now took up the challenge of providing intellectual stimulation for the very young. Like Beberman, the most zealous of these reformers sought to explore the limits of a young child's ability to absorb abstract ideas. They even rejected Piaget's well-known stage theory of development, arguing that his findings were constrained by current teaching practices and suggesting that new materials and teaching methods might change those findings. Reporting the results of a mathematics conference held in Cambridge, Massachusetts, during the summer of 1963, Zacharias and others challenged Piaget's views on children's intelligence: "Piaget is not a teacher but an observer— he has tried to find out what it is that children understand at a given age, when they have been taught in conventional ways. The essence of our enterprise is to alter the data which have formed, so far, the basis of his research . . . We therefore believe that no predictions, either positive or negative, are justified, and that the only way to find out when and how various things can be taught is to try various ways of teaching them."[30]

Stimulated by the achievements in mathematics and the sciences, the reform spirit soon spread to other areas of the curriculum. Under the provisions of the National Defense Education Act (NDEA), the U.S. Office of Education (USOE) sought to bring about a revolution in the teaching of foreign languages by helping to establish fifty-five language and area study centers at thirty-four institutions of higher education across the country. Graduate fellowships and postdoctoral awards encouraged thousands of students to seek advanced work in over sixty different languages and to become language teachers in the schools. Funds for NDEA summer and year-long institutes, installation of electronic language laboratories, and improved supervision of language instruction at all levels led to widespread improvement in this neglected area of the school curriculum. Project English, another USOE program funded by the same bill, gave support to eleven universities to establish demonstration centers, curriculum development activities, and basic research projects. Despite more time spent on English than on any other subject, American high schools were failing to graduate students who could read and write well enough to handle the growing number of white-collar and professional jobs being offered by an increasingly industrialized and bureaucratized society. Project English set about to reverse this trend.

In the early 1960s the National Science Foundation expanded its curriculum development activities to include the social sciences. In 1962 the Foundation awarded a grant to the American Anthropological Association to develop an anthropology course for high school students. In 1963 it funded a newly founded elementary social studies program at ESI. And in 1964 it provided support for two more social science projects sponsored by the American Sociological Association and the American Association of Geographers. Support for curriculum innovation expanded so rapidly during this period that by the mid-1960s curriculum projects were underway in almost every field. With funds from the National Science Foundation, the Office of Education, and numerous private foundations, scholars and teachers in disciplines ranging from math and science teaching to music and the visual arts were hard at work trying to devise new ways to improve instruction. The unprecedented availability of public funds for curriculum improvement stimulated a level of innovative activity unique in the history of American education.

The most vigorous and vocal supporter of curriculum innovation during this period was M.I.T.'s Jerrold Zacharias. Appointed to the chair of the Education Panel of the President's Science Advisory Committee in the fall of 1961, Zacharias organized a series of meetings to explore all aspects of educational reform, from the teaching of music to the problems of the deprived and segregated. Said Zacharias, "The task of educational research and development is to learn how to provide for all students the education an exceptional teacher provides for a few." He argued that effective education exists only when the grasp of a subject and the methods of teaching are integrated, and he pressed for large-scale increases in spending for both curriculum development and teacher education. After an intensive two-year review of existing educational practices, he estimated that it would take a fourfold increase in federal and private spending to solve our educational problems.[31]

Like Zacharias, most of the new reformers attacked the curriculum challenge with the confidence of those who had mastered radar and the atom bomb. Although they knew the schools were in serious difficulty, they believed that, with a fresh infusion of funds and talent, they could quickly repair the educational system. Many shared Bestor's view that the schools had suffered from excessive exposure to "professional educators" who talked vaguely about educational "methods" but lacked the substantive knowledge necessary to reform the curriculum. What was needed, said the new reformers, was the participation of professional scholars who could bring their research expertise to the precollege classroom. For a time this new breed of educational innovators had strong support from an anxious public, who had come to believe that the Soviets had opened an "education gap" as serious as the ominous "missile gap." Former worries about federal influence over the schools were drowned out by the rhetoric of national defense, and the reform movement quickly gained momentum as massive government funding attracted some of the best academic brains in the country to the task. With such impressive designers, the new reforms seemed destined to succeed.

Toward a New Vision

The curriculum reforms of the post-*Sputnik* era opened a fresh chapter in the history of American education. Never before had university research scholars taken such a deep interest in the improvement of instruction in the public schools. Zacharias and his colleagues were accustomed to working on large-scale scientific and technological problems like the development of the distant early warning system and the design of a nationwide network for air traffic control, and they brought to the work the ability to think in terms of major, systemic change. They were accustomed to approaching the federal government with major projects, and for the first time the federal government was willing to provide significant financial support for educational change. Old worries about "local control" and "free enterprise" disappeared as academic scientists united with writers, editors, filmmakers, equipment designers, and teachers across the country in an unprecedented effort to transform the curriculum at all levels. An important feature of this new movement was the leadership provided by the scientific community.

The role of the National Science Foundation in providing funding for the new reforms was especially significant. While the U.S. Office of Education, through the National Defense Education Act, funded new facilities, guidance, media development, language training, and scholarship aid, the NSF supplied the principle support for curriculum innovation. Unlike the USOE, the NSF followed a grant procedure similar to that used for scientific research, accepting unsolicited proposals submitted by academics and determining their merit through critiques supplied by scholars with backgrounds similar to the proposing individual or group. This "peer review" system had been designed to insulate scientific research from political influence and to provide the foundation with judgments based on scholarly merit alone, uncluttered by considerations of social benefit or marketing realities. Grant officers encouraged the establishment of steering committees of distinguished scholars, and during this period curriculum-making fell almost exclusively into the hands of the university community.

In the rush to create the "new curricula," few stopped to ask what effect these reforms might have upon the overall pattern of public schooling if these academic products became widely accepted. What kind of society would result if the scholar-reformers were successful in achieving their educational objectives? Might the outcome be the creation of an intellectual elite of the kind that Bernard Iddings Bell had proposed? Or would the result be that all students would learn "how to think," as Arthur Bestor had envisioned? And how would the new reforms relate to the preparation for democratic citizenship that dominated the thinking of the Progressives or the practical training called for by the proponents of "life-adjustment" education? Unfortunately, in their urgency to close the "education gap" with some well-designed courses, few of the new reformers took time to explore these broader philosophical questions or to consider the social and political ramifications of their work. This failure to articulate a clear social vision was in time to prove troublesome in a society deeply concerned with the social as well as the intellectual function of the school.

One of the few participants in the curriculum movement who did worry about such matters was Bentley Glass, who chaired the steering committee of the Biological Sciences Curriculum Study (BSCS), an NSF-funded high school biology project similar in scale and approach to PSSC Physics.[32] Glass was a geneticist with an unusually broad background in both education and public service, which suited him well for thinking about the more general implications of federally funded curriculum reform. He had begun his teaching career in a Texas high school, studied science education at Teachers College, Columbia, served as a member of a committee of the National Academy of Sciences that had prepared a report on the biological effects of atomic radiation, and was a professor of biology at Johns Hopkins University when he agreed to head the BSCS group. He believed in science instruction as a way of strengthening the intellectual and moral fiber of American society and securing America's position of leadership in the Free World.

Glass saw science teaching as the backbone of a liberal education. In a lecture delivered in New Orleans in March 1958, he spoke of science as "the greatest liberating, liberalizing force in human thought" and went on to describe its importance in contemporary society. "It is obvious," he said, "that in the modern world the strength of a nation, whether in war or in peace, resides in its science. The future solutions of the most critical problems of society . . . lie in the applications of science. The western frontier that once challenged adventurous and imaginative youth exists no longer; the frontier of today and tomorrow is that of science."[33] To achieve this meant getting professional scientists directly involved in redesigning the educational system so that science teaching would be given the attention it deserved.

The problem, in Glass's view, was to end the isolation of science from humanistic studies and place it in the center of the curriculum. To do this would mean expanding the scope of science teaching beyond a narrow concern with technical facts and mathematical concepts. New courses had to be designed that would reach all students, not just the scientifically inclined. Also, nonscientific elements of the curriculum had to be rethought in a way that integrated them with the teaching of science. All courses, he said, must be revised to instill an enthusiasm for science during the child's formative years and to expose children of all ages to the liberating power of the inductive method and the scientific point of view. Every child must be exposed to the enlightened way of thinking and looking at the world that is characteristic of the professional scientist.

Glass's panegyric for science articulated the faith in trained intelligence that dominated the thinking of the scholars who participated in the science curriculum reform movement. His essay linking science to liberal education appeared in the same year as C. P. Snow's widely heralded lecture, "The Two Cultures and the Scientific Revolution," and it offered an antidote to Snow's worries about the deep cleavage between scientific and humanistic studies. Glass was convinced that the world would be a better place if more people thought like scientists. He spoke of the rising power and importance of the university in the conduct of human affairs and emphasized the increasing dependence of contemporary society on the development of trained intelligence, a view that was more extensively developed a few years later by Christopher Jencks and David Riesman in *The Academic Revolution*. Glass, like many of his colleagues, was convinced that good science education for everyone was the only hope for the survival of society as we know it, and he minced no words in his lecture in New Orleans: "Politically it has been demonstrated that a house divided against itself cannot stand. I affirm that it must also be true that a nation of a microscopically few scientists molding and altering people's lives, and a populace uncomprehending, superstitious, and resistant to the novel ideas of the scientist while blandly accepting the technological fruits of those very ideas, likewise cannot endure. Somehow, and soon, mankind must become truly scientific in spirit and in endeavor. Otherwise we face oligarchy, and eventual collapse of our form of civilization, our way of life."[34]

To the extent that it was articulated at all, Glass defined the social vision of the new reformers. Like John Dewey they saw the teaching of science and the scientific point of view as the way to train young minds to address the challenges of the modern world. Unlike the proponents of "life-adjustment" education they believed that the intellectual capacities of all students, regardless of ability or background, could be developed if they were properly taught by people who knew the subject, and who knew how to cultivate thinking processes in the young. With Arthur Bestor, they believed that it was possible to develop an intellectually disciplined citizenry and that knowing how to think, and "think painstakingly," is the only true protection of a free society. Most shared with Bentley Glass an enduring faith in the liberating power of the scientific point of view. It was within this heady academic environment that Man: A Course of Study was born.

· 2 ·

The Origins of MACOS

The story of Man: A Course of Study properly begins at Woods Hole in September 1959. Here, under the sponsorship of the National Academy of Sciences, thirty-four scholars and teachers from a dozen disciplines gathered to review what had been learned in the newly launched science curriculum projects.[1] Jerome Bruner chaired the ten-day gathering, and his summary report, entitled *The Process of Education,* established him as an international figure in educational reform. Within a few years this slim volume of less than a hundred pages, which set forth the central ideas of the new reformers, sold over 400,000 copies and was translated into twenty languages. The popularity of the book with educators both here and abroad demonstrated that the thinking of the science curriculum innovators enjoyed the respect of a very wide audience. Encouraged by this response, Bruner continued his involvement with the science curriculum reformers as a researcher and observer, and this participation led in time to his decision in 1964 to try his own hand at curriculum development. It is to Woods Hole, therefore, that we must look for the intellectual and pedagogical foundations of MACOS.

On Learning and Thinking

The Woods Hole Conference was primarily a gathering of psychologists and research scientists who had come together, Bruner reported, "to examine the fundamental processes involved in imparting to young students a sense of the substance and method of science."[2] Many of the participants, including Edward Begle, Francis Friedman, and Bentley Glass, were already involved in course development, and they assembled to talk about how their shared experience might lead to the formulation of a theory of in-

33

struction useful to others engaged in curriculum making. The conference was divided into five work groups that considered the following topics: sequencing, teaching apparatus, motivation, cognitive processes, and the role of intuition. Each work group prepared a lengthy report from which Bruner derived his summarizing synthesis.

Perhaps the most widely discussed idea that came out of the Woods Hole Conference was what Bruner called "the importance of structure." If learning is to serve us beyond whatever pleasure it may give, he wrote, it should make future learning easier. The value of this "transfer of training," to use the language of the psychologist, is relatively obvious in the case of basic skills like knowing the alphabet or mastering the multiplication table. But it is equally true, said Bruner, for more abstract learning, such as grasping the conceptual framework of a particular discipline. According to the Woods Hole doctrine, if the student can comprehend the fundamental principles and organizing questions that give structure to a field of study, he or she can assimilate new knowledge in that field much more easily. "This type of transfer," said Bruner, "is at the heart of the educational process—the continual broadening and deepening of knowledge in terms of basic and general ideas."[3]

Bruner saw mastery of structure as the cornerstone of sound intellectual development. Knowing the structure of a discipline, he said, makes the subject more comprehensible because it permits the learner to think about facts in an organized way and provides a conceptual vocabulary for interpreting them. Moreover, research on human memory, together with commonsense experience, tells us that isolated facts are quickly forgotten unless they are placed within a comprehensible pattern. Physicists remember formulas, not the details of specific distances and times. Furthermore, structure makes future learning easier by providing a model for thinking about instances of a given case; it gives us a framework within which to place new information. Far from being confined to the natural sciences, structural thinking is equally important in the social sciences, for it offers a way of organizing highly complex information about human behavior patterns, such as the ideological differences between communism and democracy or the recurring pattern of revolution in human society. Beyond this, the organizing ideas of a particular discipline can help to create a dialogue between those who work at the cutting edge of a particular discipline and those who work with children in ordinary classrooms. Such interaction between scholars and teachers may be especially important, Bruner suggested, in an era when the growth of knowledge is rapid and factual information is often quickly rendered obsolete.

Not everyone at Woods Hole shared Bruner's enthusiasm for the importance of structure. Some feared that too much emphasis on conceptual learning could lead to a glib recitation of organizing ideas, with little knowledge of the factual context from which these general notions had been derived. Others wanted to know the age at which young children could actually grasp the organizing concepts of a particular discipline. Jerrold Zacharias, who had collaborated with Bruner in planning the conference, was particularly critical of the structural hypothesis. Recalling Bruner's account of the Woods Hole discussions many years later, he remarked, "Structure gives me the pip when you apply it to education. Jerry makes such a point that the way to remember something is to understand its structure; that's the way Jerry remembers, but that may not capture the interest of the kid."[4] In an unpublished paper written in 1965, Zacharias expressed deep reservations about Bruner's structural hypothesis. He pointed out that structures like Newton's Laws of Motion and Gravitation may be what science appears to be to the layman, but they are not what science is all about at the "cutting edge." "I have had the great good luck," he said, "to have lived through and participated in some of the great revolutions in physics, including the evolution of the great structure called quantum mechanics. But scientists are usually having their greatest sport when the structure is fuzzy, ambiguous, inadequate, or possibly just plain wrong."[5]

For Zacharias, a more important consideration for teachers was another topic of the conference, intuitive thinking, or, in his colorful phrase, "rummaging around in the intellectual attic."[6] Intuitive thinking is difficult to describe and is perhaps best understood by contrasting it with analytic thinking. Analytic thinking proceeds in carefully defined steps, can usually be described accurately to another individual, and normally involves the use of logic, deductive reasoning, or other self-conscious processes. Intuitive thinking, on the other hand, proceeds in a more casual, less organized way. The processes are less self-conscious and are based on viewing a problem as a whole. Intuitive thinkers often arrive at an answer with little awareness of how they got there. Scientists use this type of thinking when working in unexplored terrain, sometimes employing physical models to aid in visualizing relationships, just as Watson and Crick used cardboard cutouts in their search for the structure of the DNA molecule.[7] Zacharias worked this way in his own research and believed that students could be taught to approach problems intuitively. He argued that student learning should proceed from the concrete to the abstract, not the other way around, and that intuitive thinking served that objective best.

In *The Process of Education* Bruner devoted a chapter to a discussion of his views on intuitive and analytic thinking. He acknowledged the importance of intuition in scientific discovery but worried about the difficulty of cultivating intuitive thinking in the classroom. While noting the "warm praise" that scientists pour on colleagues who possess this capacity, he pointed out that it would require a sensitive and extremely knowledgeable teacher to distinguish an intuitive mistake from a stupid mistake, and to know how to encourage such thinking intelligently. He suggested that this is a great deal to ask of a secondary school teacher, and he warned that it might be the most gifted students who would suffer in a program designed to encourage intuitive thinking if it were improperly managed. "Along with any program for developing methods of cultivating and measuring the occurrence of intuitive thinking," he wrote, "there must go some practical consideration of the classroom problems and the limitations on our capacity for encouraging such skills in our students."[8]

Yet the original conference working papers reveal that most of the scholars at Woods Hole sought through their reforms to cultivate a whole spectrum of thinking styles, from logic and rational thought to intuition and creativity. All the participants seemed to agree that serious academic inquiry was characterized by a diversity of cognitive processes. A mathematician, for example, may use intuitive thinking to arrive at a solution and then check the validity of his findings through analytical methods, while a historian is likely to interpret contemporary events and trends through reasoning by analogy to the past. Similarly, scientists often construct physical models to aid their understanding of the properties of microscopic organisms or to study the laws of physics. Some thought that intuition functions best in the "hard" sciences, where analytical methods are already well worked out, but most agreed that diversity of thinking should be cultivated in all fields and that teachers should be encouraged to learn more about the range of cognitive processes involved in learning and thinking.

The concern with cognition at Woods Hole reflected the fact that the group was heavily weighted with psychologists. Ten were present, including George Miller and Richard Alpert of Harvard, Donald Taylor of Yale, Robert Gagne of Princeton, Lee Cronbach of the University of Illinois, and Piaget's colleague, Barbel Inhelder, of the Institut Rousseau in Geneva. Many of these scholars were engaged in studies of cognitive development that had significant implications for education. Bruner and two colleagues had just published a ground-breaking work entitled *A Study of Thinking,* and George Miller had recently written a very provocative paper entitled "The Magical Number Seven, Plus or Minus Two," in which he asserted that a normal human mind appears to reach a limit in its ability to remember or discriminate at about seven discrete items.[9] Some of these studies raised questions about traditional methods of teaching and suggested the need for a renewed investigation of the most effective ways to stimulate cognitive growth in the young. As one conference paper put it, "In teaching or in deciding what to learn, there is a question of getting hold of that minimum array of information that can be structured in such a way as to yield the largest range of reliable inferences."[10] If retention is as limited as George Miller's research suggests, said Bruner, we must be certain to fill those seven slots with gold.

Developmental Considerations

How the mind works was not the only psychological issue discussed at Woods Hole. Of equal concern were questions about growth, readiness, and the means of instruction. How early can a child be taught to think in a scholarly way? What are the optimum sequences for learning? Are there certain critical periods in a child's life when particular mental operations can be taught most easily? What are the limits of children's intellectual capacities? These questions were thoroughly explored and debated; some participants went so far as to argue that with proper teaching there was almost no limit to what could be taught to a child. Indeed, one of the most widely quoted statements to emerge from Woods Hole was Bruner's bold assertion: "We begin with the hypothesis that any subject can be taught effectively in some intellectually honest form to any child at any stage of development."[11]

One member set out to prove that children could be taught to think like professional academics. David Page, a brilliant teacher of mathematics who had participated in the Illinois Math project, dazzled the conference one afternoon with a live demonstration of how a group of fifth-graders could grasp the theory of functions. The performance amazed Page's audience and showed how far young minds could be pushed by a skillful teacher. Page, through his teaching experience with Illinois Math, had come to believe in the nearly unlimited intellectual capacity of children. "As far as I am concerned," he said, "young children learn about anything faster than adults do if it can be given to them in terms they understand." This, he pointed out, "turns out to involve knowing the mathematics oneself, and the better one knows it, the better it can be taught."[12] As Bruner noted, however, Page wisely avoided any attempt to explain to his class what the theory of functions was, even though their intuitive grasp of the material was plainly evident.

Barbel Inhelder expressed a more conservative view of children's intellectual capacities. When asked to comment on how early intellectual development could be pushed more rapidly, she outlined the now well-known Piagetian position regarding the evolution of mental growth from preoperational thought to concrete operations to the formal reasoning processes that emerge in early adolescence. She suggested that the most effective way to teach abstract ideas to young children is to let them discover those ideas from carefully prepared concrete experiences. She described Piaget's famous experiment illustrating how children somewhere between the ages of five and seven discover the principle of invariance by noting that water poured from a tall, thin beaker into a short, fat beaker is unchanged in quantity despite its altered appearance. Younger children are incapable of comprehending this continuity. Children's thinking, she pointed out, proceeds from concrete levels of understanding to increasingly abstract ways of knowing as they grow older. This leads, in time, to the mental mobility we associate with the reversible operations of mathematics and logic. Yet there are limits to a child's ability to grasp these matters at an early age.[13]

Pedagogical Implications

What did these psychological considerations imply for curriculum making? The consensus at Woods Hole seemed to be that a curriculum must take seriously the age-specific intellectual limitations of the child while at the same time striving to stimulate higher levels of cognitive functioning. Children at the level of concrete operations, for example, should not be expected to go beyond an intuitive grasp of abstract ideas, but such ideas should be presented concretely, through physical experiences that enable them to induce the laws of physics or mathematics or even social science by direct interaction with their physical and social environments. As Bruner explained in the original draft of his report, "It can be demonstrated that fifth grade children can play mathematical games that are premised on rules derived from very highly advanced mathematics. Indeed, they can discover these rules inductively and learn how to work with them. They will flounder, however, *if one attempts to force upon them a formal, mathematical description of what they have been doing*" (emphasis in the original).[14]

The ideal educational experience, as it became articulated at Woods Hole, is one that respects the developmental level of the child but anticipates future stages of growth and tries to prepare for them. Educational materials should be designed to match the child's level of cognitive development, but at the same time they should challenge the child to reach for the next higher stage of intellectual activity. The curriculum, in turn, should be constructed to take into account the organizing principles that give structure to the subject matter, while also encouraging students to exercise their intuition and imagination. Inductive rather than didactic approaches are best suited to these objectives. Every discipline has its own way of structuring knowledge, and this order should be implicit in the way the educational materials and teaching strategies are assembled. In each case the curriculum developer should strive for a marriage between the structure of the discipline and the psychology of the child. A curriculum so designed, said one conference paper, is "better able to concentrate on essentials and thus penetrate to the heart of the subject."[15]

The Missing Issue

So much for cognition, development, and pedagogy. What is strikingly absent from the Woods Hole discussions is an examination of the social and political implications of the proposed reforms. Toward the end of *The Process of Education* Bruner briefly suggests that there might be some "perils of success" if this academic vision for education were to become widely adopted. Here he raises the possibility that the new curricula could foster the growth of a meritocracy of the intellectually gifted with correspondingly negative consequences for slower students. In such a system, he says, there may be a tendency to push the brighter students ahead, especially those who show early promise in scientific and technical fields, and these students, in turn, may be favored for better future educational opportunities and, ultimately, for jobs. What would this mean for those left behind? "The late bloomer, the early rebel, the child from an educationally indifferent home—all of them, in a full-scale meritocracy, become victims of an often senseless irreversibility of decision."[16]

These are sobering words, and they suggest that the academics who gathered at Woods Hole envisioned a process of education that favored the development of the intellectually gifted—a product "fashioned in their own image." Such a goal was understandable given the mood of the times. The group met, after all, in an era when Soviet accomplishments in space were outstripping those of the United States, and many feared that the whole system of national defense could be in jeopardy if the United States fell behind the USSR in the knowledge race. President Eisenhower had just appointed the nation's first full-time science advisor, and the general public was becoming increasingly aware that scholarship was a resource essential to national well-being. Academics from every discipline were jetting to Washington in growing numbers to advise legislators and bureaucrats about how to manage a society of increasing technical complexity. So it is hardly surprising that these deliberations about the improvement of the American educational system stressed the cultivation of intellect.

Yet the failure of the *Sputnik*-inspired reformers to articulate in a broader way the social implications of their work may have flawed the science curriculum reform movement from the start. With the growing success of the American space program, the rhetoric of "national defense" became an increasingly flimsy rationale for educational change, yet no one emerged to articulate an alternative vision for educational reform in the post-*Sputnik* era. As the movement matured and funding became more difficult to find, the scholars who launched the new programs retreated to their research laboratories, and few of them found time to wrestle with the problems of training, logistics, and public relations faced by teachers and local school officials who were left to implement the new reforms. The innovators of this period knew little about the history of schooling in the United States and were ill-equipped to address the broader social implications of their work. They failed to understand that for most Americans the schoolhouse is not just a laboratory for training the mind; it is the place where the social outlook of the next generation is formed. Discussions of schooling, therefore, cannot avoid considering the sort of people the schools should produce. Such deliberations go beyond questions of cognitive development. They require an explicit choice of values. Unfortunately, at Woods Hole these matters never entered the discussion.

The Endicott House Conference

During the Kennedy administration Jerrold Zacharias chaired the education panel of the President's Science Advisory Committee (PSAC), and in this role he sponsored dozens of meetings to explore curriculum and teaching issues. Gathering monthly for two-day sessions during the academic year 1962–63, the panel invited nationally known educational theorists and practitioners to present their work and express their views on educational reform. These were lively sessions that often produced stormy debates. Zacharias was an outspoken and sometimes hostile critic of approaches to learning that he disliked: on at least one occasion, according to an eyewitness report, he put his fingers in his ears to block out the presentation of his guest.[17] He was openly contemptuous of educational methods that in his opinion would fail to stimulate the intellectual curiosity of the young, and some of the nation's best-known educators left those meetings shaken by the encounter.

Zacharias approached the task of educational reform with the same vigor and sense of urgency he had dedicated to the Manhattan Project many years before. His panel sponsored numerous educational conferences, including a two-week meeting on African education at M.I.T., a two-week seminar on music education at Yale, a two-week seminar entitled "Learning about Learning" at Harvard, a two-week seminar on education for the deprived and segregated, a special meeting on nongraded schools, and several meetings on teacher education held in various locations around the country. He also organized what he called "summer studies." These informal gatherings of the brightest and most gifted people he could find in a particular field were designed to break down established conventions about how to instruct the young and to get people to know each other well enough so that they might create something new together. The process typically required at least two weeks and usually took place in an isolated location where participants were cut off from their usual responsibilities and thus had no choice but to deal with the issue at hand. One favorite place for these meetings was Endicott House in Dedham, Massachusetts, the M.I.T.-owned former estate of a wealthy shoe manufacturer. Here, in a lovely rural setting far from laboratories and telephones, Zacharias sequestered his guests and attempted to extract from them their best thinking about how to improve education. Sometimes he found that even two weeks of cloistered deliberation failed to produce a useful result. Recalling the varied success of these meetings, he quipped, "Summer studies and some are not."

Of the many such meetings sponsored by the PSAC panel, one of the most unusual was a two-week seminar on the social studies and humanities hosted by Educational Services, Incorporated and the American Council of Learned Societies (ACLS) at Endicott House in June 1962. Forty-seven scholars and teachers representing a broad spectrum of social and humanistic disciplines gathered to talk about how to fix social studies and humanities teaching in the elementary and secondary schools. The participants included William Bunge, a geographer, Gerald Else, a classicist, Robert Feldmesser, a sociologist, Mark Harris, a writer, Herbert Heaton, a historian, Allan Holmberg, an anthropologist, Norton Long, a political scientist, Saul Menlovitz, a lawyer, Elting Morison, a historian, Franklin Patterson, a political scientist, Leften Stavrianos, a historian, Joshua Taylor, an art historian, Lewis Wagner, an economist and William Warntz, a geographer. Jerome Bruner and Jerrold Zacharias were also present, together with Francis Keppel, then dean of Harvard's Graduate School of Education, and Frederick Burkhardt, president of the ACLS.

By all accounts it was a spirited occasion. According to the conference report, a dispute broke out almost immediately between the historians and the social scientists. Robert Feldmesser began the debate by laying the blame for the poor state of social science teaching at the feet of the historians. "We shall make no progress in transforming the social studies into social science," said Feldmesser, "until we slaughter the sacred cow of history."[18] Arguing that history teaching had so dominated the curriculum there was no room for a scientific approach to the study of human behavior, he proposed the inclusion of social science in the curriculum at all levels, even if this meant a drastic reduction in the amount of history that could be taught. Feldmesser maintained that children from the earliest years should be introduced to the methodology and conceptual structure of the various social sciences so that they could develop a critical and questioning attitude about the social world equivalent to the attitude of mind that characterizes students of the natural sciences. The teaching of history, he said, had failed to serve that function.

The historians present were offended by Feldmesser's remarks, and the conference soon disintegrated into a shouting match between the disciplines. For Zacharias, this battle between the social scientists and the historians was an upsetting turn of events. He had been accustomed to working within the more intellectually compatible disciplines of the natural sciences, where there had been very little disagreement about content. Discussions with the scientists had centered on issues of sequencing and the exploration of innovative methods for engaging the young in the excitement of science, not on subject matter, and Zacharias was totally unprepared for the level of acrimony expressed by the social scientists and historians about what to teach. Elting Morison, who was teaching history at M.I.T. at the time, remembers Zacharias's frustration over what he saw: "That conference . . . was an experience for Zack . . . Here there was this bunch of highly verbal types, most of them from universities, most of them without a clue of what was happening in the schools . . . and most of them loathing each other's fields . . . and everybody fell into defensive postures and forlorn postures, and sad postures, and Zack had never seen anything like this—the humanities at bay."[19]

Edwin Fenton, a fledgling history professor at Carnegie-Mellon University who was doing curriculum development in the Pittsburgh schools, was one of the few historians who agreed with Feldmesser. "I thought much of what Feldmesser said made a lot of sense," recalls Fenton. "I think history has far too long dominated the curriculum of the secondary schools, and if you could get people to assess [that role], . . . maybe by threatening that role, it would be good for society."[20] Fenton shared the view of many teachers that students needed a fresh way of looking at the social world, one that would enable them to think critically about social issues and to examine their own society from the perspective of other societies and other value systems. He also saw the merit of interdisciplinary studies, which would provide students with more than one way of conceptualizing events in the social world. Only by challenging the dominance of history in the curriculum, he believed, could this new perspective be achieved.

Zacharias asked Morison, whose work at M.I.T. had brought him into close contact with scholars from many disciplines, to attempt to bring about a consensus within the meeting. After discussing the problem with Bruner, Morison addressed the assembled scholars, observing that "the intellectual processes in every discipline are very much the same" and suggesting that the group take advantage of those similarities. All fields, he said, examine data and derive conceptions from them, and in this respect both historians and social scientists employ a similar methodology. A new approach to social studies, he argued, should therefore strive to bring about a marriage of the disciplines. "I remember saying," recalls Morison, "that I thought you could write most of the history of the United States by a careful investigation of how the battleship *Kentucky* was built in 1900. And this is just the kind of remark that Zack loves, of course."[21] Morison's appeal for an integration of the disciplines around a single issue or topic helped to put the argument between the historians and social scientists to rest. In describing a proposed course on early American history, the conference report reflected the new consensus: "It was deemed not only feasible but absolutely necessary that the resources of every discipline, including geography, anthropology, psychology, sociology, art, music, literature, and the classics be brought to bear in a carefully integrated and thoroughly inter-disciplinary manner."[22]

One of the results of this effort to integrate the disciplines was a proposal that came to be called "post-holing." This approach maintained that it was better for students to concentrate on a single period of history, and to study it in depth, than to sweep through many centuries in a superficial way. This would allow time for students to develop an interdisciplinary perspective. By concentrating on the study of Athens in the fifth century B.C., for example, students could get to know the culture in great detail, going beyond the usual history of politics and warfare to consider the nature and influence of the environment, the functioning of the economy, the place of science and technology, the role of literature, religion, and the arts, and the intricacies of social and family life. This immersion in a single historical period would enable students to see interrelationships and infer general principles about the nature of society that could be applied when they studied other periods of history. Approaching the material in this way not only permitted perspectives from the various disciplines to be brought together in a single course, but it created an environment for teaching in which there were no "right" answers, and where the data supported multiple interpretations of complex events. As with the natural sciences, good answers would be answers that were supported by convincing evidence.

This consensus about *how to teach* helped the social scientists to see that their objections to history were really criticisms of how history was typically taught. It was the history that stressed "coverage" and memorization of long lists of unrelated facts rather than the history that fostered debate and interpretation that troubled the nonhistorians most. Leften Stavrianos had unwittingly provided these critics with a perfect target. Early in the meeting he had distributed copies of his recently published high school text *A Global History of Man,* a tightly organized survey of the entire sweep of human civilization from prehistoric man to the space age. The book evoked little enthusiasm. Indeed, some regarded the Stavrianos text as an excellent example of how not to teach social studies. Zacharias recalled the reaction: "What a clamor! We just raised hell with that poor thing because it was a collection of bits— everything—all of history, all of mankind. You know, Attila the Hun, dates, did this, and this—and [gesturing] that much print! You turn that loose in a school and you've got nothing."[23]

Agreement thus centered on matters of pedagogy. All shared the view that a "predigested" approach to the transmission of knowledge, in which data are presented in summary form—however economical such an approach might appear—was intellectually and pedagogically wrong. What the Endicott House participants proposed was an in-depth study of the social sciences and humanities that not only engaged students in source material and the processes of scholarship but also exposed them to the uncertainty and speculation that go along with true scientific investigation. A good example of this method was a simulated archaeological dig, where students could uncover the raw artifacts from which an archaeologist extrapolates theories about human origins and behavior. A version of this approach was a proposed "Stones and Bones" unit for the elementary grades in which children would be given a large box containing replicas of human-looking bones and chipped and broken rocks; they would then be asked to assemble the bones in meaningful patterns, to figure out why the rocks are shaped the way they are, and to speculate about how they might have been used by early man. The children would eventually discover fragments of three skeletons, one humanoid, the other two more apelike, and, having pieced them together and examined their differences, they would hypothesize about what structures and behaviors might have distinguished early humans from other primates. By examining the stones and discussing their probable function, students could speculate on the place of early tool use in the course of human evolution. As important as the materials provided would be the "missing information," the gaps in the data intended to encourage children to develop theories on their own. Following prolonged exposure to these artifacts and exercises, students would then examine current evolutionary theory.

As at Woods Hole, there was much talk at Endicott House about "habits of mind." While the interdisciplinary "post-hole" approach seemed most appropriate for the elementary and junior high school levels, the group felt that early in high school students should be exposed to the intellectual structure underlying each of the social sciences. They should understand, for example, the rules of evidence that apply to the analysis of written documents in history, the meaning sociologists give to terms like *role* and *norm,* and how archaeologists make controlled extrapolations from their materials. This was not a proposal to teach the disciplines per se, but rather the suggestion that students become more explicitly aware that scholars in different fields can view a particular period in history, or a contemporary social event, quite differently. The group also wanted students to appreciate the relativistic and speculative nature of academic knowledge, that what we regard as "true" is always changing and that intellectual inquiry is the continuous search for more powerful modes of explanation. Some proposed the development of cross-disciplinary materials so that perspectives from several of the social sciences could be presented in a single course.

The influence of Bruner's *The Process of Education* is evident in these discussions. While the scholars at Endicott House argued about the relative importance of their separate disciplines, they shared the conviction of their predecessors at Woods Hole that understanding ideas, not assimilating facts, was the prime objective of learning. Furthermore, they agreed upon methodology. A good deal was said about the importance of getting students doing things, and, in particular, having them work with original sources—artifacts, documents, maps, diaries, and so forth—much the way children manipulate physical materials in a science laboratory. Students should be asked to figure things out for themselves, to form hypotheses, to speculate, to derive conclusions from a limited array of data, to, as Bruner put it, "go beyond the information given." While the "Stones and Bones" unit was one example of this approach, others suggested that junior high school children could learn American colonial history in a similar way using the instruments, written documents, and knowledge available in the seventeenth century to sail an imaginary ship from England to America, to "prove" that the Earth is round, or to evolve a personal theory of the origins of the American Revolution.

Although there was much talk about the importance of scholarship, everyone felt that a great effort must be made to avoid academic jargon and complex terminology. Teaching should always begin by providing students with the raw materials from which new knowledge can be generated; formal analysis should follow only after those materials have been thoroughly assimilated and then only at a level appropriate to the age of the child. At one point Bruner dramatized the argument for this inductive methodology by going to the blackboard and writing the words *Action, Imagery,* and *Notation.* Children, he said, learn first by doing something and then form images and ideas from their actions, but only later does this learning take the form of "notation," that is, abstract, symbolic language. Implicit in his argument, which he bolstered with findings from research on children's thinking processes, was the proposition that the early imposition of formal language on a child's intuitive grasp of an idea is what had caused the failure of past efforts to teach abstract ideas to young children. Inductive methodology, on the other hand, could open the way to teaching concepts currently reserved for college students to much younger children. Children's minds, said Bruner, are not qualitatively different from the minds of adults; they simply lack the experiences and the associated mental imagery that support adult levels of thought.

Thus, the conference resolved the war between the disciplines by uniting behind a theory of pedagogy. Children should be immersed in concrete materials that are rich in imagery and possess the power to stir emotions and stimulate thought. Wherever possible these should be the same materials that scholars use and should be provided in sufficient richness and depth to enable children to explore their own questions about the social and cultural environment the materials portray. This process of inquiry, driven by the natural curiosity of the child, should gradually lead to deeper levels of understanding, for the mind of the child, like the mind of the adult, is energized by an innate desire to know and understand. As the child's mind grows and matures in an environment designed for conceptual learning, guided by a teacher who is attuned to how children's thought processes evolve, the child will develop increased capacities for formal thought and more sophisticated levels of understanding. The earlier controversy about which disciplines were best suited for fostering conceptual learning yielded to the view that exposing a child in depth to the raw materials of scholarship, regardless of the field, provided the best environment for stimulating the growth of young minds.

A word more needs to be said about Bruner's emphasis on imagery. If the transition from raw data to formal thought involves the creation of images in a child's head, then many of the early steps in the introduction to formalism should be handled through the use of visual materials, including films. Discussion at the conference centered on how film could be used "to add further vividness, and to [bring to the classroom] . . . learned and exciting people who could set an intellectual tone for all of the studying and learning."[24] Some thought that students could be introduced to the romance of the academic disciplines by watching specialists at work on the screen—archeologists digging up ancient artifacts, anthropologists studying preliterate peoples, historians uncovering ancient records, and so forth. The idea here was to try to give students a sense of the speculative quality of scholarship and to expose them to the way in which scholars derive inferences from often fragmentary evidence. Film, they thought, was the best medium to establish communication between scholar and student, for it could bring remote material to the classroom in a vivid form, and it could make the academic specialist more human by showing him "in his shirtsleeves." Visual information of this kind was thought to be indispensable for teaching the "New Social Studies," and almost every proposal at Endicott House suggested the use of film in some form.

The final days of the conference were given over to a series of presentations by various work groups, which had been meeting regularly during the two weeks to explore how the ideas discussed could be translated into specific curriculum proposals. The suggestions ranged from new approaches to the teaching of the classics, to a totally revised course on American studies at the eighth-grade level, to plans for the development of an interdisciplinary behavioral science course for the eleventh grade. Evans Clinchy, the ESI staffer who had coordinated the conference, reported on the deliberations of Group A, which had devised an ambitious plan for a six-year elementary school sequence called "The Human Past." The proposal envisioned the creation of six interrelated year-long courses that would take a child from the study of man's earliest origins to the dawn of modern history. The sequence began with activities designed to orient students to the concepts of "space" and "time," using aerial maps, homemade hourglasses, NASA photographs, and the like. This introduction was to be followed by a series of "post-hole" units selected to illustrate important moments in human social evolution. In the second grade students were to examine excavations in the caves of Choukoutien, using the "Stones and Bones" approach, and contrast those findings with the study of present-day hunter-gatherers, such as the Bushmen of the Kalahari, with particular emphasis on language and tool use. In grade three students would move on to study the remains of ancient Jericho and contrast that civilization with the culture of the Hopi Indian. In each case, children would be exposed to hard evidence, including bone fragments, remnants of houses, scraps of pottery that could be fitted together, early tools, art work, and the remains of the written record. Where possible, ancient examples would be played off against modern analogues. Fourth graders would concentrate on the emergence of urbanization by comparing the Sumerian city of Ur with a contrast case drawn from the later civilization of the Akkadians. When published, "hands-on" materials would be paramount, supplemented by films, readings, and games.

In grade five students would turn to a comparison of Minoan Crete and fifth-century Athens in an effort to "introduce the children to the feel, the sights, the sounds, smells, taste, thoughts and emotions of the Greek world, to show how this world came about, [and] how it differs from our own yet how much it has affected what we are today."[25] Here again the emphasis would be on using source materials and on comparing and contrasting civilizations in order to bring historical perspective to the child's understanding of the contemporary world. The sequence would end in the sixth grade with a panoramic sweep of several civilizations that came into contact with each other during the European voyages of discovery and exploration. The course would conclude with an examination of what happens when a powerful culture, Renaissance Europe in this case, collides with a group of weaker ancient civilizations such as the Mayas, the Incas, and the Aztecs. Christopher Columbus would be looked at as a symbol of this historic confrontation of cultures and as one of the founding fathers of our contemporary world.

Clinchy's presentation captured the imagination of the participants. Martin Mayer, who was writing a book about the teaching of social studies at the time, was captivated by the report from Group A, and later described the presentation as "far and away the most interesting moment" at Endicott House: "Not everything in such a sequence would work; . . . not everything in the proposal is historically or anthropologically valid; and many other patterns of elementary instruction can be imagined. But the scholars assembled at Endicott House felt their hearts lift as the sequence of these units was described in a brisk, matter-of-fact manner by Evans Clinchy; surely teachers and children should have a chance to share this excitement, if they can."[26] Clinchy, who later coordinated the early development of the project, also recalls the enthusiasm for Group A's presentation: "They all applauded at the end—and [it] gave them the feeling that maybe the whole two weeks had not been wasted. It was really on the basis of that—the enthusiasm engendered around the elementary [proposal]—that everybody [felt]: Hell, let's go on and keep trying to do something."[27]

The discussions might have concluded on this note of consensus were it not for one dissenter, a young Freudian psychologist from Brandeis named Richard Jones, who had been invited to the meeting by Feldmesser. At a time when few educators had heard of the term "affective domain," Jones worried about the emotional development of children. Following the Clinchy presentation (which Jones had helped to prepare), Jones delivered a minority report urging the group to consider the psychological impact of such materials. As he noted, "Now we have young children occupying themselves under our guidance with bones, teeth, weapons, dirt, human refuse, etc. There are no more honest materials, we feel, with which to introduce children to the disciplined study of the human past. This said, however, we can safely . . . [predict] . . . that the children will be called upon to manage highly emotionally charged images in their attempts to master these materials and the inferences to be drawn from them."[28] Jones went on to suggest that the emotions stirred by the materials created educational opportunities to be explored, not obstacles to be avoided, and that teachers should be trained to deal constructively with these emotional responses in order to deepen the child's understanding of the subject. "The alternative," said Jones, "is to expect the child to play ostrich with the very processes of imagery around which we also expect him to cultivate controlled, imaginative habits of mind."[29]

Jones's concern with emotional development was not happily received. The professors gathered at Endicott House cheerfully debated the intellectual merits of their various disciplines, but they were loathe to consider the affective consequences of social science inquiry on the young. Indeed, some were even openly hostile to the suggestion that there may be some emotional risks in the course of study proposed, and at least one participant, probably Jerrold Zacharias, urged the group to be "man enough" to disregard Jones's "psychophantasms," which, he said, only illustrated the narrowness of vision that he had come to expect from psychiatrists. "Unless they can render their data into indices of pathology and sickness," he charged, "they are helpless before it."[30]

Thus chastised, Jones appealed to Bruner, who was scheduled to speak the following day, to support his case for considering children's emotional reactions to the materials. Knowing his eloquence in addressing the needs of the heart as well as the head, Jones had reason to hope that Bruner would support his appeal for reaching the "whole child." But it was not to be. According to Jones, Bruner gave a "first-rate Piagetian talk" about the enactive, iconic, and symbolic modes of knowing, and he charmed the group with suggestions about how the latest findings in psychological research could be applied to the business of teaching, but he refused to reopen the controversy of the previous day.

So ended the deliberations at Endicott House. Given the complexity of the subject, the diversity of the participants, and the shortness of time, it was an unusually productive meeting. For the most part, the members avoided the temptation to lobby for their particular disciplines and turned their energies to the articulation of a common pedagogical style. If they failed to rise to Jones's challenge to worry about the emotional growth of the young, they responded readily to Bruner's suggestion that children should be allowed to approach a subject intuitively and inductively, beginning with concrete experiences, and only later, after much exposure to the data, be presented with the conceptual abstractions that organize that information. And the discussions were filled with the same healthy self-doubt that prevailed at Woods Hole. Although largely uninformed about earlier attempts at school reform, the scholars who assembled at Endicott House were candid about their ignorance of the schools and approached their proposals in a skeptical and experimental frame of mind. They expected their ideas and materials to undergo rigorous classroom testing and continuous modification before they would emerge as effective instruments of instruction. They knew that the meeting had, at best, produced only a few rough suggestions about where a new approach to social studies education might begin. It was not a blueprint for reform.

The Endicott House Conference generated mixed reactions among the school people who attended. Charles Keller, a historian who directed the John Hay Fellows Program, which gave scholarships for advanced graduate work to promising social science teachers, was offended by the attack on history. Keller had spent years crisscrossing the country in search of good history teachers, and he was by far the most knowledgeable person at the meeting regarding the current status of social science teaching in the country. He was upset that few of the participants, except Fenton, Wayne Altree of Newton, and Henry Bragdon of Exeter, had any understanding of the innovations in history teaching that had already been achieved, and according to Fenton, he "was so angry at Bob Feldmesser that he heard nothing else that happened through the entire convention."[31] Keller saw the Endicott House discussions as an intrusion of scholars upon a domain they did not understand. His lack of enthusiasm was costly for those who sought to build on the results of the conference, since his views carried considerable weight with the social studies profession.

On the other hand, Wayne Altree, who, next to Bragdon, was the most experienced classroom teacher at the conference, was warmly enthusiastic about the Endicott House discussions. Altree was head of the social studies department in the Newton public schools and a gifted teacher, and he brought to the conference a seasoned skepticism about the intrusion of scholars into school matters. Some years before he had observed a Ford Foundation conference in Oregon at which a group of nationally known academics attempted to prescribe educational reforms for the Portland public schools. Like Keller, Altree was concerned about the arrogance of academics and highly critical of their behavior at the Portland gathering. "It was just exactly what you would expect if a bunch of incensed, Bestor-like scholars got together and raked over the school curriculum of a large metropolitan center. [They] thought, 'This is really simple stuff. All these people need is to pull up their socks and teach good discipline-based courses.'"[32] But Altree was impressed with what he heard at Endicott House, and many years later he vividly recalled the experience:

To me it was like Paul on the road to Damascus. For the first time I began to see the possibility of going to kids in a fairly mature way and talking about the seriousness of what went on in the classroom—not pursuing my own little hobbies, not giving a course I worked up over the summer because I read a book or something—or the American Problems course where the kids say, "Oh no, not another problem!" Serious scholars never talked about the lower schools . . . And so school people had no image of the curriculum as a coherent, articulated system of ideas that accumulated . . . And there was no interdisciplinary consideration. There was no thought that we could actually teach the kids how to use their minds. There was no inquiry, no discovery, just information gathering, and it was all organized in terms of solving these goddamned problems. It was as obsolescent as *now*. Nothing is more obsolescent than *now*.

[The conference] communicated to me a vision of what a curriculum could be as a continuous enterprise from the first grade until you got out of graduate school. It was a fresh idea . . . that maybe the process of . . . inquiry was more important than the current data that we were trying to get across. [That] there were systematic ways of construing experience. Also, there was a tremendous sense of things going on in the social sciences that the schools were unaware of. This whole business of the interdisciplinary thing was new, that there was an organic way to marry the disciplines other than the crude way in the schools where you were studying the American Revolution and you sang Revolutionary songs or something like that. You just went around parasitically trying to get materials from other fields. The culture concept was absolutely absent. So this whole business about the interdisciplinary approach, and discovery, and the fruits of scholarly research that had not been available in the schools, that was good to me. The "anthropological" approach was terribly important.[33]

Altree's comments nicely summarize the important elements that defined ESI's approach to teaching the social studies: the marriage of the disciplines, the importance of fresh scholarly perspectives taken from current research, the "post-holing" approach that immerses students in original source material before asking them to assimilate concepts or arrive at conclusions, the use of the scientific method of investigation, and the introduction of the anthropological perspective to the study of human behavior. In time they were to become central features of MACOS as well as other social studies curricula produced by ESI. Later, Altree became not only a strong supporter of the ESI approach but also a major contributor to ESI's curriculum efforts.

The Gurus of Garden Street

As we have already seen, the Endicott House Conference was the brainchild of Jerrold Zacharias. The idea for the meeting had grown out of an earlier conference on African education at which Zacharias had noted the lack of clarity among American academics about what constituted effective social science education. Appalled by the "fuzzy-headed thinking" he found among American social studies educators, he decided to establish his own social studies program at ESI. In January 1962 he called together twenty scholars and teachers to make recommendations for such a program, and with the encouragement of Frederick Burkhardt, president of the American Council of Learned Societies, and support from a small Ford Foundation grant, he hosted an inaugural committee meeting, chaired by Burkhardt, on 14 February.[34] The Endicott House Conference was an outgrowth of this initial planning.

Following the Endicott House meeting Zacharias's newly formed

Social Studies group took up residence at 12 Garden Street on the edge of the Cambridge Common. During the summer of 1962, this house became the meeting place for several of the conference participants who wished to continue their discussions. Among the regular visitors were Jerome Bruner, Evans Clinchy, Elting Morison, Franklin Patterson, and Zacharias himself. By early fall a steering committee, chaired by Elting Morison, was meeting weekly to plan the ESI Social Studies Program. Soon Morison expanded the committee to include Charles Brown, superintendent of the Newton public schools, Gerald Else of the University of Michigan, a classicist, George Homans of Harvard, a sociologist, James Killian, president of M.I.T., Everett Mendelsohn of Harvard, a historian of science, and Douglas Oliver of Harvard, an anthropologist. During these early deliberations, the group was occasionally joined by Sherwood Washburn of Berkeley and Michael Coe of Yale, both anthropologists, and Robert Adams of the University of Chicago, an archaeologist.

In this illustrious and diverse assemblage there were lively debates about how the work should proceed but few doubts about ultimate goals. Some wished to fashion experimental materials immediately and test them out in the schools to see if the Endicott House ideas made any sense. Others wanted to prepare a comprehensive plan that set forth a rationale and conceptual framework for unit development at all grade levels. All agreed, however, that the final objective was to design an original sequence of courses that would encompass twelve years of schooling, and that this sequence should provide a challenging alternative to current social studies teaching. Joseph Featherstone, who served as recorder for the group, recalls the self-assurance of these scholars turned curriculum planners: "I think that all of Cambridge in those days had a sense that . . . the time had come when a lot of knowledge that had been worked up in disciplinary states was now going to affect social reality. I remember being amazed at the confident assumption of so many of these 'boffins' that the stuff would get into the schools."[35]

The first few months at Garden Street were spent clarifying objectives and preparing a proposal for submission to the Ford Foundation. The proposal reiterated and expanded upon the ideas that had been discussed at Endicott House. The course sequence should be both interdisciplinary and historical. It should provide a framework for comparing different societies and for examining the place of the individual within society. At the same time, it should give sufficient emphasis to historical process to convey an understanding of the forces that influence social change. And it should stress those features of the Western tradition that would help young people comprehend the philosophical roots of American democratic beliefs and institutions. Students should become aware that the main object of any social studies program is not to focus narrowly on a particular field of study, but rather to understand certain "basic generalizations" about what is universal in human behavior and what binds human beings to each other beyond the surface differences between cultures. As the proposal explained, "History, sociology, anthropology, may for convenience be separated into academic disciplines, but they all deal with a single thing: the behavior of men in society."[36]

With respect to the common psychological characteristics that are shared by all cultures, the proposal defined four organizing categories: tool use and technology, social organization, religion and art, and language. In defining these categories the program proposed to provide a conceptual framework that would permit and encourage cross-cultural comparisons and a model for understanding the structure of society. Study of the interplay between these features of society, which can be found in the most remote aboriginal cultures as well as in our highly technological contemporary civilization, was intended to reduce ethnocentrism and lead students to an appreciation of the common humanity that all human beings share.

Unlike the Woods Hole participants, the scholars who met on Garden Street chose to address the question of values. "We should like to have a hand in producing men as well as minds,"[37] they said, in the chauvinistic phrasing of the period. "We hope to engage each student in a search for himself," they boldly asserted, "to give him continuously a chance to exercise his own imagination, feelings, and judgment."[38] The purpose of social science teaching was not merely to teach students to think clearly, but also to engage their emotions in the great moral questions of our time. To guide the teacher in this exercise the group set out to develop a list of "gut assumptions" that might be derived from a careful study of history and the social sciences, statements that might help to define the moral lessons to be learned from these humanistic pursuits. This was obviously a risky enterprise, fraught with potential errors of omission and com-

mission, but to their credit the Garden Street group made a courageous effort to state their value positions. A few of these suffice to
illustrate the direction of their thinking:

> Man still has a very good chance, and by intelligent study of his
> own condition . . . he will measurably increase his chances.
> Men must act or have action forced upon them.
> Stay loose. The hardest thing in the world is to act "without
> attachment to results," but do your best to cultivate it.
> There is nothing that is good across the board, no value to be
> maximized at the expense of every other.
> There are human beings on both sides of every issue. So if we
> must fight, let the victors be generous.
> In any schooling worth its salt, an individual must have the op-
> portunity to find out who he is [and] what he relates to.[39]

Today, perhaps, they would have placed a greater emphasis on
communal values such as concern for others, racial equality, and
social justice.

They also discussed modes of presentation. They proposed to
replace the textbook with a loose collection of randomly ordered
materials that students could assemble for themselves. The materials would include pictures, maps, drawings, letters, rent rolls,
financial accounts, and other source documents that could provide
information, for example, about historical figures such as a Whig
nobleman, or a parish priest, or a village constable. By ordering
these materials in their own ways, students could discover significant relationships for themselves and develop insights that would
not only illuminate the historical moment but perhaps even shed
light on contemporary social and cultural circumstances. The objective of these materials was to provide a richness of detail that could
bring to life the historical period under investigation and make simplistic answers difficult. They criticized the textbook for its tendency to overgeneralize and dehumanize the material and leave an
impression of remoteness from the student's own experience. "Abstractions about the life of society, presented in isolation from the
rich disorderly *actual* tapestry of life tend to produce responses
barren and inhumane in a student."[40]

In order to implement this new approach teachers would have to
change. No longer the primary source of information, they would
have to become alert and sensitive guides for the child's direct

encounter with the original sources. To support this partnership in inquiry between teacher and student, the curriculum maker would need to prepare a guide that would suggest the variety of interpretations that could be brought to bear on a given set of materials. One solution proposed was to cultivate a relationship between scholar and teacher that mirrored the relationship between teacher and student in the classroom. The teacher's guide should be designed to create a continuing "dialogue" between the scholar who was working at the frontier of a particular field and the classroom teacher who was responsible for conveying knowledge about that field to young students. The approach should be open-ended and raise questions that would stimulate further inquiry. "Let the scholar be as candid about his doubts as he is about his organizing ideas and informing passions," said the Garden Street group. "It is more important for the scholar writing a guide to leave the teacher with a set of great and disturbing questions than to provide him with a recipe for explaining the stability of the Venetian Republic."[41]

The central pedagogical principle of the ESI Social Studies enterprise was that students should be encouraged to take responsibility for their own learning. The challenge for the teacher was to learn how to become an effective supporter of that process. The proposed curriculum exercises, and they were intended only as suggestions, "should activate the student, turn him into his own social scientist, his own historian, his own evaluator of what is wisdom and what is folly in man's conduct of his affairs."[42] It was an ambitious effort in what it demanded of both teachers and students. Its success would depend on whether or not the materials and exercises could indeed be designed to stimulate such active learning upon the part of students, and whether teachers could adjust to the freewheeling style and much less authoritarian role that this approach to teaching and learning required.

Two of the participants in these early discussions recall the experience with different degrees of enthusiasm. Everett Mendelssohn, who was teaching in Harvard's history of science department at the time, was taken with Douglas Oliver's idea that you could turn elementary students into little anthropologists, but he was appalled by Oliver's contention that anthropology could be taught in a value-neutral way. He agreed with Elting Morison that there were some real values that should be transmitted and that these values were those found in American democracy, but he thought that Morison had a tendency to romanticize the American past. At one point he exclaimed in exasperation, "Not everyone in American society was equally benefited. There were chattel slaves!" Mendelssohn pressed for more attention to non-Western civilizations and even proposed a combined unit comparing Islam and China, which was favorably received. But in the end he felt that his suggestions about the treatment of minorities and the inclusion of Eastern cultures were accepted more to humor him as a good member of the team than with any real intent to do something, and he left the group disappointed with the results of his efforts.[43]

George Homans, on the other hand, was happy with what he heard at Garden Street. Homans had written the first draft of the "Basic Generalizations," and years later he still found the proposals sound. Reviewing the list he remarked, "If I could get students . . . to understand some of these things, I would be quite pleased . . . I thought that our gut assumptions and generalizations, while not probing too hard for absolutely the bedrock equivalent of the lever or whatever it would be in physics, were something that students could assimilate and you could teach." Homans believed that the important thing to strive for in the social sciences was the lessons that have application to new situations. He was not against teaching about the glories of China, but he thought it was more important for students to learn about what makes things fall apart. "It's what goes wrong that you ought to teach the kids, in my opinion. There are no perfect institutions. If they can only grasp that."[44]

In retrospect, the essence of the ESI Social Studies Program was not so much in its content objectives, or even in the social values it hoped to transmit, but rather in the pedagogical approach itself. Here was the overriding challenge of the ESI curriculum effort. Could traditional textbook learning be made to give way to an inductive method that invited students to become excited about studying human behavior and learning how to be social scientists? Would teachers be willing to give up their authoritarian roles as presenters of knowledge and acquire new skills as tutors and guides in a learning process that was driven by the intrinsic motivation of the student? Would school systems allocate the resources to provide the sorts of materials, training programs, organizational structures, and flexible scheduling that would be necessary to conduct such an enterprise? Would textbook publishers, accustomed to seeking statewide adoptions for a single book, be able to adapt to the multimedia format suggested by ESI? And would parents approve of such unconventional schooling? However the content issues were resolved, these were key questions the new reformers would eventually have to face if their approach to curriculum design proved successful and they wished to reach students on a large scale.

The Netsilik Films

In January 1963, the Ford Foundation gave ESI a million dollars to begin implementing the Garden Street proposals. Douglas Oliver had already recruited a group of anthropologists and archaeologists to prepare plans for filming expeditions to collect materials for a series of cultural studies based upon "The Human Past" proposal at Endicott House. His plan was to begin with hunter-gatherers in the first grade, progress through the grades studying increasingly complex cultures, and conclude with an intensive study of classical Greece in grade six. Undaunted by those who worried about the implicit Western bias of his sequence, Oliver moved swiftly to launch a comprehensive filming project to create a visual data base for the elementary curriculum.

Through his friend and colleague at Columbia, Conrad Arensberg, Oliver learned about a young ethnographer, Asen Balikci, who had just completed his doctoral dissertation on the subsistence ecology of the Netsilik Eskimo, a remote group living above the Arctic Circle in a village called Pelly Bay. Arensberg recommended Balikci, as one of the most knowledgeable scholars in the world on the current state of Inuit culture, to oversee the Eskimo filming. Oliver sought him out at the annual meeting of the American Anthropological Association in Philadelphia. Balikci vividly recalls the encounter: "Doug Oliver left a message in my mailbox in the hotel where the meeting was and he invited me to dinner. He told me he had intentions to prepare educational materials dealing with Eskimo ethnography but based on ethnographic film, and he questioned me thoroughly about the state of acculturation among the Eskimos that I had been working with at Pelly Bay, and also he tried to find out . . . to what extent a reconstruction would be successful."[45]

Oliver explained to Balikci that he wanted to create an ethnographic film record of Inuit culture that would illustrate how Eskimos lived at the time Knud Rasmussen first encountered them during his Arctic trek of 1923, when they subsisted entirely as hunter-gathers using traditional stone and bone tools. He told Balikci that he proposed to recreate, as authentically as possible, the actual experience of the ethnographer viewing another culture. All films were to be made without commentary, and the sound track was to contain only the native speech of the Eskimos and the natural sounds of the Arctic habitat. He believed that the films would absorb the student viewer through the power of real activities filmed without manipulation and with no special dramatic effects. The student should feel as if he or she were actually present, observing natural sequences of behavior much as an ethnographer would. This ethnographic filming expedition was to be the first of several similar projects in which anthropologists and archaeologists would be asked to reconstruct their field work on film for educational use. While there was still time, he said, he wanted to record for posterity many fast-disappearing traditional cultural practices and preserve them for future generations of school children and anthropologists.

Fascinated by the proposal, Balikci happily joined the project. He assured Oliver that while the Netsilik people whom he had studied possessed guns and there was a Catholic mission in their settlement at Pelly Bay, many of the older members of the community remembered the ancient hunting techniques and knew how to make and use their traditional tools, and he believed that with a minimum of reconstruction authentic films of the old ways of life could be made. For Balikci, the bringing together of filmmaking with anthropology was the fulfillment of a personal dream, but he felt unqualified to address the educational aspects. Born in Bulgaria and reared in an authoritarian schooling tradition, Balikci was mystified by Oliver's pedagogical objectives, but he was impressed by this American effort to bring the research scientist into the elementary school classroom. Later he recalled that it was Piaget who first took note of this unique aspect of American educational reform, and he credited Jerrold Zacharias with the achievement: "Piaget says clearly that the originality of the Zacharias approach rests not so much on the production of audio-visuals, or the invention of dynamic or creative learning techniques, or changing the topology in the classroom environment; that has been done before many, many times . . . The originality consists in bringing the active researcher-scientist into the curriculum production process. That struck Piaget profoundly [as] a purely American achievement; it has no parallel in European education."[46]

Balikci planned his films to show culture arising from a dynamic interaction between human beings and their environment, where the behavior of the actors reflects social and spiritual as well as subsistence requirements. Not wanting to impose a rigid interpretation on the films, he proposed to follow the nomadic seasonal migrations of the Eskimos and focus on the socioeconomic integration of society. Within each camp he concentrated on the core subsistence activity: stone weir fishing in summer, caribou hunting in the fall, seal hunting on the sea ice in winter. He wanted to show each camp as an integrated whole that reflected the interrelationship between subsistence activities, technology, social life, child-rearing, recreation, ritual, and religion. Oliver gave Balikci few instructions other than that he wanted "reconstruction and bulky material."[47]

During the summer of 1963 Balikci mounted his first filming expedition accompanied by Father Guy-Marie Rouseliere, a Catholic missionary who had lived for many years with the Netsilik, and director-cameraman Douglas Wilkinson. Overcoming a variety of logistical difficulties that almost forced them to cancel the trip, they managed to expose 15,000 feet of film in two months, recording scenes of an Eskimo family living at a summer fishing camp. They depicted a small boy playing in the water with a child-sized fish spear while his father fishes with a companion nearby and his mother decorates her hair and later prepares a meal. Oliver was delighted when he saw the rushes and wrote Balikci an enthusiastic letter on 29 August:

> Two days ago . . . I saw the first fifty reels of the Eskimo film and liked it very, very much. To my untutored eye it seemed technically perfect, and the action sequences are so well done that you have left little for an editor to do. We particularly liked your chief characters. I could see no evidence of any self-consciousness on their part. The little boy, of course, completely stole the show— that alone should make the film immensely useful to child psychologists.[48]

Kevin Smith, who directed the ESI film studio, was quite pleased with the Netsilik effort, and although there were some early technical problems, such as occasional anachronisms (underpants, bandaids, nails, and so forth), and an inability to shoot synchronous sound, he viewed these as minor difficulties that could be corrected. Smith was a veteran of CBS television, and he had come to EDC in

1958 to preside over the development of the massive PSSC film effort. Having worked with scientists for many years, he knew first-rate academic work, and he was impressed with Balikci's effort because it reflected the same intellectual clarity that he had come to expect from the natural scientists and mathematicians. Balikci worried that his films would not satisfy the needs of the ESI curriculum people, but Smith, who was skeptical about whether the social scientists would ever be able to define what they wanted, urged Balikci to disregard the educators and make the films his own way. Smith later recalled his efforts to get Balikci to follow his own judgment in making the Netsilik films: "I remember long sessions with Asen . . . in which he'd say, 'But Kevin, I do not know what to do for the first-grade child.' And I said, 'Screw the first grade child. Asen, for Christ's sake, you're an ethnographer. You've got a chance to go up there and photograph those people. Forget the first grade . . . It will change over the years anyway.'"[49]

As the raw footage began pouring in, Smith asked Quentin Brown, his most experienced producer, to edit the Netsilik series. Brown was a native of Canada and a man of enormous patience and dedication, a perfect choice for a project that was to take five years to complete and, as Smith predicted, undergo several changes in leadership before taking final form as an educational project. Brown vividly remembers the early experiments with the Netsilik footage and, in particular, how Bruner sat with him in the editing room for hours making short four-minute film loops from the Eskimo material. Bruner was worried about the passiveness of most film viewing, and he wanted to explore how film could be used to get students to ask questions. Each loop, he said, should pose a question such as, "Why did the Eskimos gather moss, and what did they use it for?" This could then be followed by further material that illustrated how moss was used. Bruner called these short films "Marienbad teasers," after an inscrutable French film of the period. But Brown found that the "Marienbad" approach did not work out very well in practice, because there was no simple answer to how anything was used in the culture.[50] In the end, Bruner's loops were abandoned.

Evans Clinchy, who was staff director of the project under Oliver, persuaded Brown that longer films, without narration, could be put together in a way that stimulated the viewer to raise questions. With this in mind, Brown edited a half-hour silent film, *Fishing at the Stone Weir,* in the fall of 1963. He constructed the film from a series of sequences that showed characteristic activities: the trek of Itimangnark's family across the tundra carrying everything necessary to set up the fishing camp, two men setting up the caribou skin tent, Itimangnark repairing a fishing spear, the men rebuilding the weir, fishing together, and then dragging home their enormous catch. It also showed Itimangnark's wife, Kingnuk, braiding and decorating her hair, their five-year-old child, Umiapik, playing with a toy caribou made of bone, and the two families laughing and enjoying together a meal of raw fish. Although the film lacked sound, the viewer was strangely drawn in by the silence, and by the lack of an authoritative voice explaining the activities on the screen. The film seemed to invite the viewer to figure out what was going on, and to question behavior that seemed out of the ordinary and difficult to explain. Why, for example, did Kingnuk put ashes on the eyes of the newly caught fish? And why did Itimangnark go so far from the camp to repair his tools?

In the fall of 1963 Brown attended an Instructional Television conference at Stephens College in Columbia, Missouri, a meeting organized to discuss how television could be used for inductive learning. It was a tedious week that produced little in the way of inspiring material, and the participants became bored and discouraged. Brown's presentation was scheduled for Saturday morning, the last day, as people were getting ready to leave. He began by showing selections from ESI's physics films, but the group was fed up that the conference had gone nowhere, and even the PSSC materials could not stir this film-weary audience. Then he screened *Fishing at the Stone Weir.* The film electrified the meeting. "It was just as if the lights had gone on all over town," he remembers. "It was amazing, because the whole group suddenly said, 'Hey, this is how you get the viewer involved. Don't tell him anything! Let him try and figure it out for himself!' It was really very exciting to me because it was a vindication of some of the notions that we had."[51]

The Stephens College conference reinforced for Brown his decision to construct the films from unnarrated sequences of complete activities. These sequences, which lasted from five to ten minutes, were designed to provide enough information to allow the viewer to follow a complex event involving several participants from beginning to end. Using this format Brown made a second film in 1964 called *Jigging for Lake Trout,* but this time he added sound from wild recordings made in the Arctic supplemented by sound fabricated in the ESI studio. The addition of sound was extraordinarily effective. It added greater vividness to the films and brought the viewer even closer to the activities, almost creating the impression of being present with the ethnographer. Seeing the viewer's reaction, Brown now knew he had a powerful formula for constructing ethnographic film. These early efforts established a model for the rest of the Netsilik project.

During the next three years Balikci and his cameramen shot over 180,000 feet of Netsilik footage, recording the entire nomadic migration cycle, including summer fishing, fall caribou hunting, midwinter seal hunting, and spring ice-fishing and seal hunting. He also shot innumerable domestic activities, including igloo-building, kayak-making, sewing, cooking, games and rituals, and children's play. Brown edited this footage into more than ten hours of finished film without a word of narration. Smith and Brown were so impressed with the credibility that the addition of sound provided that they approached the National Film Board of Canada, which had one of the finest sound-recording studio's in the world at the time, to create sound tracks for the entire Netsilik series in return for worldwide distribution rights outside of the United States. The resulting collaboration greatly enriched the films and ensured international exposure through the Film Board's international distribution network. This partnership made the Netsilik films among the most widely viewed ethnographic films ever made.[52]

Quentin Brown was barely launched on the Netsilik project when Smith gave him editorial responsibility for the entire Social Studies filming program. This included several films in the Middle East under the direction of Robert Adams, an archaeologist from the University of Chicago, and a film showing how the domestication of corn led to the development of settled life in Meso-America, which was being planned by Robert McNeish of Yale. Equally ambitious was a proposed film project on free-ranging baboons that was getting under way under the supervision of Harvard anthropologist Irven DeVore. DeVore had spent many months in Kenya in 1959 with Sherwood Washburn of Berkeley doing pioneering work on baboon social behavior, and Oliver wanted to use DeVore and Washburn's data as a contrast case for his studies of social behavior in humans. The films were to be used in a human origins unit that Oliver was planning for the first or second grade.

DeVore, who was teaching a very popular undergraduate course on primate behavior at the time, was uneasy about Oliver's curriculum because he feared that it suggested a spurious evolutionary sequence which treated Western civilization as the acme of human progress. He spoke to Bruner, who was already formulating his own ideas for a course and was greatly relieved to discover that Bruner shared his reservations about Oliver's plan. Many years later DeVore explained his thoughts about the elementary program: "I felt [it] was important . . . that we look at society and behavior, and the relationship to ecology in a way which did not assume a scheme of simple to complex, or at least not that only, and looked instead for principles of behavior, and principles of social organization, and sharing, and male-female role, and ultimately tools and technology and communications and language . . . which could be treated at what I would call the horizontal or the lateral [level] rather than . . . in a vertical structure."[53]

DeVore's participation in the elementary project marked an intellectual turning point for ESI's elementary social studies program. His worries about the developmental sequence and his desire to identify unifying human behavioral characteristics gradually shifted the emphasis away from Oliver's historical and evolutionary framework to a cross-cultural and cross-disciplinary one. DeVore wanted to present biological and cultural perspectives simultaneously in order to bring out the uniqueness of human beings in contrast with other animals, and he proposed that cultures be studied in a comparative rather than an evolutionary context. He worried about the tendency to oversimplify the data, and he stressed the need for including all the significant variables in a study of social systems rather than focusing on technological development.

DeVore was especially concerned about how the study of baboons was treated in a course about human behavior. He wanted children to understand the complete texture of baboon social life and not to jump to simplistic conclusions about the nature of primates:

> If you want to tell the story [of baboon behavior] with some payoff to it, which is how things fit together, then the number of factors involved becomes quite complex. You have to have the ages of the actors in mind, the sex of the actors in mind, . . . their dominance relations in mind, and you have to get some sense of how they all fit together in a group of forty animals. My experience had led me to believe that many adults, much less kids, unless you had

an inordinate amount of time, would impose upon that complexity certain simplifying assumptions which then block you from the payoff. And a simplifying assumption, let's say, would be, well, males always act aggressively and females are always good mothers. There is a certain truth in that but it really is not true.[54]

Mindful of these concerns, DeVore proceeded to mount a filming expedition to Kenya to record the behavior he had observed in his earlier studies with Washburn. Filming turned out to be harder than he had anticipated, for the baboons at Amboseli were difficult to approach, and only the two troops that had been conditioned to anthropological observation would allow him to get close enough for effective shooting. Abandoning his plans for research, DeVore equipped a Land Rover with a specially designed rooftop hatch and observation station and devoted full time to directing the film project. He was determined to record enough information to show the variety and diversity of baboon behavior and to convey a sense of the difficulties that anthropologists face in interpreting primate behavior accurately. After two strenuous months in Amboseli and Nairobi game parks he sent back 40,000 feet of footage to Quentin Brown.

Scholars in Classrooms

While Balikci and DeVore were conducting filming expeditions, other members of the ESI Social Studies group had begun to work with children in classrooms. A summer school held at the Morse School in Cambridge in July 1964 provided the first opportunity for the academics at ESI to observe their materials in use with children. To evaluate these initial experiments Bruner formed an Instructional Research Group (IRG), which consisted of a team of psychologists who observed the classrooms and prepared an independent assessment of the ESI units. Richard Jones headed up the group that reviewed the materials on the formation of early cities that had been designed under the direction of Robert Adams. The Cities Unit materials consisted of sort cards, maps, construction projects, and written materials that were assembled in a loosely structured format. Children, using methods analogous to those used by the professional archaeologist, were asked to explain what life must have been like in ancient Mesopotamia. Adams had intended to include original films of contemporary village life in the unit, but the Iraqi revolution of February 1963 cut short his planned shooting expedition.

The creation of materials specifically designed to teach archaeological methods provided the first opportunity for Bruner's Instructional Research team to explore the way in which children's minds work when faced with a curriculum prepared by social scientists. Almost immediately children encountered problems with the materials, and after a summer of observation, the members of IRG began to raise questions about some of the assumptions on which the ESI units were based. Researcher Blythe Clinchy, for example, discovered that the children she was observing had great difficulty imagining a world before cities. "When you talked about life without cities," she recalled many years later, "they thought you meant people who lived in the country." Observed Clinchy, "It was hard for them to think of dead cities. They had a view of history that had the city as the culminating point. Cities were places with skyscrapers, and they were what came last. So . . . when you started talking about an old, dead city, that was really meaningless to them . . . If any of us had read any Piaget, we wouldn't have had to do the interviews . . . They just didn't have the same notions of time we did."[55]

Clinchy was frustrated by her work on the Cities Unit materials because of the division that arose between the scholars preparing the materials and the teachers and students who were using them. Each week there was a meeting of the whole staff, including scholars, teachers, developers, graduate students, and observers, who reviewed the previous week's work. The meetings were held in ESI's comfortable offices far from the Morse School classrooms, and she found them painful: "I remember how Dick [Jones] and I used to feel very alienated when we got into that meeting. We felt as if we had come off the firing line and back to a sort of elite, all-the-time-in-the-world, sherry-sipping type of atmosphere. I have a very schizophrenic sense of the summer. I really liked the observation group. I really liked working with the kids. Then when I got back into this group of scholars, it just didn't seem to me that what they were talking about had anything to do with . . . the real issues that were arising out of the classrooms and out of working with the kids."[56]

Dick Jones agreed. Since Endicott House, he had worried about

ESI's lack of sensitivity to the practical realities of the classroom. After observing the Cities Unit classes at the Morse School, he prepared a highly critical memorandum for an evaluation conference held at the end of July:

> The early history of this unit included an almost fatal element of precociousness: the scholar's conception of the formal structure of the subject matter was turned immediately to the task of suggesting tools and materials for implementing the teaching . . . The only pedagogical intelligence brought to bear on this quite complex (as we now see that it is) process of re-tooling was composed of casual glances . . . in the direction of the pedagogical principles expressed in *The Process of Education*. The casual leading the casual . . . in an enterprise requiring all possible explicitness.[57]

Adams Resigns

It is not surprising that this first experiment in bringing scholarship to the elementary classroom should encounter problems. Teaching archaeology to ten-year-olds was a formidable challenge for anyone, not the least for a man more comfortable working with graduate students. But Adams was a brilliant scholar and teacher, and he would probably have figured out a way to overcome these early hurdles if there had not been other difficulties. Adams shared the view that the unit suffered from an excessive commitment to scholarly priorities without sufficient consideration of the needs of students and teachers. His central interest, in fact, was in trying to find out how the new approach could be used to strengthen the performance of teachers. He later spoke about what he had learned from the ESI experience, remarking that there had been too much emphasis on materials development and too little attention to the improvement of teaching: "I think the major lessons were that teaching is interaction; that the key is the teacher rather than the materials; that the only way a teacher can be taught to be effective in some new conceptual range is by that same process of interaction as the one by which you expect him/her to work with his/her own students; and that our allocations of time were all wrong by a factor of three to one . . . We spent too much time looking over our shoulders at our academic colleagues . . . and much too little time working . . . with the teachers themselves."[58]

Adams had other problems with the ESI approach. He distrusted the Garden Street proposition that it was possible to devise a structure of generalizations that could be applied broadly to the study of all human societies. He preferred to think of human social development as in a state of evolution in which social life was transformed from one era to the next, making social knowledge impermanent. He wanted his students to "recognize the contingent character of knowledge" of the social world:

> There are very few things about which you can say $E = mc^2$, at least in terms of social and institutions and problems. For the most part, one is dealing with different levels of qualification, and how does one achieve enough certainty to act in the face of qualified knowledge? The advantage in this case is . . . precisely that the qualifications are so great. In fact, you have these busted up pots and a few little wall stubs of temples, and some tablets that are very hard to read and mostly broken, and that is the advantage here. The problem is important enough—namely, how cities began and kings and classes, and all the rest of it—that you've got to say something even though you are saying it in the face of the most formidable set of barriers you can very well imagine.[59]

This is the same uncertainty, said Adams, that confronts political leaders and governments, and yet they must decide and act, and people's lives will be changed as a consequence. It was this provisional nature of knowledge that fascinated Adams, but which he found missing in Garden Street prescriptions for the social studies.

Helping students to acquire a capacity for thoughtful action in the face of uncertainty was a worthy goal, and it was unfortunate for ESI that Adams found the working environment incompatible. Even though the first test of the Cities Unit materials uncovered some serious problems, these matters could have been corrected if he had been willing to revise his approach to make the materials more accessible to students and to work more closely with teachers. Adams had an intriguing vision for the social studies, and one wonders how a second edition of the Cities Unit might have fared had he chosen to continue the work. But Cambridge was a long commute from Chicago, he had recently acquired heavy responsibilities as the director of the university's Oriental Institute, and his differences with Bruner and the other members of ESI's Executive Committee seemed irreconcilable. Consequently, in 1965 Adams withdrew from his activities at ESI, and his Cities Unit ceased to be.

Bruner Takes Charge

In the spring of 1964 Douglas Oliver's wife died, and he lost his enthusiasm for curriculum work. Seeking time to himself, he took a sabbatical leave from Harvard and resigned as director of ESI's elementary program. Oliver's intellectual vision and his dedication to the filming, data collection, and overall conceptual design of the program had gotten it off to a brilliant start, and his leadership would be difficult to replace. The elementary program was Oliver's brain-child, and development had only just begun. Yet there was a growing debate in the steering committee about whether Oliver's evolutionary sequence was the right way to organize the materials, and classroom tests clearly revealed that attention to the needs of teachers and to the developmental level of students was essential if the program was to succeed. Perhaps it was an appropriate time for leadership that would give more attention to issues of teaching and learning.

Unlike Oliver, Bruner's primary interest was in the psychology of the child. As head of the Instructional Research Group he had spent many hours listening to children and trying to determine which of the ESI materials were most effective. He had also spent a good deal of time at the Morse School interviewing students and observing teachers working with the early units. Like Jones and Clinchy he had concluded that the materials and teaching techniques were becoming too intellectually heavy-handed, and he was beginning to develop some of his own notions about how to construct an introductory social studies course. He believed that the discipline of anthropology was insufficient in itself to address all the questions about human behavior that were on children's minds, and he preferred an approach that drew upon materials from a variety of fields to help children come to understand what it means to be human. Oliver's departure created an opportunity for Bruner to explore some of these ideas, so he agreed to head ESI's Elementary Social Studies Program.

· 3 ·

The Handmade Cadillac

In September 1964, Jerome Bruner began a sabbatical leave from Harvard and took up residence at 15 Mifflin Place, the new offices of the ESI Social Studies Program. His views on the design of a social studies curriculum for elementary students differed sharply from those of Douglas Oliver. Sharing DeVore's worries about the developmental sequence, he decided to replace Oliver's carefully structured six-year historical scheme with a topical and comparative approach organized around the question "What is human about human beings?" He proposed a cross-cultural and cross-disciplinary perspective rather than an evolutionary one, and he was content to experiment with a single course for a single grade. He believed that courses in the social sciences must be derived from moral and philosophical propositions, not the technical requirements of a particular discipline, and he set about finding out if the insights of the social scientist could illuminate for young children an understanding of themselves and the society in which they live. Bruner was less certain than Oliver that his ideas would work, so he insisted on frequent classroom tryouts to see how children responded to the proposed materials. Under his influence the emphasis at ESI began to shift from course creation to the study of children, and he challenged the developers to find better ways to bridge the gap between the organizing conjectures of a field of knowledge and the developing intelligence of the young.

This change in emphasis brought new people to the enterprise. A staff once dominated by university academics, especially anthropologists and archaeologists, now gave way to a mixture of disciplines and talents in which scholars were joined by teachers, researchers, writers, artists, designers, editors, and media specialists. If the course was to be rich in its definition of what it means to be human, said Bruner, the staff itself, must reflect that diversity. He expected

72

every member of the staff to contribute to an understanding of how to convey the meaning of "humanness" to the young so that the answer to his central question would be given the broadest possible construction in the classroom.

In one sense Bruner's goal of developing a year-long experimental prototype was more modest than Oliver's effort to create a finished six-year sequence. But in another sense, his aim was more ambitious, for he proposed to create an interdisciplinary course that drew upon many perspectives and many media—a course which, in both format and conceptual design, was without precedent in the schools. His aim was to construct a new model for social studies education that would change the existing pattern in both form and content. He wanted to draw upon the latest findings from the "behavioral sciences," including evolutionary biology, animal ecology, developmental psychology, cultural anthropology, and structural linguistics, and he was also concerned about including perspectives from the arts and humanities. He believed in using a diversity of instructional media, including film, games, graphics, sound recordings, "hands-on" materials, and a variety of print, including original sources, fiction, and poetry, not only to accommodate a variety of learning styles, but also to emphasize the immense range of what it means to be human. Like everyone else at ESI, he had little use for the authoritative "text."

The Westtown Speech

In early October Bruner described his thinking about this new course in an address to a group of elementary school teachers at the Westtown School in Philadelphia at a meeting sponsored by the Friends Committee on Education. He began by setting forth four bases for redefining social studies education: increased understanding of man as a species, new knowledge about cognitive development, the results of the recent curriculum experiments, and the changing nature of modern society. He noted that he did not presume to speak as an educational policymaker but rather as a scholar who wished to share his knowledge with those who are responsible for deciding social questions. "The psychologist," he remarked, "is the scouting party . . . of the political process today where education is concerned. He can and must provide a full range of alternatives to challenge the society to choice."[1]

He began by stressing the importance of tool-making in the evolution of intelligence. The human brain, he pointed out, has evolved through the use of tools, which have amplified the powers of the mind. The ability to make tools, in turn, has developed through the coordination of hand and brain that was a consequence of bipedalism. The resulting technologies, and their associated social patterns, enabled our ancestors to prevail over their physically more powerful hominid cousins, and all of human evolution since that remarkable turning point, he reminded his teaching audience, has proceeded through the pool of acquired characteristics that we have come to call "culture." Herein lies the significance for educators, said Bruner, for, since the advent of tools, human evolution has become wholly dependent upon how effectively we are able to transmit the cultural memory from one generation to the next. "If you lose the means for amplifying the mind, you lose the race; the genes don't carry it. Memory now is in the culture, not in the genes. All that the genes have is an enormous capacity for taking advantage of technology and skill."[2] Like the Mayans and the Easter Islanders, he remarked, we may lose our cultural heritage if our educational system fails to transmit what is important from one generation to the next.

Expanding on this theme of the importance of education Bruner set forth the view that formal education will become increasingly important as society becomes more complex, and, because of this, educators must become more self-conscious about what they do. No longer will the casual teaching interactions of a simpler society suffice to prepare today's children for the world they will face, he pointed out. Modernization and increasing technological sophistication have made the formal educational processes of the school increasingly important, and as this development is still relatively new, we have much to learn about how to bring it off effectively. We would do well, he said, to cultivate the participation of the best brains in the country, and to allocate significant financial resources to the task, if we wish to define instruction that is appropriate to our complex times.

He went on to discuss the relevance of recent work in child development to the formulation of educational programs. Studies all over the world, he said, had now confirmed that learning in children is not a steady acquisition. "It is quite clear that mental growth is simply not a building of a storehouse full of stuff." Rather, learning in the young is more like "a staircase with sharp risers," and certain capacities have to unfold before others are possible. He pointed out that children cannot understand the concept of ratio, for example, until they are able to hold two objects in mind simultaneously, and he reiterated the Piagetian view that children's intelligence evolves from sensory motor experience to more abstract understanding at particular ages, illustrating his point with a discussion of Piaget's famous water beaker experiments, which showed the difference between five- and seven-year-olds in their ability to comprehend conservation of quantity across transformations in appearance.[3] The significance of these "stages" for educators, he said, is not that they are rigidly fixed but that teachers who take into account the mental stage of the child can do a more effective job of preparing the child for the next stage.

Bruner noted that the stage of development that was particularly relevant to the work of the ESI elementary program was the transition from "concrete" to "formal" operations that occurs between the ages of eleven and thirteen. This is the stage, he said, when children begin to speculate about the possible, "to deal . . . in terms of logical propositions rather than things." He emphasized that, as recent research has shown, mental levels can be "drastically affected by the nature of the environment in which the child lives," and he suggested that the judicious use of "replacement therapies," which have proved effective with children from deprived environments, could raise the mental capacities of all children to new levels. While this prospect, he said, raises the troubling possibility that improving the effectiveness of instruction "increases the distance between the head and the tail of the academic procession," it also means that the less able child will go much farther than he would otherwise. Bruner supported his plea for strengthening instruction with an evolutionary argument: "Any species that does not increase variability is on its way toward extinction. This is one basic rule."[4]

In discussing the contributions of the recent curriculum projects to an understanding of the learning process, he noted that they had put to rest certain cherished educational myths. "The idea of readiness," he said, "is a mischievous half-truth," because readiness, in fact, must be taught by providing students with the simpler skills that make higher skills possible. If you want a child to learn calculus in the eighth grade, you had better begin by teaching the concept of limits in the first in some appropriately intuitive form, like acting out the myth of Sisyphus, for example. The concept of readiness, he suggested, implies the ability to define a hierarchy of skills and abstractions that will permit a child to proceed from the simplest levels of understanding of a subject to the most comprehensive order of things.

Another lesson of the curriculum movement, he said, was the discovery that intellectual mastery is self-rewarding in most children. If students experience the cumulative power of learning by finding out that mastery of one skill fits them to acquire the next, no amount of external praise is as satisfying as the recognition of their own achievement. Good coaches, he remarked, have understood this since the first Olympiad, and we must find similar techniques for exercising the growth of mind. The trick is to bring the students to the point where they control their own sources of reward and punishment rather than relying on external symbols of praise or blame. When they reach that point students will have learned how to learn, and life-long intellectual development will naturally follow. This, he said, is the logical objective of all instruction.

The curriculum movement also demonstrated the need for systematic classroom evaluation. Most educational experimentation had been conducted without benefit of any formal feedback other than after-the-fact assessments that permitted little significant alteration once the program had been developed. Bruner argued for including evaluation as an integral part of the curriculum design effort "as a form of intelligence operation to help the curriculum maker in his choice of materials, in his approach, in his manner of setting tasks for the learner, in his sense of where the booby-traps are and where the snipers live."[5] He spoke of the need for a "theory of instruction" to guide educational experimentation, and he saw the whole curriculum movement primarily as an opportunity to learn more about how young minds worked, and how they could be made to grow more effectively. Knowing this would help to make teaching a more professional pursuit.

Finally, Bruner turned to a discussion of the relationship between education and society. The central feature of our highly complex culture, he noted, is the accelerated pace of change and the likelihood that we will continue to experience major scientific and technological breakthroughs that will alter the relationship between human beings and their environment. These circumstances, he said, demand that we reorganize learning around the fundamental ideas and principles that allow us to see the continuities underlying these powerful and disturbing changes. In such an age, he remarked, it is not enough to have good technicians; we must have first-rate philosophers as well. This means that all students must learn how to think, and think critically. In proposing the development and teaching of more generalized ways of thinking about things, Bruner suggested that social studies teaching was likely to move toward increasing instruction in the "sciences of behavior" and away from the emphasis on history. He noted that to adapt to change we must focus on "the possible rather than the achieved": "It is the behavioral sciences and their generality with respect to variations in the human condition that must be central to our presentation of man, not the particularizations of history."[6] In closing, he made a brief plea for the return of psychologists to the field of education in order to work with teachers and to make their own contribution to humanity's further evolution, for it is psychology, he believed, more than all other disciplines, "that has the tools for exploring the limits of man's perfectibility."[7]

In the question period that followed Bruner spoke more specifically about his ideas for an elementary course of study. He criticized Oliver's Human Origins sequence as overly content-oriented and "just too longhair for words." While granting its scholarly merit, he said it lacked other critical ingredients of a proper curriculum, such as attention to skills and values. He referred to the earlier discussions at ESI about the concepts and values the content units should address, but he said these objectives had been obscured in the rush to develop specific materials. He proposed to lead the program back to the original objectives set forth by the steering committee. The skills Bruner sought were those that would help children learn to use their minds in more powerful ways. He spoke about cultivating an understanding that behavior is interconnected, that "things cohere," and that you "don't have to eat the whole apple to know it is an apple." The idea, he said, is to help children see that you can get maximum travel from minimum information if you use your head. Making the "intuitive leap," learning how to "go beyond the information given" to grasp the meaning of things—these were the important skills in Bruner's view.[8]

Another goal of Bruner's new curriculum was to help children see that human life has certain "tragic invariances," and that all behavior makes sense. He wanted them to understand that no matter how different individuals may seem, all human beings are born, reproduce, get sick, and die. Similarly all cultures, however diverse they may appear on the surface, must respond to certain biological imperatives, and therefore there is a discernible purpose behind all human activities, no matter how bizarre they may seem from our own cultural perspective. Bruner wanted children to learn to ask "What's that for?" when looking at another culture, to become little functionalists, so to speak, and to suspend premature judgment until they had a thorough understanding of the behavior of other people in their own terms. He also sought ways to encourage children to speculate about the meaning of things and to appreciate that "It's okay to have a theory." He wanted them to understand that theories are tentative ways of simplifying, and so long as the theorist knows that the theory is tentative, theory-making can be a powerful way of bringing order to the world.

In these informal remarks we can see Bruner's first gropings toward a conceptual design for his elementary program. Although he found Oliver's content sequence too heavy-handed and academic, his own scheme, beyond a few general objectives, was still far from clear. The strength of his approach lay in his effort to articulate some organizing ideas and cognitive skills that could be developed through new curriculum approaches, although he offered the Westtown teachers little in the way of a blueprint. For some who heard him, his way of thinking about the education of young children was fresh and challenging. At least one participant remembered the occasion vividly years later and came away impressed by Bruner's open, exploratory approach:

> One of the fascinating parts of Bruner was that he was so willing to say that there were questions that were unanswered, and he would get so excited about watching the interaction between children and the ideas . . . I remember his enthusiasm as well as the content of the course from that meeting. And I remember wishing that I could work with him, feeling that he had such curiosity about children. The questions that he had seemed to be ones that I had about youngsters also, and I just felt him to be a terribly exciting man.[9]

Defining a "Course of Study"

During the next few months a plan for the elementary program began to take a more precise shape in Bruner's mind. By the end of the year he had drafted a working paper entitled "The Emergence of Man: An Elementary Course of Study." His struggle to be sure that the course gave equal weight to both content and learning objectives is reflected in the opening paragraph:

> There are instructive difficulties in describing a course of study. Shall one begin with an assessment of the intellectual substance of what is to be taught? Indeed, one must, for without it one can give no sense of what might challenge the curiosity and provide the activating mystery. Yet, so soon as one gets deep into those particularities of a subject that one wishes to "get across," at that moment one loses the ingredient of pedagogy. For it is only in the most trivial sense, really, that one gives a course to "get something across" in the sense only of imparting information. Unless the learner masters . . . what he has learned in exercising his taste, or viewing his world, or converting his difficulties into manageable problems, the "something" that got across was surely not worth the effort of transmission.[10]

The overriding objective of the course was to help children understand what it means to be human. "We seek exercises and materials," he later wrote, "through which our pupils can learn wherein man is distinctive in his adaptation to the world, and wherein there is a discernible continuity between him and his animal forbears." The course was to examine the emergence of man as a species with particular attention to what Bruner called, in language reminiscent of the Garden Street discussions, "the five massive contributors to man's humanization": tool making, language, social organization, prolonged childhood, and "man's urge to explain." The fourth category, prolonged childhood, which had not been discussed at Garden Street, had been added at the urging of Richard Jones. The course was to be organized around three questions: What is human about human beings? How did they get that way? How can they be made more so? Materials and exercises, he said, must be designed to keep all three of these questions in the forefront of children's thinking. In Bruner's new course, asking questions was to be as important as finding answers, and new knowledge about human nature was to be coupled with issues of value, namely, how human beings can improve the quality of human life.[11]

In this early effort to describe the course we can see how far Bruner's thinking departed from the earlier work of Adams and Oliver. Unlike his predecessors, he was searching for an intellectual framework that would permit the integration of insights from several disciplines to address basic human questions. He was less interested in imparting specific bodies of knowledge than in devising new and powerful strategies for helping young minds grow. He proposed to undertake a broad inquiry into the nature of man as a biological, psychological, and cultural creature, and he wanted the framework for this investigation to be as comprehensive and diverse as human life itself. Some of the staff regarded Bruner's third question about becoming "more human" as inappropriate for a social science course, but Bruner contended that a proper study of mankind must include philosophical as well as technical questions. To achieve his cross-disciplinary objectives he set out to attract people from varied backgrounds to the enterprise. He welcomed actors, designers, writers, artists, linguists, folklorists—even a business school professor—and some even claimed that he deliberately included people with no experience in education in order to bring fresh perspectives to the work.[12] Both content and grade level placement were thrown open to debate, and these choices were to be resolved through classroom experimentation and evaluation.

Pedagogical Considerations

In another break with convention Bruner rejected the popular notion of the time, set forth by Paul Hanna and others, that the most effective way to teach young children about society is to begin with the familiar surroundings of home and neighborhood. Speaking of this approach, he wrote: "It is a thoroughly commendable ideal; its only fault is its failure to recognize how difficult it is for human beings to see generality in what has become familiar." The "friendly postman," he pointed out, may indeed be "the vicar of federal powers," but to understand that role would involve excursions into the meaning of power, how it is constituted, and how power and force differ. "We would rather find a way of stirring the curiosity of the children with particulars whose intrinsic drama and human significance are plain—whether close at hand or at a far remove." He preferred to rely on children's sense of "mystery, human relevance, and order" as a means of engaging them in the study of society rather than on "the lure of the familiar."[13]

More effective than the study of the familiar, said Bruner, is the power of *contrast*. To this end he proposed the use of three comparisons: man versus the higher primates, man versus prehistoric man, and technological man versus "primitive" man. Later he added a fourth comparison: man versus child—perhaps again at the urging of Richard Jones. By the use of comparison and contrast he hoped to sharpen children's awareness of the uniqueness of man as a species and to help them see the behavior patterns we share with cultures that seem very different from our own.

A second teaching strategy was the use of *models*. Bruner was always looking for ways to extract the general features from a particular instance in order to get educational "travel" from a classroom lesson or exercise, to "go beyond the information given," as he liked to phrase it. However captivating a set of materials might be to students, Bruner was never satisfied unless the lesson taught something of general value that could be applied to new situations. Early on he engaged Clark Abt, a bright young economist who had devised military simulations for the Pentagon, to create games that simulated problem-solving situations in simple societies. In the spring of 1965 Abt designed a game that reconstructed the hunting practices of the !Kung Bushmen of the Kalahari Desert. Although this particular game had some drawbacks, it demonstrated that properly designed educational games that are easy to play and generalizable to other situations can be a very effective device for teaching transfer of learning. Children could easily recognize the logic of the Bushman hunting strategy, and the experience of playing the game generated respect for the intelligence and resourcefulness of people who on the surface seemed very different from themselves.

Another pedagogical technique that Bruner endorsed was the "case study approach," or "post-holing" as it had been called at Endicott House. Although he had a passion for avoiding extraneous detail, Bruner saw that by concentrating on the study of a single culture in depth, children could figure out for themselves how the various elements of that culture relate to each other without being "told" in the fashion of a textbook. "We are keen that our pupils get a sense of the integral structure of a culture," wrote Bruner, "the fact that parts of it fit together in a way that is extraordinarily non-random."[14] He mentioned in particular the way that Eskimos fashion beautifully designed and specialized tools, such as the fishing leister or spear, and that each man is responsible for making his own and must learn to get by with the materials at hand. Unlike our own society, where tool-making is a specialty that falls to a certain group and where resources are plentiful, each Netsilik male must learn to be technologically self-sufficient in an environment of scarcity. Bruner wanted children, through viewing and studying the Netsilik films in particular, to come to understand the internal order upon which Netsilik society was built and how that order was equivalent to, though different from, our own. Only an in-depth study could accomplish this.

Bruner also wrote about helping children to become "self-conscious about assumptions." He hoped to foster the skill of *inference-making* by designing materials that raised questions and invited theorizing. His "Marienbad teasers" were an early example of such materials, but, as it turned out, the longer unnarrated films were more successful in this regard because they encouraged students to come up with multiple explanations for an observed behavior. He wanted to stimulate children to become detectives searching for clues to explain the culture before them. To do so required students to formulate their own theories, to devise their own explanations, and to test their assumptions and conclusions in the light of fresh information. In short, he wanted children to trust the power of their own minds. He was not proposing that children be asked to "discover" the whole corpus of social science knowledge, but he suggested that "two ideals should be respected": "The first is that we want to give children enough of an opportunity to discover generalities on their own so that they can develop confidence in their ability to do so . . . Also [we want to give] children an opportunity to discover the connectedness of knowledge, that knowing one set of things, they are able to infer another set. It is this kind of discovery, internal discovery, that is of highest value to us. The second objective, the cultivation of a sense of connectedness, is about as central to our curriculum effort as any single thing that could be named."[15]

Organizing Themes

Having defined his pedagogical objectives, Bruner set about assembling working parties to collect data, devise organizing frameworks, and construct lessons and classroom activities that explored the five central themes. Although most of the staff accepted the logic of Bruner's interdisciplinary approach as a replacement for Oliver's evolutionary sequence, generating materials for an interdisciplinary course raised many new and troubling questions, and creating materials that addressed these themes in ways that were easily accessible to young children proved more difficult than anyone had anticipated. Developers were asked to put aside the simple organizing scheme provided by the historical and evolutionary approach and seek out ways of structuring material that would provide a cross-cultural and cross-disciplinary frame of reference.

Anthropologist Ted Dethlefsen, who had developed the Human Origins unit for Oliver, set to work on *social organization*. Abandoning the comfortable concreteness of the fossil record, Dethlefsen now sought to devise a way of teaching about social behavior that would enable students to compare subsistence cultures, modern technological society, and nonhuman primates. He decided to focus on roles and to contrast role behavior in Eskimos, urban Americans, and free-ranging baboons. He proposed to examine the function of the group (defense, economy, cooperation, politics, care of the young, and so forth) and the place of the individual within the group. From case studies and comparisons between groups, students would be asked to derive some general propositions that would enable them to make educated guesses about behavior in new settings.

In devising a unit on social organization Bruner wanted children to see that every society has a structure and that if you change one part of the pattern, other parts are also likely to change. He also wanted them to understand that social organization is as much a reflection of the belief system as it is of the physical environment or the requirements of a particular technology. He wanted to teach children that societies are made up of many different relationships—kin and nonkin, ethnic and corporate, face to face and secondary—and that, beyond family, social continuity depends more on roles than on specific people. He especially wanted children to understand the concept of reciprocity: "Social organization is marked by reciprocity and exchange—cooperation is compensated by protection, service by fee, and so on. There is always giving and getting. There are, moreover, forms of legitimacy and sanction that define the limits of possible behavior in any given role. They are bounds set by a society and do not depend upon the individual's choice. Law is the classic case but not the only one. One cannot commit theft legally, but then too one cannot ignore friends with impunity and law has nothing to do with it."[16] In short, he wanted children to see that *reciprocity* is the glue that holds society together.

While Dethlefson was struggling with social organization, Bruner invited linguist Gloria Cooper to join ESI to begin work on *language*. The goal of the language unit was to get students to discover the differences between human language and communication in other animals, particularly in the capacity for generativity. Since most young children are naturally attracted to animals and are impressed with animal sounds, the study of animal communication seemed a useful point of departure for examining the uniqueness of human speech. Cooper had hoped to introduce the design features of human language, notions such as *arbitrariness, duality of patterning,* and *productivity,* but although students seemed to have an intuitive appreciation of the uniqueness of language, her approach proved too abstract for them to comprehend. She therefore introduced the study of bee language to provide contrast. Drawing on the work of Karl von Frisch, she prepared materials that illustrated how worker bees signify the location of nectar finds to their hive mates through "round dances" and "waggle dances." With the help of Michael Sand, a designer, she devised a "High Seas Game," which simulated some of the encoding and decoding features of human language on a simple chesslike board. But despite some brilliant teaching by Cooper, the central concepts of the language unit seemed beyond the grasp of ten-year-olds. Betsy Dunkman, a Newton teacher who had helped to prepare the materials, was pessimistic about the likelihood of the language unit ever achieving its objectives: "The subject is sophisticated and abstract for teachers as well as children. I still have reservations about developing with fifth graders notions of 'the design features of human language.' We can, however, work toward a threshold sense of the power in human communication."[17]

Dunkman touched on two issues that were to become a persistent problem for the developers of MACOS: the sophistication of the concepts and the limited background of teachers. Bruner's proposition that "any subject can be taught effectively in some intellectually honest form to any child at any state of development" was now facing the practical reality of the classroom, and the language unit represented a particularly difficult challenge. Even Bruner was forced to recognize that there were limits to what the unit could effectively achieve. Describing children's struggle with the language materials, he said, "What comes hard is . . . to go beyond the intuitive grasp of the native speaker to the more self-conscious understanding of the linguist. It is this task—getting children to look at and to ponder the things they can notice in their language long enough to understand them—that is most difficult and it should not be pushed to the point of tedium."[18]

Elli Maranda, a Finnish anthropologist who was a fellow at the Radcliffe (now the Bunting) Institute, joined ESI at Bruner's invitation to put together the unit on *mythology,* or "man's urge to explain." Maranda wanted to show the interrelationship between belief systems and the rest of society, so she devised the simple model in the accompanying diagram to illustrate how mythology can be viewed in relation to Bruner's other four aspects of culture.[19] Each of these five aspects of culture, said Maranda, represents an independent system, and, taken together, they comprise the whole system we call "culture." She wanted students to understand that these systems are interdependent, that they continuously influence each other, and that such interactions help to explain cultural change or a culture's failure to change. Developments in technology, for example, may transform social organization, or, conversely, the strength of a belief system may retard social change. Comprehending the dynamics of these interactions was one of the objectives of the mythology materials.

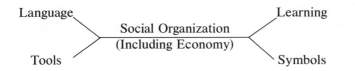

In developing the myth unit, Maranda especially wanted to know whether exposure to the belief systems of other cultures could lead young children to an appreciation of the intellectual awareness that is characteristic of all human beings. Ten-year-olds, she found, were surprised to discover that Eskimos were as curious as we are about the underlying order of things—about what explains conflict, or the availability of food, or the changing of seasons. By reading myths children could begin to see that even so-called "primitive" people grapple with the same philosophical questions that trouble advanced societies, and that their explanations, though perhaps different, are equally plausible in their own context. She quoted Claude Lévi-

Strauss's argument that "primitive" explanations are as rigorous as so-called "scientific" ones, that the difference lies mainly in the "materials available to the thinker": "In a sense, we can even maintain that all cultures are created equal. What this means is that all societies, given sufficient time, make sensible choices and adjust to their environment so that theirs is the best of all worlds possible for them. Structurally, a simple culture is as complete as ours: there is a balance between the functions and the 'elements' of culture."[20]

Maranda sought to communicate to children the universality of the human need to know, and through this awareness to help them understand that we can share an intellectual kinship with apparently remote civilizations. To accomplish this she assembled a collection of the most important Netsilik stories collected by Knud Rasmussen and others who had studied Inuit people. She also put together for teachers a collection of readings about how anthropologists view the function of myth in society. She pointed out that myth plays the role in simple societies that philosophy plays in Western tradition by providing an explanation for the underlying nature of things: "It may reflect what is believed about the celestial bodies and their relation to man, it may tell how man came into being, how social life was founded, what is believed about death and about life after death, it may codify law and morals. In short, it may give expression to the group's basic tenets on astronomy, theology, sociology, law, education, and even esthetics."[21] She wanted students to see that the "need to know" is found in all societies.

Maranda made a persuasive case for the value of myth as teaching material. Not only can the study of symbol systems provide an intellectual challenge for the student, she said. They also convey a sense of the universality of the human search for understanding, thus bringing remote civilizations into closer relationship with our own society. She was not proposing an uncritical romanticism about simpler societies; rather, she was looking for a way to help students grasp the notion that all people, regardless of the surface differences that may appear, share an intellectual curiosity about the world around them. "Between idealization and contempt," she wrote, "there is a thin fragile line: that of seeing clearly and appreciating without sentimentality. In other societies, men succeed in coping with their environment, their companions, and themselves; but we do too."[22]

Concern with teaching about *technology* had been a persistent theme from the beginning at ESI Social Studies. Elting Morison had proposed a course on the impact of technology on Western society to be taught at the high school level. Douglas Oliver wanted to teach about the role of technology in human evolution. Bruner linked technology to the development of man's conceptual powers. "What is most characteristic of any kind of tool-using," he wrote, "is not the tools themselves, but rather the program that guides their use. It is in this broader sense that tools take on their proper meaning as amplifiers of human capacities and implementers of human activity."[23] He wanted students to see how technology enhances human physical, sensory, and thinking capacities, and that tools are components of a system that permits substitutability and innovation. Tools reveal how the human mind works, he said, and it is through tool use and technology that human beings have taken over responsibility for their own evolution. Therefore we must now learn to adapt not only to the physical world but to an environment of our own invention. Examining the impact of technology on our lives today and speculating about the implications of technological development for the future of human society were to be a central concern of Bruner's course.

Early efforts to define the technology unit and translate these general notions into effective classroom materials bogged down in debates over how broadly to define the term *tool*. Should the discussion of tools be restricted to physical objects, or is a logarithm a tool? Is the Magna Carta a tool? Is $E = mc^2$ a tool? Should the technology materials include perspectives from disciplines as diverse as mathematics and history? One of the difficulties in trying to construct a unit on this topic was the lack of a clear conceptual structure for defining what technology is and for considering its social implications. Here, as with the other topics, some of the most interesting issues and questions fell outside of the framework of established academic categories. To wrestle with this problem Bruner hired Richard Rosenbloom, a professor at the Harvard Business School, who took over leadership of the technology unit in the spring of 1965.

Rosenbloom brought clarity to the technology materials. He looked for simple examples in the films, like the Eskimo bow drill, to illustrate general principles. To fashion the drill a man secures a length of thong to the ends of a caribou rib bone and loops it over a bone shaft with a metal point. A back and forth motion of the handle spins the shaft, which is secured at the upper end by a wooden socket held in the user's mouth, leaving the driller's hands free to hold the work. "You see," said Rosenbloom one day while demonstrating the technique, "the principle here is the conversion of reciprocal to rotary motion, the basis of a good many of our own mechanical systems, like the internal combustion engine." Rosenbloom saw many basic technological principles illustrated in the Netsilik materials. Ingenious methods of joinery, for example, are found in the many tools and implements Inuit people fashion from small bits of skin and bone. A serviceable hunting bow is made from seven pieces of caribou bone, and a sled from skin, antlers, thong, moss, and the bodies of frozen fish. The way an igloo is built reflects an intuitive understanding of the laws of physics, the design of a parka reveals a knowledge of the air-capture principle for trapping heat, and a seal-hunting kit how much the Netsilik know about the behavior of seals. It didn't take Rosenbloom long to discover that a careful examination of Netsilik technology was about as good an introduction to the place of technology in society as anything he could hope to find.

Hans Guggenheim, an anthropologist, joined the MACOS development team at about the same time as Rosenbloom, and his first assignment was to help with the development of the technology materials. Guggenheim added the insights of the ethnographer to Rosenbloom's contemporary perspective. Referring to the bow drill he remarked to Dick, "You may see this as a crude ancestor of our own tools, but what is intriguing to the anthropologist is how human beings managed to invent a freely rotating joint when there is nothing comparable in nature. The drill looks simple enough, but it must have taken an enormous act of imagination to think of it." Working together in this way, the business school professor and the anthropologist set out to structure a technology unit for ten-year-olds drawing mainly on the opportunities provided by the Netsilik materials. Guggenheim kept the discussion honest with respect to the ethnographic facts while Rosenbloom pressed for general points that related Netsilik technology to that of contemporary society. Guggenheim was also a gifted artist, and his illustrations enlivened some early versions of the student materials.

Under Bruner's new regime, even Richard Jones got a chance to try his hand at curriculum-making. To his surprise, Bruner asked him to head up the *prolonged childhood* unit, and after many frustrating months of classroom observation, he jumped at the opportunity. Jones had prepared a memorandum that detailed how he proposed to modify "the ESI way" based upon what he had seen at the Morse School during the summer of 1964. He proposed more participation of teachers at the beginning of the curriculum development process to ensure that knowledge about children was incorporated into the materials and exercises. He questioned the "inquiry approach" because he had often seen it degenerate into an undisciplined "fun and games anarchy," with little clarity on the part of either teachers or students about where the lesson was going. He called for more explicitness in both the definition of conceptual objectives and in the articulation of pedagogical assumptions. And he challenged the group to proceed "at all possible speed toward a theory of instructed learning" that would bring together "the conceptual objectives of the scholar, the materials objectives of the unit-maker, and the interpersonal objectives of the teacher."[24]

As at the Endicott House conference, Jones was skeptical from the beginning about the heavily cognitive emphasis in Bruner's approach to curriculum-making. He felt that Bruner stressed mastery of external knowledge without at the same time seeking to cultivate the natural creative responses of the child. He believed that the materials of MACOS had the potential to evoke powerful emotional reactions, and if these reactions were taken seriously, the child could move to new levels of self-knowledge. "A comprehensive theory of instruction," he later wrote, "should seek to prescribe not only optimal levels of intellectual uncertainty, risk and relevance but also optimal levels of emotional involvement and personal curiosity . . . Find a way to engage his heart in the problem and you are likely to see the child rise naturally to his own optimal levels of uncertainty, risk and relevance."[25] In other words, said Jones, we learn best when we care most. He noted, however, that this proposition is more often honored in conferences than in classrooms because what the child cares most about may also be the most threatening, both to himself and to his teacher.

Jones took the development of the childhood unit as an opportunity to test his convictions about the emotional basis of learning. Aided by researcher Kathleen Sylva, he began work on a unit that examined the role of childhood in human development. Bruner did not share Jones's enthusiasm for the unit, and he supported Jones's efforts with some reluctance. In his first working paper on the course, Bruner had expressed uncertainty about what form the materials should take, and he worried about the possible risks in teaching children about childhood: "How much self-consciousness do we want to encourage in children of what age about the processes of growing up? We are not yet clear in our own mind and will not be until we have some opportunity for preliminary tryout of material in small classes."[26] According to Sylva, Bruner had agreed to include the childhood unit only because of strong pressure from Jones. She recalls, "I personally know that there were great arguments with Bruner about this, because Bruner's course . . . was on structuralism, and Dick Jones was bringing an orange into a crate of apples . . . It is my recollection that Dick threatened to quit . . . [unless] the final version of *Man: A Course of Study* had prolonged childhood in it."[27]

During the winter of 1964–65 Jones and Sylva, together with Phyllis Stein, another researcher, set about developing an intellectualer framework for the childhood unit. After considerable discussion they hit upon an idea that turned out to be one of the most productive organizing concepts of the course, the study of comparative life cycles. Sylva recalls the process of discovery:

We found it together . . . Dick and Phyllis and I were looking at baboon movies in the month of March, and we saw some Eskimo movies, but they were very rough cut, and we knew . . . that we wanted to teach the kids about life cycle variables. We hadn't called them that then, but we wanted to have a course that would focus on the fact that through evolution man had, by his immaturity at birth and his need for a long period of dependence, become an animal that could be a culture-bearing animal by that lengthening of immaturity. We knew that our focus was going to be on the lengthening of immaturity making culture possible.[28]

Jones was eager for feedback from the classroom, so Stein and Sylva, with the help of Catherine Motz, a teacher from Germantown Friends School who had joined the working party in February, drafted some booklets about baboon infant behavior that brought out the similarities and differences between the way baboons and humans grow up. Topics included nursing, weaning, play, parental care, dominance, and adaptation with a particular focus on dependency and learning. In April Motz tried out the materials at the Underwood School in Newton, and the student response was electric. Not only were children fascinated by the relationship between infant baboons and their parents, but they raised questions about reproduction, gestation periods, and birth, and additional booklets had to be prepared to deal with these pressing topics. *Life* magazine had just published a remarkable photographic essay on uterine development, which provided excellent supplementary material, and the childhood unit became an instant success.

Jones was ecstatic. Never before, in countless hours of classroom observation, had he seen kids so engaged. His convictions about the power of materials that touched upon the emotional concerns of children was vindicated: materials that dealt with issues of growth and development had spoken directly to the interests of ten-year-olds. Motz particularly recalled the impact of the childhood materials on a boy named Kevin, who had been an indifferent student until the discussion turned to birth and reproduction. Now Kevin's hand was often in the air with questions about miscarriages, about abortion, and about what causes some children to be born unhealthy. Later, Motz learned that Kevin's mother had recently had a miscarriage, and Kevin, who had not been particularly happy about the prospect of a rival sibling, was worried that he had somehow caused the problem. In a parent conference Kevin's mother explained that the course materials had helped her to talk with Kevin and to convince him that the miscarriage was not his fault. Such incidents convinced Jones that he was on the right track, and, Bruner's worries notwithstanding, he pressed ahead with the development of the prolonged childhood unit.

Underwood Summer, 1965

With a new course design in the making and several working parties busily generating materials, the development of MACOS was now in full swing, and Bruner began planning a five-week summer school to be held at Newton's Underwood School. The purpose of the summer session was to provide an opportunity for intensive testing of the new course design in three full-sized classrooms with the participation of several of Newton's regular teachers. University professors were more readily available in summer, and Bruner could conduct curriculum experimentation without interfering with the regular school program. This was the first chance to see if his new approach made practical sense in ordinary classrooms and to find out if the ideas underlying the course were accessible to elementary school students. The "gospel according to St. Jerome," as Bruner's ideas were referred to jokingly in some quarters, was now to receive its first comprehensive test.

The summer session at Underwood in 1965 was my first direct exposure to MACOS, since I had moved to Cambridge only a few days before it began. It was a unique event even by ESI's lavish standards. To teach seventy-five students from grades four to six, Bruner had assembled a staff of seventeen teachers, twelve scholars, seven research assistants, ten instructional researchers, four audio-visual specialists, and eleven clerical people and administrators—sixty-one in all. He sought maximum exposure for the ideas and materials that had been generated by the five working parties, and he wanted to record and evaluate every lesson in each classroom to prepare for the work of revision and retesting that was planned for the coming fall and winter. As always, he was eager to learn from the children, and he charged the instructional research group with providing a rigorous evaluation of the ideas, materials, and teaching methods of the course and reporting their findings each day to the working parties.

Mornings were devoted to classroom instruction, afternoons to critiques of the morning's work, and evenings to preparing materials and lessons for the following day. Each classroom had a working party consisting of a head teacher and several assistant teachers, as well as curriculum writers, scholars, media specialists and evaluators. The working party shared responsibility for the preparation of each lesson, and the members were expected to observe the use of the materials in the classroom. Probably never before had such a diversity of talent been assembled to fashion a single social studies course for the elementary schools. The cross-disciplinary backgrounds of the participants provided for a heady exchange of ideas, and many later recalled this summer school as one of the most stimulating experiences of their academic lives. After a two-day visit, one outside observer from Yale's MAT program, who had a reputation for being a tough critic, called it "the most successful and spirited educational innovation that I have ever seen in operation."[29]

Each of the three classrooms concentrated on a few topics with briefer treatment of the remaining lessons. The fourth grade, taught by Catherine Motz, studied life cycle, baboon behavior, and language, and ended up with a short unit on Netsilik cosmology. The fifth grade, under Betsy Dunkman, studied cultural adaptation, examining topics such as environment, technology, social organization, language, myth, and learning. Dunkman used films and other materials on the !Kung Bushmen of the Kalahari as her main source of data and introduced the baboon materials during the fourth week for contrast in the discussion of group organization and communication. David Martin, a veteran Newton teacher who had worked with ESI before, headed the sixth grade. Martin organized his class around a comparative study of Netsilik and Bushman culture, looking at ecology, technology, cosmology, social organization, and learning, and concluded with a few days devoted to the study of language. The Netsilik materials received the most intensive study, with Bushmen brought in for contrast. Thus each classroom had a decidedly different focus, and this made it possible to try out a great variety of materials, lessons, and teaching strategies in a few weeks.

The Bushman Materials

The materials on the !Kung (now generally called San) Bushmen require a word of explanation. Prior to ESI's Netsilik project the most complete film record of a hunter-gatherer society was John Marshall's Bushman footage. During four expeditions to the Kalahari Desert between 1951 and 1958, the Marshall family had assembled the most extensive written and filmed record ever made of a subsistence culture. John Marshall's film footage (which included the award-winning film, *The Hunters*), together with Elizabeth Marshall Thomas's best-selling book, *The Harmless People,* and the meticulous monographic work of Lorna Marshall—all made possible by the financial support and organizational genius of Lawrence Marshall, the founder of Raytheon—provided a touching and intimate view of a gentle people who had managed to survive in one of the harshest of Earth's habitats. The resourcefulness of these people living with almost no water, harvesting a nutritious diet from a hostile desert, carrying out a rich and varied social life, deploying a remarkably sophisticated hunting technology, and maintaining in these extreme conditions a disarmingly nonviolent outlook on life, provided a perfect contrast to the Netsilik study.

With the hope of including this material in the course, Bruner approached the Marshall family in the spring of 1965, and they generously released their materials for experimental use in the Underwood summer school. The Marshalls were pleased to have the materials used with children, and they were interested in finding out what our students' reactions would be to the experimental lessons. John's interest in other cultures had first been kindled at the Shady Hill School in Cambridge, and the Marshalls were intrigued by ESI's effort to make anthropological materials available to the nation's elementary schools. Both Lawrence and Lorna Marshall visited the school on several occasions, and one day Mrs. Marshall taught a moving class on Bushman social life that entranced Betsy Dunkman's fifth graders.

Other Bushman experts also took part. Nicholas England, an ethnomusicologist, came from New York with his collection of Bushman musical instruments to perform for Betsy Dunkman's class and to discuss the significance of Bushman dance and trance performances. And Richard Lee, a Canadian anthropologist who had just completed a doctoral dissertation on Bushman gathering practices, stopped by on his way home from field work in the Kalahari to help plan some lessons on Bushman cosmology. He shared with us his new data on food consumption, which showed that the women were providing most of the food in the Bushman diet by gathering nuts, roots, and berries while the men were off hunting, often without success. Lee was a gifted teacher and his command of the Bushman language, and his ability to imitate Bushman story-telling and act out Bushman joking and avoidance relationships, captivated the children.

The Lessons of Underwood

The Underwood teaching experience profoundly shaped the development of MACOS. During those five intensive weeks we tried out materials and teaching techniques of every description, including games, films, slides, booklets, dance, improvisational drama, story-telling, demonstrations, construction projects, small- and large-group activities, even lectures on occasion. Classroom discussion was the dominant mode of instruction as we set about exploring the students' ability to grasp the central concepts and questions of the course. The diversity of the staff made it possible for us to try out an immense variety of approaches and to present many points of view, and no idea, however bizarre, was denied a trial. In considering formats, subject matter, and types of materials we paid little regard to the realities of the everyday classroom or the imperatives of the commercial marketplace. These accommodations could come later. We were engaged in putting together what Bruner called "The Handmade Cadillac."

The Power of Film

Children almost universally found the ethnographic films engaging. Whether or not the deeper lessons were learned, unnarrated films about baboons, Eskimos, and Bushmen had the power to capture the attention of ten-year-olds and to stimulate their desire to learn.[30] Quentin Brown's experience with adults at Stephens College was reconfirmed with children at Underwood. By providing information to all students simultaneously, and by inviting inquiry instead of providing authoritative commentary, the films were a breakthrough in inductive pedagogy, and the staff came away from the Underwood experience deeply impressed by the power of ethnographic films to stimulate learning. Like laboratory studies in the natural sciences, ethnographic films allowed students to subject behavior to repeated observation and analysis. Instead of telling students how people in other cultures behave and why, the films permitted children to figure things out for themselves through direct observation. This was a giant leap forward in our effort to get students to take responsibility for their own learning. Following Underwood, MACOS became a film-based course.

The Importance of Data

While we were discovering the power of film we also learned that children of this age need to absorb a great deal of information before they begin to grasp a concept. A unit on baboons may be a study of social organization from a teacher or scholar's point of view, but ten-year-olds need a lot of exposure to the daily activities of a particular group of individuals before the "logic" of their behavior toward each other becomes plain. Why, after all, should we expect young children to grasp insights quickly that have taken scholars years of training and observation to discover? This finding reaffirmed the Endicott House "post-hole" theory that to know the general significance of a body of information one must first become intimately acquainted with its details. The Underwood experience caused us to question Bruner's topical organization and reconsider a more content-oriented, "case study" approach. This would allow children to spend much more time absorbing factual information about baboons, Eskimos, or Bushmen so that concepts could then arise from a deep familiarity with the specifics. This meant a departure from Bruner's goal of getting "maximum travel from a minimum array of information," but such immersion seemed essential to achieve our conceptual objectives.

Engaged Learning

Another lesson of Underwood was the reaffirmation of the ESI dictum that abstract ideas are best taught to young children through concrete materials and experiences. Catherine Motz hit upon a brilliantly successful approach to teaching the concept of life cycle one day when she used lengths of rope to represent the life times of different animals. Seeing how the different lengths compared, children became deeply engaged in discussing why some species live longer than others, how interdependence relates to life span, and why certain key events occur at different stages in the life cycle. When she turned the discussion to human beings, the rope, when compared to the deer and the salmon, extended the whole length of the hall, dramatically illustrating the difference between the length of human life and that of most other animals. Motz invited her students to act out the human lifetime from death to birth, with suitable postures that indicated the differences between old age, middle life, and infancy, and she was impressed with how this experience enabled children to identify with what life might be like at different stages of the life cycle.[31]

Kathleen Sylva had a similar experience with a lesson on Netsilik cosmology when she asked a group of children to act out the Eskimo myth about Nuliajuk, the goddess of sea creatures. Nuliajuk, the Netsilik believe, tries to hide seals from Eskimo hunters because the early Eskimos were cruel to her when she was an orphaned child. According to ancient legend, they cut off her fingers when she tried to climb on a raft to save herself from drowning. Her severed fingers became the seals, which she now controls from her home at the bottom of the sea. One child who played Nuliajuk became so engaged in the part that when Sylva offered her a ring to decorate herself, she replied, "But I have no fingers!" Identification turned out to be an important step in getting children to comprehend Netsilik values and to appreciate the centrality of religious belief in a culture where people face great danger daily. To perceive Netsilik culture from the "inside," we learned, required more than intellectual engagement. To be maximally effective, as Jones foresaw, the lessons must stir the heart as well as the head.

New Methods and Materials

One of the most productive features of the Underwood summer school was the opportunity it provided for experimenting with new materials. Our gifted designer, Michael Sand, produced innumerable ideas for engaging youngsters in the subject at hand. He supplied modular cardboard pieces from which students could construct "environment boards" of their own design that simulated the savannah habitat of DeVore's baboons. By placing cutouts of the various troop members (adult males and females, juveniles, and infants) in different configurations on these boards, children could speculate about troop organization, intratroop relationships, and defense against predators. Sand also created a life-size baboon troop out of cardboard and began work on some highly innovative formats for children's textbooks. He set about proving that sophisticated concepts could be taught simply and powerfully by capturing the creative imagination of the student and by using inventive graphics. Sand's visual sense, and his flair for the invention of physical materials that captivated children, had a major impact on the course design.

Timothy Asch, a photographer, filmmaker, and anthropologist, brought a special combination of skills to the social studies program. Asch believed that film should be made as accessible to students as written materials, and he often worked late in the night editing footage from the Netsilik, baboon, and Bushman archives to respond to the latest pedagogical whim of a classroom teacher, developer, or scholar. He produced carefully structured sequences that illustrated technological processes and short clips that focused on important social interactions such as conflict situations, parent-child interactions, or children's play. Asch's "sequences" were designed for close and repeated study, much like a written text. One example showed Bushman string-making, illustrating how an elderly man removed the fibers from sansevieria leaves with his digging stick and then spun the fibers into a length of rope by twisting them against his naked thigh. By repeatedly observing this sequence, Dick Rosenbloom and I were able to construct a unit on Bushman string-making in which we used similar methods to produce a rope strong enough to lift a chair.

One of Asch's most effective creations was his "environment chamber," a device for simulating life in the Kalahari desert in an ordinary classroom. By rear-projecting scenes from the Kalahari on a huge translucent screen and accompanying these images with a tape recording of desert sounds, Asch took children on a trip through the Kalahari seasons of the year and exposed them to the cycle of a Bushman day. Seated on the carpeted floor of their darkened classroom, the students at Underwood could imagine themselves side by side with the people they were studying, hearing the soft Bushman language, absorbing the sounds of the Kalahari environment, and listening to a Bushman musician playing mournful songs on his hunting bow. Fashioned from inexpensive paper and cardboard tubing, and using a single carousel projector coupled to a tape recorder, Asch's environment chamber was designed to be easily replicated by a resourceful teacher in an ordinary classroom.

Midway through the summer, Paul Schmidt, a linguist and professional actor, joined the ESI staff and entertained the children at Underwood with dramatic recountings of Netsilik myths and stories. Schmidt's expert renditions of traditional Eskimo tales demonstrated the power of the oral tradition from which they sprang and illustrated how much could be lost in the transition to the printed page. Schmidt's performances were so effective with students that we later reproduced them as professional sound recordings and distributed them with the published course. To capture some of this poetic quality in the written versions, Bruner asked poet Edward Field to translate Rasmussen's accounts into blank verse, which became a student book entitled *Songs and Stories of the Netsilik Eskimos*. He also invited a young novelist, Carter Wilson, to create a fictionalized version of traditional Netsilik life based on Rasmussen's ethnography. Wilson produced a compelling series of stories about the adventures of a young Inuit boy and his family called *On Firm Ice*. Captivated by the Netsilik story, he later wrote a classroom drama entitled *The True Play of How Itimangnark Got Kingnuk, the Girl He Always Wanted,* an authentic account of the events leading up the marriage of the central characters in Asen

Balikci's films. These efforts to translate ethnography into an idiom that children could enjoy and easily comprehend were an outgrowth of the interdisciplinary curriculum development process that began at the Underwood School.

Even movement and role-playing became teaching mediums at Underwood. Amy Greenfield, a professional dancer, helped children appreciate the physical rigors of Arctic life by teaching them to use their bodies the way the Netsilik do. Under Greenfield's tutelage children stalked seals by crawling across the floor of the gymnasium in seal-like fashion, much the way the Netsilik stalk seals on the spring ice in their effort to deceive their wary prey. They practiced dragging the heavy catch homeward and sharing it, and tried to imagine how they would entertain themselves huddled in an igloo, often with little to eat for months at a time. These activities were enhanced by role-playing exercises designed to help students identify with the hardships imposed by arctic life and appreciate the humanity of the Netsilik response. According to those who observed and evaluated these lessons, the children who were exposed to the dance and role-playing were better able to relate to the Netsilik experience and to comprehend more of what was being taught in the formal classroom.

Games

Another discovery of the summer experience was a new way of looking at educational games. The problem with elaborate simulations, like Clark Abt's Bushman hunting game, was that they took too much time to play, and children became engrossed in "winning the game" without reflecting on the problems the game was supposed to simulate. We found that for teaching purposes we needed simpler devices that would permit children to replay the game often, trying different strategies and recording the results of each attempt. In this way they could gradually discover the patterns or rules that governed successful play. In the caribou game, for example, students needed an easy way to compare the results of several plays in order to figure out the factors that influenced the success or failure of a hunt, such as the movement of beaters or the placement of stone decoys. We also found that games that promoted winning did not serve our teaching purposes, since we were more interested in getting children to solve a problem, or invent a strategy and test its effectiveness, than to best an opponent. Our hunting games were usually tests of group strategy, not individual skill, and the most effective solution often required collaboration not competition.

One of the most successful simulations of the summer turned out to be a simple corkboard exercise that Betsy Dunkman used to help her students visualize Bushman social relationships. Corks representing various band members, color-coded to indicate kinship ties, could be moved about to represent the behavior patterns of a Bushman band during the course of the day. With the aid of this simple device, together with excerpts from Lorna Marshall's journal, children could track the duration and location of subsistence activities, note the division of labor, perceive patterns of interaction and avoidance, and examine the relationships between parents and offspring, males and females, kin and nonkin. Visualizing behavior in this way made it easy for children to grasp the patterns of Bushman social life. Like Sand's environment board exercise, the use of a physical model to map social behavior enabled children to assimilate facts quickly and to explore alternative possibilities in a concrete way.

Anthropomorphism

We were surprised to discover the inclination of many children to identify with the baboons. Despite our efforts to develop materials that brought out the contrasts between humans and the other primates, the more familiar children became with the details of baboon life, the more similarities they seemed to find between baboon and human behavior. The helplessness of baboon infants at birth, their long growing-up period, their group social life in which males shared with females the care of the young, and their frequent displays of aggression and affection all seemed reminiscent of human behavior, and our efforts to emphasize the differences between humans and other animals fell on reluctant ears. Even the lessons that attempted to contrast the two dozen or so baboon sounds and gestures with the complexity of human speech were met with youthful skepticism. "Their way of communicating is probably just as complicated as ours," the children insisted. "We just don't understand it." Troubled by this tendency to anthropomorphize the baboons, we began looking for case studies of animals that would provide even sharper contrasts to human behavior. We were baffled by the inclination of children to impart human characteristics to animals, and we came away from Underwood determined to find ways to get across the uniqueness of man.

Further difficulties with the concept of humanness turned up in the student response to the language materials. Bruner had especially wanted children to understand the crucial importance of language in defining what makes humans human. It is the human capacity for symbolizing, he liked to point out, that particularly distinguishes people from the higher primates and makes possible the invention of culture, including tool-making, social reciprocity, and the formation of beliefs and values. Without language it is difficult to imagine a significant distinction between humans and other animals, yet our efforts to get across this central idea proved frustratingly unsuccessful. Determined to solve the problem, Bruner went to class one day armed with an invention of his own called "the sentence generating machine," a device that Sand had fashioned according to Bruner's instructions from several large ice cream containers fitted to a length of wooden dowel so that the drums could turn freely. Each drum had been inscribed with a separate category of words—articles, adjectives, nouns, verbs, and objects—ordered in such a way as to create a simple sentence. Bruner then spun the drums to illustrate that, whatever "nonsense" sentence might appear, the sentence retained a logical order and organization. Meaning, he tried to show, is conveyed by the structure of a sentence, not just by the words alone. But the subtlety of this linguistic argument was lost on ten-year-olds, and Bruner left the classroom more perplexed than ever about how to transmit the design features of human language to the young.

Our First Evaluation

One of the most dedicated and outspoken observers of the Underwood classes was Howard Gardner, who was a graduate student in psychology at Harvard at the time. Gardner had observed David Martin's class throughout the summer, and he conducted a five-session tutorial with six of Martin's students. He was keenly interested in finding out whether students of this age could grasp the ideas that Bruner was trying to teach, and he was disappointed with the results. With his associate, Judith Krieger, Gardner had spent many hours devising ways to figure out how children were actually thinking about the issues raised in the course, and he concluded that despite the strong interest shown by students in the materials, we had failed to get across much of what we were trying to teach. In the summary report of their findings, Gardner and Krieger concluded: "It is our feeling that very few of the youngsters came significantly closer to an understanding of the concepts cited in *Man: A Course of Study;* nor do they have much of an inkling of good strategies or responses to the question: What makes man human?"[32]

Gardner and Krieger found that most of the lessons failed either because the teacher pushed too hard for abstractions before the child had assimilated enough specific information to give the concept concrete meaning or because teachers were unclear about what concept they were trying to teach. Ambivalence on the teacher's part between open-ended discussion and directed teaching was a persistent problem. They cited only two occasions on which they saw students coming to grips with the basic questions of the course. One was when David Martin told his class he knew a man who did not believe that the Netsilik were human and asked if they could prove him wrong. This challenge produced a lively and focused discussion on the nature of humanness. The second occasion was in Gardner's tutorial when he asked his students how they thought Bushman life would change if three of the men used a steel trap to capture large game. Given such a question, Gardner found, sixth-graders could begin to think about how the parts of a culture fit together.

Despite these weaknesses, however, Gardner and Krieger concluded that the course had promise. They found that the goals of the summer had been excessively ambitious given the time available and suggested that with better teacher training and a restructuring of the units, much might be achieved. They were impressed with the quality of the source materials and with the overall impact of the summer experience on the children, and they were persuaded that a good deal of educational value, in time, could be extracted from the course. As they noted, "Because of the excellence of many of the films, lectures, materials presented, etc., we feel that the students have accumulated a far richer collection of impressions, notions, and ideas than are normally accrued in a far longer time in a regular classroom . . . We feel that much valuable conceptual training and understanding can be built in such lessons and exercises."[33]

In a thoughtful memorandum entitled "On Sequencing," prepared on 5 August, Gardner reflected on how the summer effort had identified some optimal ways for ordering educational experiences to minimize confusion and maximize the potential for comprehension of concepts. He conjectured that in conceptual learning at this age, ego involvement on the part of the child must precede engagement with the problem or task. Unless children identify with what is being taught, said Gardner, we cannot expect them to comprehend abstract ideas. "As far as the relationship of the material to the youngster is concerned," he wrote, "it is essential that the youngster's interest be piqued. *A student's curiosity is our greatest asset:* we must channel this curiosity toward the question."[34] This means, he said, that we must begin with the youngster's own concerns and seek material relevant to his own experience. It does not have to be familiar material. Exotic materials can capture students' attention; they may identify with another society, or a species, or even with their teacher. What is important is capturing the child's ego and then slowly transferring this involvement to the material itself. Wrote Gardner, "It is not optimal for the youth's ego to remain the chief tie to the material. A gradual transition should take place, whereby the youngster becomes increasingly intrigued by the task or material itself until finally it has achieved 'functional autonomy'; just as interest will not endure unless the youth identifies or is ego-involved with the material, interest will not be transferable and the mind will remain unexercised unless the material itself begins to hold fascination for the student."[35]

Using the example of teaching about Netsilik technology, Gardner posed the problem of seal skinning. The lesson begins with the children trying to peel an orange with their fingers while watching a film of the Eskimos skinning a seal. Then they are asked to design a tool for skinning their "seal" from a few simple materials—popsicle sticks, fragments of pencils, or other materials readily available in the schoolroom. As the lesson evolves the student becomes engaged in the task of designing and using a tool, and the value of the lesson is finally realized when the student sees that there are many ways to make a tool and many ways to skin a seal. At this point the information under consideration is no longer linked to the Netsilik example, and children begin to grasp more general points, such as how tools work, how technology functions as a programmatic system, how human beings control their physical environment, and so forth.[36]

Gardner's observations captured the message of Underwood. MACOS contained some powerful materials that engaged the curiosity of children, but the transition from powerful materials to conceptual learning still needed more work. To succeed we would have to clarify our objectives, develop a comprehensive training program for teachers, and order the materials so that they progressed from early ego involvement to the abstractions we wanted to teach. We were encouraged that the raw materials of the course consistently piqued children's interest and made them feel that they were engaged in a study of uncommon importance. Their enthusiasm, coupled with our own fascination with the ideas and materials of the course, drove us on.

The Winter of Discontent

The fall and winter of 1965–66 were a time for regrouping, soul searching, and reflection, and for putting the lessons of Underwood to work in the development of new and revised materials. After two weeks of intensive review of the summer results we undertook preparations for a second trial teaching cycle to begin in December. This test had to yield the program we would present to a considerably expanded group of teachers in the summer of 1966. These teachers, in turn, would try out the course in twenty-five experimental classrooms in the greater Boston area during the following academic year. The staff now consisted of twenty full-time researchers, teachers, and curriculum designers and sixteen part-time specialists and consultants. Four new members brought important skills to the work: Marilyn Clayton, a psychologist, who had joined IRG; Barbara Boylan, an editor who brought textbook editorial experience from D. C. Heath as well as substantial writing skills; Anita Mishler, a sociologist who headed up teacher training; and Anita Gil, also an editor and a gifted writer. Gil later recalled the exhilaration of her first ESI meeting in the basement of Mifflin Place: "It was one of the most exciting moments of my life, intellectually. It was at that big meeting where we all sat down and met each other . . . And Jerry was just talking. What caught me was not the notion of educational process, but the substance, because I had never bumped into this notion of the world, and specifically man, being millions of years old, and it just bowled me over. I started reading, and I was socked . . . I still am."[37]

The Problem of Structure

The original working party organization based on Bruner's five "humanizing forces" had proved unsatisfactory as a framework for creating materials for the classroom. His five-part conceptual design made sense from a logical point of view, but it failed to capitalize on students' intrinsic interest in the specific course materials. From the students' point of view the course was about people and animals, not abstract ideas, and we needed a way to imbed our conceptual goals in a learning context that was engaging for children. The search for a curriculum design that worked in the classroom and at the same time fulfilled our learning objectives dominated the work of the fall.

The staff was divided between two points of view. One group thought that children would relate best to materials that emphasized issues most closely linked to their own experience. They suggested organizing the materials around the concept of the life cycle and selecting examples from the animal and cultural materials that dealt with issues like growing up, socialization, status and role, the crises that accompany transitions between life cycle stages, and comparisons between the life cycles of human beings and other animals. They argued that the study of life cycles would provide both a conceptual bridge between animal studies and the cultural materials and a framework for comparing the Netsilik and the Bushmen. The process of growing up, they argued, is a theme that any child can relate to, and it could provide an integrating conceptual framework for the course. DeVore's footage on baboon infants, Balikci's material on Eskimo childhood, and the extensive Marshall data on children's activities would provide plenty of information from which to construct materials and lessons.

The other group was equally convinced that the concept of "adaptation" provided the best way to integrate the materials. As they saw it, children would respond to an approach that immersed them in the study of all aspects of a society and then looked at how a culture reflects the way human beings deal with the challenges of their environment. Netsilik behavior, for example, can be understood by examining the interaction between the Inuit people and their Arctic habitat, and how this interaction is reflected in their social patterns, in their child-rearing practices, in their system of beliefs, and in their technology. The study of animal morphology and behavior, they argued, can be used for contrast; students will see that, while most animals are adapted to a rather narrow environmental "niche," human beings have managed to survive in a great variety of environments through the medium of culture. Drawing on examples from both the Netsilik and Bushman studies, together with the animal materials, the "adaptation" group proposed to help children discover for themselves what it means to be human.

Given the plausibility of both approaches, dividing the staff into two working parties to test these convictions seemed to make practical as well as theoretical sense. The life cycle group could expand on the animal materials, especially the baboon studies already developed in Motz's summer school class, while selecting from the Bushman and Netsilik archives for materials on growing up, rites of passage, child-adult interactions, personal histories, stories told to children, animal myths, and other materials that focused on the socialization of the individual within society. The adaptation group, on the other hand, could develop the cultural materials in depth to illustrate group behavior, links between technology and social organization, the importance of belief systems, the nature of ecological adaptation, and the similarities and contrasts between Bushmen and Eskimos. We knew that eventually the two perspectives would have to be integrated, but for the moment it seemed a sensible way to get on with the task of developing specific materials and lessons.

As the work progressed, the course gradually began to take on a new shape and content. To cope with the problem of anthropomorphism that had arisen in the summer school classes, the life cycle group examined other well-researched animal studies in which the contrast with humans was more pronounced than it had been with the baboons. Birds, fish, and even insects were considered, and after much discussion and a prolonged search for appropriate material, they selected the Pacific salmon, whose dramatic life cycle had been well-documented on film, and the carefully researched herring gull studies of William Drury of the Massachusetts Audubon Society, which also included some excellent film footage. Since both salmon (arctic char) and herring gulls appeared in the Netsilik films, these seemed particularly appropriate choices for behavioral comparisons.

The expansion of the animal studies created new problems and challenges. Comparisons between animals brought out certain critical life cycle variables, such as length of lifetime, infant mortality rates, the number of offspring that survive to reproduce, the amount and quality of parental care, and the role of males in raising the young. The impact of parental care on infant survival rates was dramatically illustrated in these comparative studies and led to classroom discussions of sensitive topics such as parental neglect and parent-offspring conflict. Examining animal behavior also raised questions about sexual promiscuity, the role of parents, the relationship between innate and learned behavior, and the process of natural selection. The animal studies dramatized the uniqueness of prolonged immaturity in humans and the overwhelming impact of parental nurturing on survival. They also raised some sensitive questions about cultural differences. We found that it was a mistake to have children selectively looking at child-rearing behavior in an unfamiliar culture without understanding the total cultural context of that behavior. Examining how a child learns how to kill in Netsilik culture, for example, without understanding the scarcity of food in the arctic and the role the hunter plays in ensuring the survival of his family, could create misleading impressions and negative attitudes toward the people being studied.

Meanwhile, the adaptation group concentrated its efforts on developing the Bushman and Eskimo materials in depth. Adopting the "post-holing" approach discussed at Endicott House, they immersed students in the details of Netsilik and Bushman life before attempting to extract general points. They spent hours viewing the entire archive of Bushman and Eskimo films, and constructing sequences of study that proceeded from the concrete to the abstract. Starting with the Bushman camp, for example, and examining the activities of a single family and band, they encouraged children to become familiar with each individual, to know individuals by name and how they were related to each other. Children would first see Bushman gathering practices or Netsilik hunting techniques as specific activities carried out by individuals they knew and cared about. Only later would they talk about them as elements in an orderly economic and social system. Drawing on Howard Gardner's observations, the adaptation group treated the experience of identification as crucial to the learning process and introduced abstractions, such as the interaction between technology and social structure or the relationship between belief and behavior, only after students had become closely identified with the Bushmen as people.

The Debates of January

Because the two units were evolving in quite different directions, it soon became plain that we would have to address the issue of a unified course of study. The Executive Committee, chaired by Elting Morison, met weekly to review the progress of all ESI social studies projects, and it began to press for a report on the status of MACOS. Some of the more conservative members of the committee were skeptical about Bruner's interdisciplinary approach to curriculum development, and they wanted to know how the course was progressing. The NSF grant that supported much of the work of ESI Social Studies group was due for renewal in the spring, and the committee was looking for evidence of a coherent course with proven results. Under growing pressure from the Committee to defend our work, we formed a "link group" of staff drawn from both working parties to examine the differences between the two approaches and to make proposals for combining the units into a single course.

At the first meeting, early in January, Bruner opened the discussion by calling for a rethinking of the overall course design. In an obvious reference to the activities of the adaptation group, he warned against the danger of getting bogged down in "interesting things" and expressed concern that the organization and selection of materials had been overly influenced by the thinking of "content experts." He called for a conceptual framework based on a more general theory of human behavior than could be provided by ethnographers and presented a matrix for structuring the selection of material that looked suspiciously like a return to his original pre-Underwood plan, which featured technology, social organization, cosmology, and language.

Bruner's new scheme received a chilly reception. Rosenbloom, who had worked with the adaptation group, proposed focusing on activities like hunting, cooperation, and storytelling, topics that could be supported with significant amounts of data, and suggested that Bruner's more general concepts could best be derived from a thorough exploration of these specific activities. Schmidt, although a linguist, said that the materials at hand did not easily lend themselves to the study of language and pointed out the success that his group had achieved with the study of life cycles. Others argued for beginning with our most intriguing material and letting the concepts evolve after the children had become emotionally engaged. All seemed to agree that the experience of working with ten-year-olds had led them to the conclusion that the abstract ideas we were trying to teach, if teachable at all at this age, must evolve gradually through deep immersion in specific materials. The conflict with Bruner was not over goals but over how best to reach his ultimate objective.

As the month progressed the debate crystallized into two opposing points of view. One held that a strategy of cross-cultural and cross-species comparison would keep the focus on Bruner's general points. The other argued that an in-depth study of a single culture, using ecological adaptation as the integrating concept, was the most effective way to get across Bruner's themes. The first approach would employ contrast to maximum effect, while the second would rely on the ego involvement of students and their emotional engagement with the people they were studying. Underlying both points of view was the conviction that Bruner's urgency in making general points risked overintellectualizing the course at the expense of pedagogical techniques that had proven effective in classrooms. Emotions ran high as the staff struggled to reconcile their experience with children and Bruner's aspirations.

The debate was finally laid to rest in a meeting on 1 February when Bruner presented a second proposal for a new course sequence. He suggested that we begin with the life cycle unit, which had proved so successful in all our tests, together with some materials developed by Marilyn Clayton that were designed to clarify how animals had become physically adapted to their environments. He then proposed a five- or six-week unit on baboons that would focus on maturation, troop organization, and territoriality, followed by another Clayton-developed unit on social adaptation. This, in turn was to be followed by an in-depth study of the Netsilik, especially the winter camp, which would be structured to emphasize the adaptive systems inherent in hunting, group organization, child-rearing, and myth. Possibly some Bushman materials could be included for contrast, but he suggested that we not rely on the Bushmen due to possible complications in getting publication rights.

The course would close with another adaptation unit that would examine the meaning of culture. Perhaps language could be featured at this point. This time his proposal was more warmly received, for it appeared to provide a happy marriage between concrete materials and general points.

Trial by Fire

Agreement on a basic outline for the course had come none too soon. The Executive Committee was becoming increasingly impatient with the turmoil they sensed in the Elementary Program, and they asked us to make a series of presentations during March to clarify our goals and articulate our accomplishments. Franklin Patterson, who directed the Junior High Program, and Morton White, who headed the High School Program, were openly skeptical about our ability to produce an intellectually respectable course, and even Elting Morison, who had been Bruner's strongest supporter, was beginning to lose confidence in the Elementary Program. Staff turnover had been high, expenditures excessive, and conceptual reorganization too frequent to encourage the belief that we would ever produce a coherent product. Only Charles Brown, who presided over the school system where much of our classroom experimentation had been taking place and who had regular contact with the teachers who had used our materials, remained convinced that Bruner was on the right track. Although we had more classroom time than any of the other ESI social studies programs, classroom experience counted for relatively little in the heady fireside deliberations that took place over sherry in Morison's spacious, book-lined office at 55 Brattle Street. A coherent conceptual presentation that made sense to scholars was crucial for the future of MACOS.

We had planned that Bruner would open the first meeting with an explanation of the new course design, but he had an attack of the flu the day before and was forced to send a tape recording of his presentation from his sickbed. As the tape rolled, the committee listened politely to Bruner's mellifluous descriptions of yet another approach to transforming social learning for the young, but they remained unmoved. They had been dazzled by his eloquence before. Their mood was skeptical and the atmosphere tense. Some had reservations about his "three questions," and they were put off by his failure to meet with them face to face.

Irven DeVore followed with a discussion of the value of animal studies in a course on Man. He stressed the importance of Bruner's first question, played down the second as difficult to teach to ten-year-olds, and dismissed the third as "Brunerian rhetoric." DeVore read his audience perfectly. Marshaling the considerable forensic skills he had acquired as a Texas high school debating champion, he confidently described his pioneering fieldwork on free-ranging baboons, and the group visibly relaxed as he spoke authoritatively about the many new perspectives on human behavior that can be derived from the study of animals in the wild. DeVore's obvious command of the material together with his practical sense about what worked with young children, bolstered by examples taken from the classes that he had taught himself at Underwood the previous summer, were warmly received by the Executive Committee.

Then Motz and Sylva took the floor. Their presentation was also impressive: knowledgeable about children, articulate about how the materials could be used to bring out the themes of the course, and warmly enthusiastic about the power of the program to deepen children's understanding of themselves. They described the "Life Ropes" exercise in which they had introduced children to the life cycle theme by having them create cards describing the important events in a human lifetime and hang them on ropes so they could be easily compared to those of other species. They spoke about the value of the salmon film as a way of dramatizing for children the contrast between the lack of parenting in the salmon case and the long period of dependency in humans, and how it helped them introduce the discussion of the relationship between instinct and learning. And they illustrated with examples from their teaching experience how children were able to relate general ideas, such as life cycle, innate behavior, and learning, to their own lives and thus deepen their understanding of what it means to be a human being.

Marilyn Clayton concluded the session with a discussion of her materials on adaptation. She spoke about the process of concept formation in children and described how her proposed materials, when added to the specific case studies, would help to clarify and reinforce the general ideas of the course. She showed how the animal studies could be used to illustrate the contrast between morphological adaptation in animals and the development of tools in man. And she explained how other materials she was planning would address issues of learning, social organization, and communication. Clayton's presentation made clear to the Executive Committee how Bruner's general themes could be integrated with the individual case studies, and they could begin to see how his conceptual objectives could be worked out in practice. Her proposals, as it turned out, laid the groundwork for a series of "concept books" that were later developed to accompany the "man and other animals" section of the course.

This meeting was an important turning point for the Elementary Program. For the first time the Executive Committee began to see that MACOS was progressing from a collection of heady ideas to a course that worked in the classroom. In the succeeding weeks they sat through four additional presentations during which they saw baboon materials taught in class, observed Eskimo films, listened to dramatizations of myths, played hunting games, and even sat on the rug in the basement conference room at Mifflin Place to experience Tim Asch's environment chamber. Asen Balikci, Lorna Marshall, and Richard Lee discussed the teaching power of the Eskimo and Bushman archives, Dick Rosenbloom explained the power of the materials to illuminate children's understanding of technology, and Anita Mishler and Dick Jones described our plans for teacher training. In the end, the committee seemed persuaded that MACOS had a chance, and their support gave the elementary staff renewed confidence that we were on the way to producing a workable course.

These presentations to the Executive Committee brought further clarity to the course design. In discussing their materials and strategies, the life cycle group began to realize that the main emphasis of their work was the comparison of people and animals. By April they had decided to rename their part of the course the "Man and Animals Unit." Turning to DeVore for help in designing the unit rationale, they constructed a sequence that compared salmon, herring gulls, and baboons, using the concepts of life cycle, parental care, innate and learned behavior, social organization, ecological adaptation, and communication. DeVore opposed introducing the concept of evolution, because he thought it would be controversial and too difficult to teach to young children. He preferred a series of comparative studies that drew upon animal behavior to provide a contrast for the study of man.

Similarly, in presenting their ideas and approaches, the adaptation group began to realize that their principal focus had been on trying to clarify the concept of "culture." Dividing into two working parties, they developed both the Netsilik and Bushman units as comparative culture studies, and they asked anthropologists Balikci, Guggenheim, and Marshall for help in defining the conceptual framework. They wanted to be able to compare and contrast behavior across two cultures with similar subsistence patterns and to relate both to our own in order to bring out the aspects of human behavior that transcend the boundaries of culture. The proposal submitted to the National Science Foundation in April described the course as having two parts: a "Man and Animals" unit that examined man as a species, and a "Primitive Cultures" unit that looked at what it means to be human by comparing the Netsilik, the Bushmen, and ourselves. Learning about abstractions like life cycle, adaptation, ecological balance, innate and learned behavior, technology, social organization, child-rearing, and belief systems would derive from an immersion in the details of the human and animal case studies.

The Summer of 1966: The Acid Test

Our second summer school provided the first opportunity to try out the new units in sequence. Using six experimental classrooms we were able to test different combinations of the animal and human units and begin to experiment with teacher training under the supervision of Anita Mishler. Mornings were devoted to working with children and afternoons to scholar-led seminars on different content areas: DeVore on "Primatology and Evolution," Rosenbloom on "Man and Technology," Jones on "Theories of Instruction," and Balikci on "Cultural Anthropology." We rotated teaching, evaluation, and interviewing responsibilities between new and experienced teachers and had our first opportunity to learn about the reactions of teachers who had not participated in the development of the course. We had much to learn, it turned out, about how to reach teachers.

To ensure objectivity Bruner sought outside evaluation. He selected Sylvia Farnham-Diggory, a tough-minded cognitivist from the Carnegie Institute of Technology, to handle the task. Farnham-Diggory was fond of Bruner, but she was skeptical about his effort to teach psychological and anthropological concepts to ten-year-olds and was determined to use rigorous methods to see if MACOS really worked. During a preliminary visit to ESI in May, she closely questioned each working party to find out what content and conceptual information they hoped to get across so that she could construct proper pretests and posttests. She decided to administer intelligence tests to all students at the beginning of the summer session in order to measure the effectiveness of the materials with students of different abilities. "I do not know what evaluation ought to be," she later wrote. "My rule is simply to get as much information as possible, from as many different sources as possible, as systematically as possible."[38] Only after two or three years, she said, can you begin to know what sort of evaluation to use with a project of this kind.

Farnham-Diggory's evaluation was our first formal effort to find out what children were learning, or failing to learn, from MACOS. She gathered intelligence data on all children and administered a carefully designed pretest that provided baseline data against which she was able to measure the degree of content and conceptual learning students acquired during the summer school. Some staff members opposed this approach, which was far more structured than anything we had used before, protesting that emphasis on test-giving would instill negative attitudes in the children. One teacher even refused to administer the tests, claiming that testing might be damaging to the learning process. Farnham-Diggory had little patience with those who resisted formal testing in an experimental project, and she bluntly pointed out that her results would be meaningless without such tests.

Her findings, in fact, were to prove quite useful and instructive. She discovered, for example, that a "containers unit," which challenged children to create from simple materials durable carrying devices that would allow safe transport to and from school of two raw eggs and a cup of water, failed to produce a measurable impact on children's thinking about technology, even though it was hugely popular with students. On the other hand, a booklet entitled *Structure and Function,* a derivative of Marilyn Clayton's work that used simple line drawings to illustrate the contrast between animal morphology and human tool use, significantly strengthened student's ability to conceptualize important differences between humans and other animals. The responses of children in a control classroom that had not used the booklet further confirmed this finding. Clearly Clayton's approach to the handling of concepts was on the right track.

Other results were also encouraging. On the pupil rating scales administered midway through the summer school, students uniformly rated the clarity and interest of the reading high and the projects almost as high, and they were enthusiastic about the teaching. Boys rated the "ESI way of teaching" 83 percent different from public school, while girls rated it 62 percent different. Farnham-Diggory was particularly excited by this discovery because it suggested that our methods appeared to involve boys in the learning process more intensively than a traditional elementary school curriculum. "We all know," she wrote, "that there is a subtle discrimination against boys in a traditional setting. The girls get higher grades, have higher IQ's, are liked by teachers better, make better social adjustments, etc. . . . All of which goes to show that our traditional way of teaching suits girls better than it suits boys. Everybody knows this; nobody knows exactly what to do about it. The ESI curriculum is apparently doing something about it. That may be why the boys feel (even more strongly than the girls do) that 'the teaching is very different here.'"[39]

Parents, too, were almost universally enthusiastic about the course. They answered a lengthy questionnaire with such comments as, "It has been completely enjoyable for Richard," "Nancy seems to have gained considerable knowledge in a very short time," "Has especially enjoyed 'thinking things out,'" and "Extremely satisfied." One parent commented, "Each morning my daughter was up early and waiting for the time to go to school, which is most unusual for her. Never realized she could be so enthusiastic about a program of this type."[40] From the responses to the questionnaire, Farnham-Diggory concluded that the parents "were overwhelmingly pleased with the course, and so were the children."[41]

But Farnham-Diggory was not happy with the way teachers had been handled at ESI. She urged that we be much more candid with teachers, both about our methods and about alternatives open to them for the use of the materials. In drafting her formal recommendations at the end of the summer, she proposed that a closer relationship be established between the Instructional Research Group and the working parties. She suggested that the curriculum developers be trained in the techniques of evaluation so that they would become more inclined to experiment with alternative ways of presenting information, and she urged ESI to become more explicit with teachers about the rationale behind our way of teaching. She recommended that we develop a specific program for preparing teachers in the ESI curriculum philosophy and pedagogical techniques, and scolded us for our tendency to regard our methodology as some "mysterious 'mystique'": *"Giving the teacher the feeling that she has failed, when, in fact, curriculum development teams have failed to provide clear instruction, rationale and goals, is shockingly irresponsible."*[42]

To solve the teacher training problem Farnham-Diggory proposed the development of a "Sampler Training Workshop," a four-week seminar that could be implemented nationwide as the standard method for bringing the ESI curriculum into new schools. She recommended that teachers be selected on the basis of interest and special qualifications for teaching ESI material, and that no ESI materials be released unless such training had been completed. She urged immediate development of such a seminar series, suggesting that "it will probably save a dozen years of headaches in the introduction of the curriculum to the outside world."[43] Farnham-Diggory's teacher training suggestions made sense, and under Anita Mishler's direction, we set about developing a series of workshops along the lines she proposed, which became in time the backbone of the MACOS dissemination program. Although the "headaches" were to come anyway, the teacher-training needs that Farnham-Diggory identified were to prove critical to the success of the course.

The summer school of 1966 provided new evidence that the development of the course was on the right track. Students were uniformly enthusiastic about the materials, and at least parts of the curriculum had proved effective in getting them to transfer insights and ideas gained in the MACOS classrooms to other learning situations. The success of *Structure and Function* led to the expansion of the "concept book" idea to include other topics. One sunny day at Underwood a few of the staff gathered for lunch at a picnic table in the school yard and listened to DeVore sketch out some ideas he thought would be suitable for concept books: life cycle, innate and learned behavior, animal adaptation, information and behavior, and possibly even natural selection. Researchers Malcolm Slavin and Robert Trivers were especially enthusiastic about this idea, and they set to work, under DeVore's guidance, to develop some testable prototypes. Their approach was to keep written material to a minimum and make extensive use of carefully crafted illustrations to help carry the message of the text. Slavin and Trivers illustrated the early versions themselves to show that it was possible to integrate words and pictures in the transmission of a complex idea. Like *Structure and Function,* the new concept books were also successful and provided a conceptual vocabulary for relating the animal case studies.

The Form of the Course Evolves

We spent the ensuing academic year testing and revising the materials in classrooms in Newton, Boston, and several other schools in the Boston area. The course divided naturally into two parts. The first part we now called the "Man and Other Animals" unit. Because of complications with the Bushman material, the second part was narrowed to an intensive study of the Netsilik Eskimos. The course opened with a study of the life cycle of the king salmon. The salmon study introduced children to a species in which the parents die before their offspring are born and the young must survive without their aid. A comparison of salmon and human survival rates quickly pointed up the importance of parental care. The low percentage of salmon fingerlings that survive to adulthood, about two in six thousand, dramatically illustrated the contrast between humans, who invest a great deal of time in the care of their young, and a species that endures by maximizing the number of offspring. Parental investment proved to be a sensitive topic, particularly among children of broken or dysfunctional families, but it brought us directly to an examination of the importance of nurturing in humans, their prolonged period of immaturity compared to other animals, and the enormous percentage of time, comparatively speaking, that human beings devote to learning. For grade school children this was a topic of great relevance, and in the hands of a sensitive teacher discussion could become quite intense. Learning about how salmon achieve adulthood without reliance on parents enriched the discussion of humans and led to an examination of the difference between innate and learned behavior. While we made no value judgment here—salmon, in fact, have proven to be a very durable species—the uniqueness in the way humans go about the business of survival became vividly plain through the salmon materials. The responsibility of humans for the well-being of other species also became a topic as students considered our intrusion on salmon survival rates through overfishing and pollution.

Following the salmon materials came the study of herring gulls, one of the most durable creatures on Earth. Here students encountered a species in which two parents, mated for life, invest a great deal of energy in the protection and feeding of their offspring. Herring gull chicks are extremely vulnerable to predation at birth, but through constant feeding they grow as large as their parents within six weeks and are relatively free from danger once they learn to fly. The materials examined how herring gull chicks are adapted to their environment through protective coloration and how they are born with an innate response that enables them to induce their parents to regurgitate food for them by pecking at a red patch on the side of the parent's bill. A film about herring gulls showed that gull chicks will readily peck at any similar red object in the environment and that parents may mistake their larger young for hostile intruders if they do not duck their heads in submission. By studying the film and related booklets, our students learned that what appears at first to be "caring" as humans know it is actually innate behavior. The instinctive nature of these responses, in a species that appears on the surface to display such parental devotion, further illustrates the uniqueness of the way human beings relate to each other.

Yet children are not always quick to accept these differences. During one memorable class at Underwood students were asked to "role-play" parent-offspring interactions among the herring gulls. We were startled to discover that ten-year-olds in Newton were quite accustomed to begging for cookies and lowering their heads in deference to parents. Submission did not strike them as behavior confined to herring gulls. One of the most striking results of the use of these animal behavior studies with young students was our recognition of the degree to which human beings tend to anthropomorphize animals and to see in them reflections of their own experience. To our surprise we found that it was impossible to deal with animal-human comparisons in an unambiguous way. The animal material was valuable not only for the perspective it brought to the discussion of human behavior but also for the reminder it provided of the biological kinship of human beings and other creatures. We may be uniquely gifted learners and communicators, but we share many social and behavioral characteristics with our nonhuman companions, and the need to understand these relationships seems deeply rooted in the human psyche.

The salmon and herring gull units provided important introductory material for our more extensive case study of free-ranging baboons. These early studies gave students a background in the biology of behavior, which they could now apply to an examination of one of our closest primate relatives. For the purposes of the course, the most striking feature of baboon life is their highly developed social organization and the process of socialization and system of communication that accompanies it. Through their field studies DeVore and Washburn uncovered a dominance hierarchy and complex social structure in troops of forty to over a hundred members, which had enabled baboons to defend themselves against large predators in the open African savannah grasslands where food was most abundant. During the process of growing up, young baboons must learn how to behave effectively in this environment, including the social environment, since the most socially skillful have the greatest chance for survival and the greatest likelihood of maximizing their reproductive success.

The baboons materials were an instant hit with students. They identified with the baboons, invested them with humanlike qualities from the outset, and were especially intrigued by how baboons grow up. It was not hard to see why. Infants are born black, have pink faces, and are enormously attractive to other members of the troop. They are nursed, groomed, cuddled, and carried clinging to their mother's stomach until, at about four months, they learn to ride "jockey style" on their mother's back. At about eight months of age, when they begin to turn the tawny brown color of the adults, the weaning process begins, and soon they are pushed out into the world to begin foraging for themselves. As the young males begin to leave their mothers, the adult males, particularly the large dominant males of troop, begin to care for the young, grooming them and watching that they don't injure themselves in the rough play-fighting that takes place among the juveniles. Maturing females are more inclined to stay with the mothers and infants.

Growing up for a young baboon, male or female, is fraught with the struggle to establish a position of dominance within the troop hierarchy while also learning to cooperate with others. Aggressiveness in baboons must be tempered by the ability to collaborate, for it is only by acting together that adult baboon males can protect the troop against their most dangerous predators, leopards and cheetahs. To observe a group of young male baboons play-fighting is to watch a highly volatile wrestling match, a wild mixture of aggressive, playful, and affectionate exchanges, the object of which seems to be to establish who is dominant. In one memorable sequence of DeVore's Amboseli game park footage, children saw three young baboons playing in a thorn bush, climbing up, swinging out on a branch, and then dislodging each other from the highest perch in a game that looks remarkably like "King of the Castle," all under the watchful and protective eye of a nearby male.

The baboon study also examined social organization, individual differences, and the relationships between individuals. The children received a copy of DeVore's original field notes in which individuals are named and identified by their unique physical and behavioral characteristics. By studying these notes they could see how the behavior of individual troop members contributed to the survival of the troop as a whole. They learned about the dominance hierarchy within the troop, which establishes the social order, and about the way in which troop members coordinate their behavior to ensure protection in time of danger. They saw how the troop is organized so that its most vulnerable members receive the greatest protection and how the young juveniles, who are expected to protect the troops flanks, are considered somewhat expendable. And they studied how baboon communication relates to social behavior. DeVore and Washburn identified twenty-two distinct sounds and gestures, which express different levels of emotional arousal, anger, fear, and threat and serve to modulate social relationships, alert the troop to the presence of danger, and maintain the stability of the social order. Eyelid threats, ground slapping, baring of the canine teeth, and various barks are all well understood by each troop member. Study of these nonverbal forms of communication and their function in a social context provided a basis for children to consider the importance of human language. While this topic was never fully developed in the course, the baboon materials, with their emphasis on learning, social organization, and communication, provided an excellent starting point. Here, the differences between animal communication and human language are beautifully illustrated.

The animal studies gradually built up a conceptual vocabulary and a body of data that helped children think about the biological nature of man, about the characteristics that we share with other animals, and about the features that make us unique as a species. We stressed the importance of understanding behavior in relationship to environment, and how humans have been able to overcome many of the limitations imposed on other animals by creating their own environments. For the teachers, this biologically oriented approach was a unique way of teaching social studies, and for many of them it required a good deal of rethinking about what was appropriate material. In an introductory piece for teachers, DeVore explained our rationale for the use of animal studies in a course about human beings:

> It may still seem to you that what we are asking you to do is to teach biology in the early part of a social studies course. Actually, at colleges and universities today, the old barriers that once stood between biology and social studies are disappearing very rapidly. One often hears these days of the "behavioral sciences." In a sense, the behavioral sciences are dedicated to the notion that to understand behavior, human or animal, you must take into account something of the organism's biology, something of its life strategy, its life cycle, its social organization, and the length of time parents care for the young. What we are trying to do is to bring into the classroom these new behavioral ways of approaching a perspective of man's human nature and some of the intellectual ferment that goes with them.[44]

A Culture Study: The Netsilik Eskimos

Following the biological perspectives provided by the animal units, we introduced the study of culture. At the outset we had hoped to use both the Bushman and Eskimo materials to build on the strategy of comparison and contrast we had developed in the animal units. We were fortunate to have two well-documented examples of hunter-gatherer societies that occupied very different habitats. Hunter-gatherers had been selected originally because of the simplicity of studying small-scale societies and because the hunter-gatherer way of life represented the oldest and most enduring form of human adaptation. What better way to begin the study of human beings than by examining the few surviving fragments of the way of life that sustained our species for most of human history? Furthermore, the Bushman and Netsilik film archives represent the most extensive visual record of hunter-gatherers available anywhere. While we did not have a firm commitment from the Marshalls to include the materials in a final published edition of the course, they were strongly supportive of our work, and we expected, if the unit proved successful, that they would eventually agree to publication. Lacking that commitment, however, Bruner had cautioned us to design the unit with a "zipper" so it could be removed if necessary.

Unfortunately, Bruner's worries proved prophetic. After two years of work and extensive classroom testing, we were forced to abandon the Bushman materials, not because the Marshalls opposed its use, but for political reasons. Despite great success in our classroom tryouts, including many inner-city classrooms in Boston and Philadelphia, by 1967 it had become politically unacceptable to use materials that showed partially naked, dark-skinned "primitives" in a public school classroom. Students and teachers who had used the materials had been almost universally enthusiastic about the Bushman unit, and some even thought, because of the appeal of the central characters and the lack of reconstruction, that the Bushman study gave us a more intimate and engaging view of a subsistence culture than the Netsilik materials provided. The special quality of Bushman life—their delightful stories, their gentle way of dealing with each other, their resourcefulness in coping with a very hostile environment, and their sense of humor—endeared them to children, and it was only with great reluctance that we withdrew the Bushman materials from the course. The teaching power of MACOS was diminished by their loss.

The Bushman decision left us with the Netsilik materials as the remaining resource from which to construct our study of culture. Balikci's film series, as we have seen, was designed to reveal the way the Netsilik lived when they were first encountered by Knud Rasmussen in 1923, before the introduction of guns, Christianity, and other Western influences, and to show, without commentary, how this traditional hunting society sustained itself under the harshest conditions on Earth using nothing more than the rocks and snow and the bones and skin of the creatures that inhabit their barren arctic habitat. Children came to know the central characters in this stark drama: Itimangnark, father and accomplished hunter; Kingnuk, his stalwart wife, whose domestic activities equal her husband's in importance; Umiapik, their six-year-old stepson who must learn how to survive from his parents; Tunglik, Itmangnark's hunting partner; Irkowagtok, his brother; and Iluitsok, the old grandmother who tells the children stories about how things used to be. Through prolonged exposure to these people and their rigorous way of life, students identified with the resourcefulness of this extended Inuit family, and by studying the details of their lives, began to understand the general features of their culture that make survival possible with such limited resources under such difficult conditions. It is plain from viewing the Netsilik films that their society is based upon a network of mutually interdependent relationships.

The simplicity of the Netsilik material culture, and the small scale of the social system, made this case study ideal for teaching young children about the nature of human society. Each adult man and woman possesses the knowledge necessary for carrying out his or her role successfully in this demanding environment. A married couple living and working together, perhaps accompanied by a few friends or relatives, constitute a self-sufficient economic unit in the summertime when stone weir fishing is the primary subsistence activity. The fall caribou hunt requires a more extensive collaboration between hunters and beaters, and here we find larger family groups living together. But it is in winter, the harshest time of year, when we see the culture in its most elaborated form and experience its power to sustain human life. Winter presents the greatest challenge, since food is scarce, darkness prevails, and snow, wind, and bitter cold are a constant danger. Survival depends almost entirely on mutual support and the success of the seal hunt. Here kin and nonkin collaborate to pursue this highly intelligent and elusive creature upon which their lives depend, which lives in a world concealed beneath the sea ice, occasionally surfacing for air at one of fifteen or twenty widely separated breathing holes. To locate and harpoon a seal through one of these hidden breathing places requires enormous patience and skill, and anyone who has witnessed it in Balikci's films comes away with a deeper appreciation of the enormous ingenuity that has made human life possible under these extreme conditions. The successful hunter ritually shares his catch with the rest of the camp according to patterns established by ancient custom, thus ensuring that, if one hunter triumphs, no one will starve during this brutally difficult time of year.

Children studying this material were amazed to discover the resourcefulness of Netsilik technology. They were impressed by the unique design of the fishing leister, which can snare an arctic char with a single blow, and the clever strategy of the caribou hunt, which employs stone decoys called *innukskuk* as "scarecrows" to divert the fleet-footed caribou into the lakes where they can be easily speared from kayaks. They were fascinated by the intricate set of tools used by the seal hunter to prepare the breathing hole, to detect the seal's presence when it comes to breathe, and to harpoon and capture him. And they were captivated by the ingenuity of the skin sled made from caribou hide, leg bones, and the carcasses of frozen fish, and the efficiency of the igloo with its spiral construction, its insulating properties, its classic design, and its use of the air-capture principle for retaining warmth. They could see in these deceptively simple devices the means by which these clever people had transformed an otherwise hostile environment in a way that had made human life possible.

They also came to appreciate the logic of Netsilik social behavior: the sensible division of tasks between men and women; the way children learn what they need to know without benefit of formal schooling; the emphasis placed on sharing and reciprocity; the importance of play for both children and adults, including contests of strength and skill; and the many ways in which the Netsilik's daily activities reinforce the bonds of mutual obligation and provide both economic and psychological support within the society. They were surprised to discover that in winter, when the environmental pressure is most severe, the Netsilik work hardest to help each other, affirming the importance of collaboration in the struggle to survive. Although the Netsilik face difficult choices, especially with regard to the old and infirm who are incapable of supporting themselves, the anthropological literature contains few more impressive examples of the centrality of reciprocity in human society. The Netsilik study provided an impressive reaffirmation that human beings are fundamentally social creatures.

Children also learned something about the relationship between belief and behavior. Initially, the students tended to regard Netsilik myths, such as the story of the orphaned sea-goddess Nuliajuk, as exotic and primitive, and they were put off by the practice of shamanism, the use of amulets, and the exploits of the legendary hero Kiviok, who could transform himself into an animal at will. But the more they examined these curious stories, the more they began to see parallels in the fairy tales and religious rituals of their own lives and in the many ways we attempt to manage uncertainty. As one sixth-grader sagely remarked after a long discussion about whether Netsilik beliefs were more primitive than ours, "We believe, some of us, in a male god that lives in the sky; they believe in a female goddess that lives under the sea. Are they so different?"

Our most difficult design problem in this unit was to find a way to present the culture that avoided a simplistic interpretation of Netsilik behavior as solely a response to the problems of survival in a harsh environment. Cultures arise from social and spiritual needs, not just subsistence requirements, and like ourselves, the Netsilik had evolved a way of life that provided for their psychological as well as their physical well-being. In our first version of the unit we trapped ourselves by beginning with technology, following with social organization, and concluding with belief systems. The progression was logical, proceeding, in a sense, from the concrete to the abstract, but the problem with this approach was that students came to think of Netsilik culture as technologically and environmentally determined. To the children they appeared as hunters first and people second, and since the unit followed the study of baboons, we ran the risk of making them appear more like clever animals than human beings.

To counter this impression we reordered our lessons and began the course by examining the Netsiliks' "inner world" as well as their external behavior. The teacher's guide made the point in the first lesson:

> Man lives in two worlds, one of things he can touch and another of things he cannot touch. The world of the intangible includes the meanings that man attaches to his environment and his actions. To know man, we must inquire into these meanings; to know the Netsilik, we must listen to their stories, legends, and myths.[45]

From the first day we discussed the way Kingnuk beautifies herself with a bit of fur braided into her hair, the meaning of the ashes that she places on the eyes of the fish her husband has caught, the stories that she tells her child, and how this inner life relates to the way the Netsilik make tools, catch fish, instruct their children, and define the network of social obligations. We wanted the students to realize that to understand another culture we need to comprehend how they perceive and interpret the world around them, not just how they behave. We therefore set out to present all aspects of the culture at one time so that children would get a sense of their interaction and not be misled into believing that there is one primary cause that shapes the way people live. We wanted them to see that in understanding the forces that form a culture, as Dick Rosenbloom once said, "there is no unmoved mover."

For children fully to appreciate the humanity of the Netsilik, or of the members of any culture, including their own, they must become conversant with the values that underlie the behaviors they observe. For the Netsilik the dominant values are cooperation and sharing. Men and women collaborate, dividing their labor so that both benefit equally from the partnership. Activities like working and playing together, telling stories and joking, sharing responsibility for protecting and teaching their children, and sleeping together as a family so that everyone keeps warm, create powerful social and psychological bonds. Cooperation extends beyond the family to the seal-hunting partnership that unites two unrelated men in a lifelong web of reciprocity that protects both families. By stressing these values we wanted children to see the Netsilik as human beings on their own terms, neither better nor worse than ourselves but cultural equals. By coming to know the resourcefulness of their technology, the sophistication of their social relationships, the quality of interaction between parent and child, and the spiritual strength of their belief system, our students, we hoped, would learn to respect a culture quite different from their own, and by getting to know another culture well, come to understand the common humanity that all humans share.

We concluded the course with a brief study of acculturation called *The Netsilik Today*. Using materials gathered by Balikci in the 1960s, together with a film made by public television station WGBH in Boston in the early 1970s, students examined life in the modern village of Pelly Bay, where the Netsilik now live in heated houses supplied by the Canadian government, receive welfare checks, play pool and basketball, listen to disco music, attend Mass, and make soapstone carvings for the tourist trade. Parents learn to house their infants in separate rooms, and teenagers are sent off to high school hundreds of miles away. Seals and caribou are hunted with rifles and motor boats, but many of the traditional ways of living remain: the ceremonial igloo continues to be used on occasion for celebrating Mass, fur parkas are preferred to nylon because nylon is too noisy for hunting, and ancient skills are still required to locate the illusive seal. Pelly Bay has a store run by the Catholic mission where women can buy sewing materials and tea, and men can buy guns, tobacco, liquor, and steel tools. The materials included interviews and biographical information, and provided the basis for a consideration of what happens when cultures change. Discussion of the impact of our culture on theirs, and both the positive and negative results of that interaction, provided a fitting close for the Netsilik study.

The Uses of Media

Although I have discussed ESI's approach to pedagogical film-making at some length, of equal concern was the pedagogical design of the rest of the course materials. For Bruner it was not enough to get the ideas straight and the teaching strategies properly worked out. For the course to be successful, he liked to say, "the materials themselves must be human." By this he meant that they should convey in their design and in the plan for their use a respect for the humanity of the student. They must be esthetically pleasing, must contain drama and pathos and humor, and must engage and respect the intelligence and curiosity of those who used them. He wanted the materials to offer students a variety of ways of getting into the subject and to provide teachers with a powerful alternative to the textbook by replacing it with a highly diversified library of curriculum materials. He believed that in design, format, style, and illustration the materials should reflect a wide imaginative range and standards of artistic excellence not normally found in the elementary classroom.

Games and Simulations

Bruner saw design as an integral part of the development process, and he argued that the substance of an idea and the medium in which it was expressed were equally important curriculum concerns. In the spring of 1965 he had hired Michael Sand, a student of Charles Eames and a recent graduate of the Rhode Island School of Design, to head up the MACOS design effort. By charging him with examining every aspect of the Elementary Program, Bruner hoped to include the designer's perspective from the earliest stages of the development process. Sand had designed materials for the Boston's Children's Museum, and he was particularly interested in creating physical materials for use in the social studies. He later reflected on these early discussions with Bruner:

> Jerry conveyed to me [a vision] that social science teaching in this country has special obstacles to overcome that science teaching

was not faced with. It was so accepted by then that [in science] kids should learn from their own experience, the whole laboratory-learning approach of getting kids to explore phenomena and try out hypotheses . . . and having demonstrations and models and examples of things that you could observe . . . Jerry felt that with social science teaching . . . you're dealing with students who are not really in control of social situations, so he was very anxious to . . . see if there were ways we could invent models or invent methods that would give kids a chance to try out things and see the consequences of them.[46]

Sand explored many ways of bringing "laboratory learning" into MACOS. I have already discussed his High Seas Game and sentence-generating machine for teaching language concepts, his baboon silhouettes and environment boards for helping children to imagine life on the African savannah, and his "container's unit," which attempted to give children a sense of how the Bushmen solve their transportation problems. With Hans Guggenheim he developed a full-sized "take-apart seal" to help students simulate the Netsilik meat-sharing ritual. And to help children develop an appreciation for how a hunter thinks, he created a little classroom exercise called "Stalking the Paperclip," which invited children to find, approach, capture, and retrieve their paperclip "prey" in the classroom. But his proudest accomplishment was his participation in the development of the Eskimo hunting games.

Before Sand's arrival at ESI Clark Abt had been responsible for game design. Abt's approach, as we have seen, was derived from his Pentagon experience. It relied heavily on a detailed replication of the situation being modeled and employed competition between game participants to create interest. In the work he did for MACOS we found that although his games stimulated student involvement, they did not create the process of reflection we were seeking. One evaluator in the summer of 1965 described the problem with Abt's Bushman hunting game:

The class then played the hunting game again, apparently with great enthusiasm. New rules to allow for cooperation were used and each table played as a unit. But it still seems that there is a separation in the children's minds between how they play this game and how real hunting is done. I suspect it is because a game is, by definition almost, something entered into purely for fun—it is not classified as a way of learning anything except how to play it better, and perhaps the importation of the seriousness of real life into it is something the children resist. The relationship between the game and their understanding of the problem of hunting needs exploration, however, by explicit discussion.[47]

Subsequently, Abt's designers set about constructing a simulation of the Netsilik caribou hunt, but this game turned out to be even more elaborate than the Bushman game. The rules were so complicated that the teacher had to serve as referee, which meant that only one group of students could play at a time. The map was a detailed simulation of the arctic environment, and to play the game properly the students needed a comprehensive knowledge of Netsilik hunting practices. In effect, the game was an elaborately staged role-playing exercise in which students were required to act out a proper Eskimo caribou hunt. Jerry Fletcher, a researcher we had hired to evaluate the game, was disappointed by what he saw. While observing the game Fletcher began to formulate some fresh ideas about how our hunting games should be designed:

> In its present form the game is not very well designed to teach a sense of strategy or planning. This is primarily because there aren't any alternative strategies that are acceptable or discernible. The point of the game is basically replication, to act out a predetermined pattern, to get the players to catch a caribou the way the Netsilik do. In order to have a game teach strategy, in order to make "planning" a conscious concept, there have to be several ways of playing the game all with some chance of success but some better than others, and these alternative strategies have to be consciously recognizable. This game does not even potentially have this.[48]

Following this experience we abandoned Abt's approach and decided to design our own games. Under the guidance of Dick Rosenbloom, a team consisting of Sand, Fletcher, and a Newton teacher named Don Koeller began to develop some games that more nearly reflected our teaching objectives. First they established their design criteria: pare the game action to the bare essentials; simplify the map, drastically cut the cycle time, reduce the number of players, and construct a record-keeping system so that students can keep track of the progress and the results of their play. Role-playing and analysis had proved incompatible, so they discarded the former in favor of the latter. Their objective was to construct an exercise that would enable children to reflect on the strategy of the hunt, not necessarily to experience it; to do this children must be able to experiment with alternative approaches, compare them, and evolve through successive plays an optimal hunting strategy. The result would not be a competitive game in the Abt sense but an exercise in contemplation and invention. In time, every child would be able to discover an appropriate strategy for catching a caribou. Having accomplished this, the game would have completed its teaching job and further play would be unnecessary.

The new caribou game introduced a disposable board on which students tracked moves with magic markers. At the end of each play they had a record of the movements of both Eskimos and caribou that served as a ready reference for working on improving their strategy in the next cycle of play. Through several successive plays students could chart their progress as they advanced toward comprehension of the optimum hunting strategy. Fletcher evaluated the new game in three classrooms during the summer of 1967 and he was amazed by the results: "The overall improvement on the post-test—3.417 right answers per student on a twelve question test—is significant beyond our wildest dreams. Providing the questions test material which is also taught in the body of the unit, and which is important to more than just the game, the game is a great learning device."[49]

Even more challenging was the development of the seal-hunting game. The problem for the seal hunter was quite different from that of the caribou hunter. To catch a seal in winter, the Netsilik must locate an active seal breathing hole, one of perhaps twenty tended by a given seal, and harpoon the seal when it surfaces for air. Seal hunting is thus in part a game of chance—of picking the right hole to wait by. Sand first designed a prototype game in the form of a kind of roulette wheel, a board perforated with holes under which he mounded a disk fitted out with randomly placed dots. When the student spun the disk, "seals" appeared at a few of the holes. Sand plugged the holes with corks so that the students had to guess where the seals were. Successful hunters got fed; unsuccessful hunters went hungry.

From this first design the game progressed through several versions to its final form, which consisted of a laminated board with 144 holes. "Seals," represented by printed "meat stickers," were loaded into the back of the board prior to play, and students hunted for them by puncturing a disposable paper cover in their search. One seal could feed a hunter for five days, a hunter could survive three days without food, and the object of the game was for each hunter to try to remain alive for twenty days. As with the caribou game, there was a record-keeping system, a pad of score sheets the players used to keep track of their individual hunting performance. The contest here was between man and nature, not between players. To "win" hunters had to figure out how to beat odds that favored starvation. Two strategies, students discovered, maximized the chances for all to remain alive: cluster hunting and sharing. By cooperating in the hunt to saturate a given area of the board and by sharing the catch of the successful hunters, the whole group had a good chance of surviving. If the outcome were left wholly to chance, however, some hunters would live—perhaps in abundance—and others would almost certainly starve.

In the seal-hunting game, as in the caribou game, students were free to decide how they wished to conduct the hunt, without adult intervention. Left alone, most students began by competing with each other, giving little thought to sharing or cooperation. When they realized that their survival might depend upon collaboration, however, they began to share, make deals, and discuss cooperative hunting strategies. Playing the game usually produced a range of responses and solutions. Some children were inclined to "go it alone" and risk starvation for larger rewards, while others preferred the lower risk-lower gain strategy of cooperation and sharing. Because of the chance factor in the game, sharing usually proved to be the most consistently successful survival strategy. Playing the game gave children a new perspective on the importance of Netsilik hunting partnerships and seal-sharing practices and often led to a discussion of differences between Netsilik and American values.

"Seal Hunting" turned out to be a powerful teaching tool for helping children realize why the Netsilik social system is structured as it is, and by extrapolation, why all cultures employ some system of exchange and reciprocity. The "insurance" provided by the Netsilik sharing system suggests that selection for cooperation is deeply rooted in our evolutionary history. Eskimos hunt together and share their catch, not because they are more virtuous or altruistic than other people, but because it is the way of living that has proved most successful in ensuring their survival under the conditions in which they live. Sharing and cooperation are behaviors that people value because people that have practiced such behaviors have managed to prevail under extremely harsh conditions. This is the message that we hoped our students would retain from the seal-hunting game long after they had forgotten the details of the hunt.

Written Materials

Much has already been said about the ESI aversion to the textbook and commitment to the use of original sources in the design of written materials for children. Sharing scholarship with elementary school students, however, created some special problems. It was one thing to translate anthropological field work into ethnographic films; it was quite another to take the field notes, diaries, monographs, and theoretical papers of Rasmussen, Balikci, DeVore, Drury, Tinbergen, and others and turn them over to young children. Barbara Boylan and Anita Gil worked closely with Michael Sand to create written materials that drew upon these resources while at the same time making them attractive and accessible to ten-year-olds. They tried to achieve maximum integration of text and illustration to convey as much information as possible with a minimum of reading, thus making the ideas of the course comprehensible to the widest possible range of students.

An early result of this collaboration between the design and editorial departments was a set of baboon booklets that combined a brief descriptive text with a profusion of illustrations, diagrams, and charts. These booklets covered topics like growing up, the organization of the troop, baboon communication, and the animal ecology of the African savannah. The booklets began with the most easily assimilated information, and the weightiness of the text gradually increased as the students progressed through the unit. For source material Sand prepared a convincing facsimile edition of DeVore's field notes, typewritten on yellow lined paper with handwritten corrections, glued-in photographs, and DeVore's original "Reward if Returned" notice in the front. (Some children actually sent their books to DeVore in hopes of claiming the reward.)

The strategy of using pictures to teach ideas worked particularly well in the concept books. Complex notions like structure and function, or natural selection, were presented in a series of cartoonlike drawings, which helped to carry the concept. Trivers and Slavin provided examples of appropriate illustrations with their original manuscripts for these booklets, and Sand then reworked these drafts using professional designers and illustrators. The designers thus became direct collaborators with the writers in the development of the material. The success of these booklets bore out Bruner's conviction that design should influence development and not be treated as a cosmetic afterthought. The booklets turned out to be a very economical and engaging way of getting across complex ideas, and DeVore was so impressed with the results of these efforts that he assigned some of the booklets in his undergraduate animal behavior course at Harvard.

Another influence in the development of the materials was Bruner's notion that the written material of the course should be presented in different forms so that children could develop an appreciation of different literary genres. Anita Gil remembered a discussion with Bruner about this:

> He came to me . . . and he said, "I want the children to get more out of this course. I want them to get more out of it than substance or inquiry. They've got to learn that, or they'll be illiterate, but on top of that they have to learn style. Can you go through Rasmussen and pick out four or five very different styles of writing? They exist in Rasmussen. I would like them to exist in the course so the children can begin to perceive that you write myth in a different language than you write history, than you write description." His notion [was] that each mode of expression has its own language, and that a really well-educated person knows how to use these differentially.[50]

So we created written materials for the Netsilik unit that reflected the variety of styles Bruner proposed. I have already noted that Edward Field translated Netsilik legends into poetic form and that Carter Wilson created fiction from Rasmussen's ethnography. In addition, Barbara Boylan wrote two factual books on arctic life, an ecology handbook entitled *The Arctic,* and a mini-encyclopedia of Inuit artifacts entitled *The Data Book.* We also created a children's edition of Rasmussen's journal called *A Journey to the Arctic,* and even Bruner tried his hand at transliteration by reproducing in mythic form a book about a legendary Netsilik hero called *The Many Lives of Kiviok.* Through this range of written materials, each cast in a different literary form, we attempted to reach children with different learning styles and show that a given body of information can be expressed and interpreted in different ways. This was a long way from the typical textbook.

The diversity of written material in MACOS was one of the important ways the course differed in form and style from a traditional course. Boylan, who in her former editing job had been exposed to the rigidities of "readability formulas" and "word counts," found the ESI approach a refreshing change. As she commented, "The problem was that the readability formulas were so arbitrary. They tested for long or 'unfamiliar' words, long sentences, and number of personal pronouns. They did not test for style, humor, grace in the use of language, any of the more subjective things that make us love or hate what we are reading . . . I didn't think that readability meant readableness, and of course we know that is true because most of what we consider children's classics score much higher [on the readability formulas] than the age at which they are generally read."[51] Boylan suggested that by letting the material take its natural literary form and by providing for variety and increasing difficulty as the course evolved, we might have achieved many of the "readability" objectives that publishers were looking for in their more restricted approach. "It would be possible," she wrote, "to do a nice, rigid little set of readings for ten-year-olds on an Eskimo culture, but you would have to work at it. The data . . . just naturally demand different modes, different styles."[52]

Postscript to Development

By the fall of 1967 we had created a workable course with content, teaching methods, and student materials well in hand. After two years of development and three summer tryouts, we had a program of study that appealed to teachers and students. We still had to clarify lessons, rewrite booklets, complete some of the films, and redesign and test some of the games, but the basic course was in place. In its final form it consisted of nine teacher's guides, thirty children's booklets, sixteen films, four records, five filmstrips, three games, fifty-four artifact cards, two wall-sized maps, a caribou-hunting strategy chart, a kinship chart, a sea ice camp chart, eleven enlarged photographs taken from the Netsilik films, several poster-sized photo murals, and a take-apart seal.

The challenges remaining were to complete the program of

teacher education, to develop an implementation plan that would provide for widespread teacher support, and to find a suitable publisher. We approached these tasks confident that we had developed a powerful new way to teach social studies, and that teaching it to others and making it available on a large scale would be relatively easy. We knew we had an exciting course that worked with children, and the school systems using it were uniformly enthusiastic. As one school administrator put it after evaluating the program in his school, "the best suggestion I could give to those who might want to consider whether the investment is worthwhile would be that they take an opportunity to talk to the students themselves. I have yet to see a course of study as enthusiastically received."[53] With this sort of response, we were certain that publishers would leap at the opportunity to distribute it. We couldn't have been more wrong.

Yet for a brief time MACOS became something of a cause célèbre in educational circles. School system after school system in both the suburbs and the inner city gave the course glowing reviews. In a study of twenty national social studies curriculum projects in 270 California classrooms between 1968 and 1971, MACOS was rated by both teachers and students as clearly superior to all other programs.[54] In 1969, when we were at the height of our struggle to find a publisher, Bruner received an award jointly from the American Educational Research Association and the American Educational Publishers Institute for his leadership in the development of a course that the citation called "one of the most important efforts of our time to relate research findings and theory in educational psychology to the development of new and better instructional material," and "enormously suggestive of what we could and should be doing to equip the instructional process adequately."[55] He spent most of the cash prize on a lavish party for the staff who, as they downed champagne, joked about the irony of recognition from those who by then had turned down our publishing proposals. Someone called the award "hush money."

But did the MACOS of 1970 fulfill Bruner's original objectives? To what extent was his hoped-for marriage between the insights of academia and the intellectual development of children actually achieved? This question is not easy to address, partly because of the enormous range of his ideas and partly because his aspirations for the course changed in response to the findings of our research and classroom experience. It is fair to say, however, that MACOS turned out to be much less cognitive than Bruner, ideally, would have liked. Anxious to get "the maximum degree of travel from a minimum array of information" he was surprised to learn that ten-year-olds needed so much data in order to discover an idea. He preferred his "Marienbad teasers" to the longer films and brief units like Marilyn Clayton's adaptation exercises to the full-blown units on salmon or herring gulls. Almost anything can be made interesting, he had said at Westtown, but the trick is to be able to help children grasp the ideas that have intellectual "travel" and bring clarity to new situations. He had spent a good deal of time brooding about how education could be designed to give children new and more powerful ways of dealing with the explosion of information that is characteristic of contemporary life, and he was impatient with the amount of time it took to make a measurably significant impact on the structure of children's thinking.

He was especially disappointed by our failure to devise lessons to help children appreciate the power of human language. For Bruner, one of the most important things about what makes human beings human is their symbolizing capacity. He wanted children to understand that language is what makes culture possible, and that it is culture that has enabled humankind to escape from the iron laws of natural selection. To understand the true meaning of humanness, he said, children have to appreciate the enormous breakthrough that language represents in setting human beings apart from other creatures and in making it possible to create and adapt to an environment of their own devising. It is through their symbolizing capacity more than anything else, he stressed, that humans have taken control over their own evolution. In failing to get across this crucial idea in ways that could be measured conclusively, MACOS fell short of Bruner's most cherished hopes and expectations.

Yet to appreciate Bruner's true feelings about the course we have to consider his commitment to the "left hand" of human development as well as to the right. Although he is most cited for his references to "the importance of structure," he had also spoken and written extensively on the importance of intuitive understanding, even though this aspect of knowing is much more difficult to assess. In a little book of essays published in 1962 he wrote:

> Since childhood, I have been enchanted by the fact and the symbolism of the right hand and the left—the one the doer, the other the dreamer. The right is order and lawfulness, *le droit*. Its beau-

ties are those of geometry and taut implication. Reaching for knowledge with the right hand is science. Yet to say only that much of science is to overlook one of its excitements, for the great hypotheses of science are gifts carried in the left hand . . .

It is an approach whose medium of exchange seems to be the metaphor paid out by the left hand. It is a way that grows happy hunches and "lucky" guesses, that is stirred into connective activity by the poet and the necromancer looking sidewise rather than directly. Their hunches and intuitions generate a grammar of their own—searching out connections, suggesting similarities, weaving ideas loosely in a trial web.[56]

Much of MACOS was based on this looser, more intuitive way of knowing. The primary source of information, unnarrated ethnographic film, stimulated speculation and aroused student curiosity in a way that permitted multiple lines of inquiry rather than the linear presentation of a single idea. It encouraged intuitive as well as cognitive responses and gave all children equal access to information, regardless of their reading ability. It turned out to be a superb catalyst for discussion and for wide-ranging speculation. Aroused in this way, students were motivated to search for answers in the many other materials provided. The ability of the course to engage children's curiosity was one of its most significant cognitive achievements. How that curiosity was kept alive and gradually channeled from intuitive ways of understanding to more explicitly conceptual ones became the task of the sensitive teacher, and we had much to learn about how to cultivate that sensitivity. To put intuitive understanding first was a reversal of the normal teaching process, for it assumed that understanding was already within the child and that teaching was a matter of teasing out and making explicit what students already intuitively knew.

Finally, we must consider the emotional power of the course. It contained materials that dealt with some of life's most central issues—birth, death, reproduction, mate selection and marriage, conflict and cooperation, caring and sharing, learning, surviving, explaining, believing—and brought to the classroom topics central to the psychological well-being of the child. As Richard Jones had often pointed out, when handled by a sensitive and well-trained teacher, the MACOS materials were especially well suited to addressing emotional issues. By distancing these issues through a strategy of comparison and contrast that drew upon the study of animals as well as very different cultures, the course was especially strong in helping children address some of the central questions of their own personal lives. While this pedagogical power of MACOS proved to be controversial in some communities, the course frequently succeeded in reaching children "where they live," a rare achievement in social studies courses.

But what about "the importance of structure"? Contrary to much that has been written about his educational views, Bruner was not especially interested in teaching the "structure" of a particular "discipline" for its own sake. What intrigued him most was the power of a clear idea and how it permitted the learner to achieve transfer of understanding. The ideas that particularly excited him were not those that defined the narrow vocabulary of a particular field of study but rather, the larger organizing conjectures that made it possible for the thoughtful person to transcend his discipline. He never thought of MACOS as a course designed to teach the concepts of anthropology or behavioral biology as an end in themselves. That may be sufficient for the specialist but not for the student in pursuit of a liberal education. Bruner looked for powerful ways of thinking, wherever they could be found, in order to deepen children's understanding of the nature of their humanity. The ideas that particularly intrigued him—such as the principle of reciprocity within a social system or substitutability within a technical system, or the concept of arbitrariness as it applies to our understanding of language, or the synthesizing power of myth—did so precisely because they had the capacity to draw information from many fields of study in support of a deeper understanding of ourselves. He was in search of a vocabulary of thought that would make the language of our humanness more comprehensible to everyone, not just the professional academic. In seeking this objective, the reach of MACOS often exceeded its grasp, when measured objectively. But by striving for this more universal level of understanding the course stimulated the imagination of educators about what a powerful social studies course might be.

· 4 ·

From Widener to Wichita

There was ambivalence about teachers at ESI. On the one hand the Social Studies Program viewed its work as a panacea for teachers, a liberation from the drudgery of textbook materials and didactic lessons. On the other, professional educators were seen as dull-witted people who conversed in an incomprehensible "middle language" and were responsible for the uninspired state of American education. Much of ESI's experimental work in mathematics and the sciences had resulted from direct interaction between scholars and schoolchildren, and there had even been some loose talk in the early days about developing "teacher-proof" materials. Some scholars had adopted the Bestorite view that all you had to do was serve up the most stimulating fare that Harvard's Widener Library had to offer, and the materials would carry themselves. Even in the rarefied environment of Cambridge, however, those who became involved in school reform soon learned that significant change in the public schools would come about only when the great mass of American teachers was enlisted in the curriculum redesign effort. The challenge, as Elting Morison was fond of saying, was to get "from Widener to Wichita."

Reflections on Teaching

Bruner was not especially interested in teacher training. Although he had great respect for good teachers and a knack for attracting able teachers to his work, he never gave much thought to the design of a teacher-training program. In *The Process of Education* he barely discussed the subject, and then only to point out the hazards of poor teaching: "Somebody who does not see anything beautiful or powerful about mathematics is not likely to ignite others with a sense of the intrinsic excitement of the subject. A teacher who will

139

not or cannot give play to his own intuitiveness is not likely to be effective in encouraging intuition in his students. To be so insecure that he dares not be caught in a mistake does not make a teacher a likely model of daring. If the teacher will not risk a shaky hypothesis, why should the student?"[1] He believed that for teachers to be effective they must "be free to teach and to learn." That is, they should be treated like professionals, be encouraged to take risks in their classrooms, and be engaged in a process of continuous intellectual growth. He left to others, however, the task of figuring out how to achieve these worthy objectives.

ESI's first discussions of teacher education in the social sciences began at Garden Street. Here there was talk about preparing a "teacher's guide" for each unit, which was to be "a very special kind of literature that needs much searching inquiry." A scholar should write it, and it should convey different interpretations and perspectives on the subject as well as suggest useful supplementary materials. The guide, at its best, would encourage intellectual risk-taking and stress student inquiry and, unlike the conventional "cook book" teacher's manual, it envisioned a partnership between scholar and teacher that would bring the teacher in on the kind of intellectual speculation that takes place in the university. The guide would encourage teachers to approach their material in the same questioning and critical way the scholar does and to model for their students the spirit of inquiry that is characteristic of university research. To assume that this could be accomplished with a teacher's guide alone was perhaps naive, but we can see in these early proposals a conception of the teacher as a respected professional capable of engaging in a productive dialogue with a scholar and bringing to that discussion ideas about the most effective ways to involve schoolchildren in the excitement of academic learning.

In a piece entitled *The New Curricula,* undated but written probably in the spring of 1964, Evans Clinchy discussed ESI's emerging notion of teacher education. He pointed out that, since the new curriculum materials were being prepared to engage the imagination of the student, the role of the teacher is no longer one of "telling students" or assigning chapters in a text, but rather one of "guiding the student through material that had been designed to engage his interest, to present him with intriguing problems, and to enable him to work through to at least tentative solutions largely on his own."[2] Clinchy described the new role for teachers as "more important than ever" because they are now responsible for seeing that students develop the ability to work and think independently. To do this, teachers must become models of active learners themselves and share in the process of inquiry with their students. How teachers were to be trained to perform in this way, however, Clinchy did not discuss.

In 1965, when Bruner first described his goals for MACOS, he reported little further progress on teacher training. He spoke of wanting to bring together a group of master teachers to provide advice and guidance, but he was clearly too involved in materials development to give the matter much thought. His main contribution was a description of what he called "Talks to Teachers," which he suggested putting on records for a "Sunday Night Series" so that teachers could listen before starting the week. These were to consist of "lively accounts of the nature of the unit—particularly the nature of its mystery, what about it impels curiosity and wonder." He proposed to draw upon the writing of the best scholars in a particular field—Hockett on language, Radcliffe-Brown on kinship, perhaps Margaret Mead on child-rearing—and to present their work in an abridged form. He suggested that the language of these talks should be "at once science and poetry" and proposed that the materials be made available to interested students as well.[3] Yet there still was no serious discussion about how teachers were to be brought in on the process of educational reform.

During the summer of 1965, members of the Instructional Research Group had many opportunities to view teachers in action at the Underwood School, and their observations led to some new thoughts on teacher education. Howard Gardner and Judy Krieger proposed that special attention be given to those moments when classroom instruction went especially well and suggested that they be analyzed and shared with other teachers for training purposes. Arguing that no curriculum, however well-designed, could replace the vital ingredient of teacher judgment, they proposed a program of "education by teachers," pointing out that the insights of outstanding teachers would be essential to our success: "To put across these college level concepts we need teachers who can note on the spot the degree of task and ego involvement of the student, the degree of identification with the material, the personal feelings of the students as they relate to students, teachers, or the material, the boredom or attention of the students. We need teachers who can both draw out and direct questions and discussion into fruitful channels which we will feed back into the heart of the curriculum."[4]

At ESI this was a fresh view of the role of teachers. For Gardner and Krieger, teachers were vital participants in the curriculum-design process who must assess at every stage the proper relationship between the age-specific needs of children and the ideas and insights contained in the materials. They envisioned a dynamic interaction between teacher, material, and student, which they called the "educational triangle." For a curriculum to work the materials must be sound and appropriate for the age and ability of the students, the teacher must be a competent professional who has a comprehensive grasp of the subject matter, and the students must be engaged. Student motivation, they said, is crucial for this type of instruction, since the student must develop a heightened degree of self-awareness in relationship to the other parts of the triangle. And the teacher is critical in making this process work: "A teacher must not only know the material, he must know the material as it relates to his students. The students cannot know the material only abstractly; they must know it as it relates meaningfully to their own background, interests, needs, and desires."[5]

Gardner and Krieger pushed us to consider the psychology of teaching. Their arguments for the early involvement of teachers in the curriculum development process, particularly when introducing emotionally charged materials, were reinforced by our experiences at the Underwood School. Their concern with the role of the teacher in the "educational triangle" increased our awareness of the need to address the problem of teacher training and teacher development before the course was completed. Their identification of the psychological role of the teacher gave new meaning to Bruner's focus on intellectual "risk-taking" and to Jones's worries about the dangers of placing teachers and students in an emotionally threatening environment without giving them proper support. Both the nature of the materials and the methods of instruction placed demands on the teachers that needed to be addressed. Jones's Endicott House admonitions were beginning to sink in.

A New Approach

Anita Mishler, a sociologist with little background in education, which may have been why Bruner selected her for the job, had joined ESI in the fall of 1965 to direct teacher education. Mishler shared the Gardner-Krieger position on the centrality of teachers in the curriculum-design process. During the orientation meetings held in September, Mishler was shocked to learn that Bruner was thinking about his "Talks to Teachers" as a set of records for Sunday-night listening. She opposed the plan on the grounds that it made assumptions about teachers' needs without consulting them and placed them in a passive role with respect to the curriculum. She proposed that we involve teachers in the development of the course immediately by setting up a teacher-training program before the program was completed. Bruner liked the idea and moved to involve Lesley College, a local teacher-training institution, where he negotiated a collaborative training program with the dean.

Mishler began designing and implementing a teacher-training program that would run concurrently with course development, thereby permitting the needs and perceptions of teachers to be incorporated in the course design. She proceeded on two levels at once, engaging college students who were preparing to enter teaching as well as experienced classroom teachers. With a professor at Lesley College she designed and taught a course for ten selected seniors during the spring of 1966, and, in collaboration with Betsy Dunkman, she launched an in-service program for fourteen experienced elementary teachers in the Newton Public Schools. She worked with the groups separately during the 1965–66 school year and then brought them together during our second summer session at Underwood in July 1966 for further training and for trial teaching of the experimental units of the course.

Involving a cross section of teachers in MACOS as early partners in the course design produced some surprising results. The feedback from our teacher training sessions was spirited and sometimes sobering. The Newton teachers, for example, immediately began raising questions about the goals of the course and expressed concern about children's reactions to some of the materials. Jones, who was an observer in some of these sessions, reported one teacher's response to the baboon unit:

A major question I would like to raise . . . has to do with family and sex relationships among baboons . . . To what extent do children look at baboons as "people," not as animals like their pets? To what extent will they assign human attributes to these animals?

I anticipated from reading the duplicated article on baboons that a problem might exist because the biological father is never identified and never assumes a paternal role. I have since learned that in fact the problem did occur in summer school when the children tried to organize the troop in such a way that family units—mother, father, and children—were together . . . Is this problem avoidable, or would we want to avoid it, or is there a better answer?[6]

A lively discussion ensued in this seminar. One teacher spoke of the obvious concern that both adult males and females showed for the infants. Another reported on the enthusiasm her students expressed when she used some of the baboon material in her classroom. But most of the comments stressed the potentially threatening aspects of the materials and the need for clarity about the purposes of the course. Was the role of the baboon unit to point out the similarity between baboons and humans (care of the young, social organization, communication, and so on) or the differences (lack of social fatherhood, absence of reciprocity, absence of language, and so on)? There were no easy answers. The purpose of the unit, of course, was to raise all these questions and to consider what we can learn by comparing ourselves with one of our closest primate relatives. But teachers would have to come to grips with these issues themselves, be comfortable with their own views on the subject, and be convinced of the value of these materials for their students before they could teach the course effectively.

Similar problems arose when we introduced the cultural materials. In a discussion of the differences between baboons and humans that Bruner conducted in January, in which he contrasted the "home base" activities of the !Kung Bushmen and the "range" inhabited by the baboons, the teachers wanted to talk about broader issues. The discussion soon turned to questions about the influence of culture on behavior and to a consideration of all the features that distinguish humans from the higher primates. Although Bruner tried to narrow the discussion, the teachers insisted on talking about the basis of cultural differences, whether mankind is continuing to evolve culturally, and in what ways our culture is more advanced than so-called "primitive" societies. They wanted to discuss feelings and attitudes as well as the prejudices that people express when talking about social behavior and cultural values different from their own. They wanted to know whether issues of this kind could be discussed honestly in a social studies classroom. It was obvious that we needed to provide a forum for the continuous consideration of such issues by teachers.

While our initial goal for the Newton and Lesley seminars was to provide content preparation for the teaching of MACOS during the upcoming summer school, we soon realized that for the participants they were an opportunity for serious discussion of the purposes of social studies education. The materials proved so challenging to accepted social studies practice that the teachers insisted on exploring their own feelings about the issues raised before they attempted to handle the materials with children. We recognized that we had uncovered some deep anxieties about addressing emotionally charged issues and value-laden questions in the classroom. Anita Mishler's commitment to teacher involvement in the course design forced us to think more deeply about how to design a well-planned program of teacher education, one that would provide plenty of time for teachers to explore their concerns about what issues were appropriate to raise in a social studies classroom.

The Message from Teachers

This first encounter with teachers taught us some useful lessons. We found that we could not expect elementary school teachers, many of whom had had very little training in anthropology and biology, to take on MACOS without both subject matter training and an opportunity to debate our conceptual and pedagogical objectives. Both the animal studies and the cultural materials had stimulated teachers to think in new ways about how to teach social studies, but without a clear plan for addressing their questions and anxieties, most would be unable to handle the course comfortably with children. The materials were laden with value issues that simply had to be faced and discussed. We also learned that the questions and concepts addressed by the course made most sense to teachers when examined in the context of their teaching experiences. Discussions of topics such as innate and learned behavior, aggression and territoriality, social organization and dependency, or technology and belief systems engaged teachers most when they could see their relevance to the questions that were important to children.

Mishler brought this out in a paper summarizing her observations of the summer of 1966:

> It seems quite clear that teachers are not likely to become involved in difficult reading or serious consideration of the instinct-learning issue at the start . . . but after discussion of . . . a classroom situation in which this issue was the stumbling block, they are likely to become engaged in the problem and will be willing to hear a lecture, or read a paper prepared to this point.
>
> Similarly, the teachers this summer would have been . . . ready for seminars, discussion [and] readings on the issues of culture change and social evolution . . . after they had been confronted by children who asked, "Why haven't the Bushmen developed as we have?"[7]

This experience with teacher training taught us that we must address the psychological needs of teachers and develop a strategy for teacher education that would provide for a proper transition from the rarefied environment of the curriculum laboratory to the culture of the public schools. It was not enough to expose teachers to heady new ideas in our academic seminars. Teachers needed to be convinced of the value of these ideas for the intellectual and emotional growth of children. We were sobered to find that both the content and the teaching methodology of MACOS sometimes made teachers less comfortable and less confident in the classroom than they were with their regular courses. If the course was to succeed, we needed to deal seriously with teacher concerns and teacher anxiety. In order to address these issues we decided to develop a "parallel curriculum" for teachers that could be taught in a series of workshops during the implementation of the course. This would give teachers the opportunity to learn the course while teaching it and to bring their substantive and pedagogical concerns, drawn from their direct experiences with children, to the workshop sessions.

Workshops for Teachers

During the fall of 1966 we began work on a teacher education program to integrate teacher training with the teaching of the course. Classrooms were to serve as a curriculum "laboratory" where teachers could experience and study children's responses to the material while they were learning about the course themselves.

Teachers could bring their observations and concerns to the in-service seminar, where they could share and discuss them with other MACOS teaching colleagues. Under this plan, the first year of teaching MACOS became an integral part of the teacher-training program. To make the plan work we needed a curriculum for teachers that could be taught by an experienced MACOS teacher or administrator who could lead the workshops and assist teachers with the introduction of the course in their classrooms.

This in-depth, "on-line" approach to teacher training offered benefits that we did not at first anticipate. Teachers learned the content of the course in a setting where they were comfortable, working with children, and in association with trusted colleagues from whom they could receive support and encouragement. When problems arose, there were others nearby to commiserate with. When things went well, sympathetic friends were there to applaud their success. As it turned out, many teachers rejoiced at the opportunity to discuss issues of teaching with their colleagues and to learn new subject matter in association with their peers. Given the usual isolation of teachers, many of them found this opportunity for closer professional association and exchange extremely stimulating, and it had a positive effect on teacher morale. In the teacher workshop, as in the classroom, shared experience turned out to be an important ingredient of the learning process.

To help us develop and implement this new plan we set out to find one or two highly qualified educators from each of a dozen carefully selected school systems in different parts of the country and to invite them to a summer workshop at EDC (ESI had now become Education Development Center) during the summer of 1967. We approached the administration of those school systems expressing interest in the course and negotiated a commitment to establish an in-depth training program that would include released time for teachers, salary credit and course credit for the seminar, and assurances that the school system would provide all the necessary administrative support to make the program a success. Each system was to structure the workshop to fit its own particular staff-development patterns, but all agreed to provide time for at least twenty hours of workshops that would parallel the teaching of the course. Some systems scheduled workshops every two weeks, while others preferred to cluster their training in intensive sessions spaced at wider intervals (see Figure 4.1).

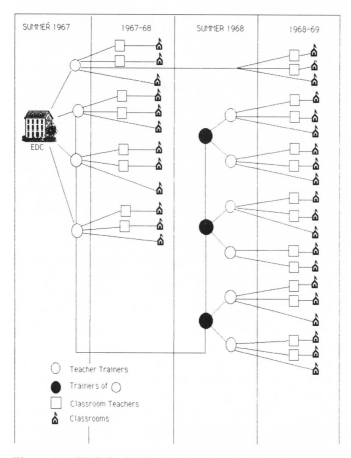

Figure 4.1. EDC Social Studies Teacher Training Program.

Eighteen educators from twelve school systems representing a mix of urban, suburban, and rural communities from a wide geographic area attended the 1967 summer school.[8] Richard Jones presided over the first week of the workshop, which was held at Themis House in Weston, Massachusetts, a conference center owned by Brandeis University. Jones led a week of intensive discussions about the philosophy, pedagogy, and content of MACOS, which also included generous amounts of time with Irven DeVore and Asen Balikci. In the relaxed atmosphere of this rural estate, scholars and educators were able to exchange ideas about the goals and purposes of the course, and examine their reasons for deciding to join us in training others to teach the program. Many of the participants had prior exposure to the course, and they came to Themis House committed to helping us develop the teacher education and dissemination program. Following this first week of immersion in the thinking behind the course, the participants spent the balance of the summer observing classes at the Heath School in Brookline and drafting plans for the in-service programs they intended to run on their return.

Planning these in-service programs proved more problematic than we had anticipated. Despite our efforts to provide appropriate background, many of the participants did not feel qualified to design an effective training program without knowing more about the course and its pedagogical intent. When, under considerable pressure, they finally submitted their plans, many of the workshop proposals turned out to be disappointingly conventional and didactic. We were surprised to discover that exposure to the open-ended, exploratory approach characteristic of EDC classrooms and workshops, where participants were encouraged to express their opinions and air their concerns and criticisms, did not automatically cause our workshop leaders to create similar approaches in planning their own teaching. The same anxiety about our methods we had encountered among classroom teachers now appeared among these higher level professionals. How, we began to wonder, could the same spirit of inquiry and intellectual risk-taking that had inspired the development of the course and characterized our work with teachers be perpetuated when the responsibility for teacher training passed out of our hands?

Lessons from Teacher-Trainers

Working with prospective teacher-trainers gave us a new perspective on MACOS. At the outset we had been caught up in the ideas of the course and in the challenge of creating workable materials for children. We believed that if we got the ideas straight and the children excited, other educators would embrace the course with enthusiasm and understanding. The staff that built the course consisted of a group of like-minded academics, bound together by the challenge of creating the course and sharing a common point of view about the education of children. When the course began to take shape, however, and we tried to convey our teaching philosophy, we found that we were not only challenging conventional notions of what and how children should be taught, we were also challenging accepted patterns and practices of staff development in the schools. To address the problem of implementing MACOS in hundreds of classrooms across the country we needed to know much more about the culture of the public schools and how to interpret the course to educators who had never before seen anything remotely like it.

What became increasingly plain as we worked with teacher educators was that MACOS was more than an unusual set of materials about animals and Eskimos. It represented a different point of view about children, learning, and society. More important than the specific units on territoriality in herring gulls or making a skin sled from frozen fish was the way the course confronted conventional assumptions about how children learn and about the kind of subject matter that is appropriate for the young. For educators encountering the course for the first time, this exposure could be a troubling experience. Administrators who were responsible for implementing the program in their school systems needed time to think through their own reactions to the materials, to the organizing ideas, and to the value issues of the course, just as the developers and teachers had, before committing themselves to incorporate MACOS into their existing school curricula.

The Problem for School Systems

One of the program's most challenging ideas, as we learned in our discussions with potential workshop leaders, was the notion that human behavior can be subjected to rational analysis. Underlying the animal studies was the implicit notion that human beings, like other animals, have evolved through millions of years of natural selection, and that human behavior, like that of other species, can be understood, in part, as a successful response to selection pressures. This point of view holds that it is instructive to compare humans to other animals, particularly our primate relatives, not because we have evolved from them, but because we share a common biological history and our ways of coping can therefore be usefully compared to theirs in biological terms. This is where the pedagogical power of examining similarity and difference comes in.

What results from this comparison that is important for educators is a deepened appreciation of the limited repertoire of innate responses in humans compared to all other animals, and the enormous capacity that human beings have for thinking, communicating, and learning. Prolonged immaturity and a capacity for language seem to have a lot to do with these differences. These ideas have major implications for schooling, as Bruner had pointed out at Westtown, since they reinforce the idea that it is through thinking and learning, through invention and education, that we preserve, transmit, and renew our culture. In this way, unlike other animals, we have taken charge of our own evolution.

Equally unsettling for newcomers to MACOS was the notion of cultural relativism. Few elementary teachers in the 1960s had much formal training in anthropology, and most had been educated in a social studies tradition that views Western culture as the most advanced of human civilizations. The Netsilik materials, on the other hand, were designed to illustrate that there is no discernible difference between the intellectual and creative capacity of Eskimos leading a traditional hunting way of life in the Arctic and contemporary Americans. In MACOS cultural differences were treated as a reflection of environmental circumstances, the availability of information, and shared values. To impose the standards and values of one culture upon another, the course suggested, was to deny those people their humanity. This point of view challenged the deeply held belief in the notion of "progress," particularly technological progress, or what is sometimes thought of as the "advancement of civilization," regarded by some as central to understanding the American way of life. Many school people had not encountered these alternative ideas before, and the teaching implications of this new "behavioral science" perspective took time to assimilate.

Still another disturbing feature of MACOS was its implicit attitude toward learning. The inductive pedagogical approach presumes that knowledge is tentative and changeable, and that the development of human intelligence is a process of unique individual growth. What MACOS tried to communicate was that truth, especially in the social sciences, is transitory, and that provocative questions are often more illuminating to the inquiring student than settled answers. This provisional stance toward knowledge, which had been so eloquently defended by Bob Adams and others, left us vulnerable to the criticism that we really didn't know what we were trying to teach. What was difficult to get across to professional educators until they had been exposed to the experience was the power of an approach to teaching that took seriously the natural curiosity of children and that trusted their ability to learn from the exercise of inquiry using materials designed to provoke thought and speculation rather than revealed truth.

This attitude toward learning contained specific implications about how we expected teachers and teacher-trainers to behave toward the material, toward children, and toward each other. Cultivating a questioning attitude toward knowledge and respecting student diversity were primary ingredients of a good MACOS teacher, and we expected these same qualities to be reflected in the design of the teacher workshops. In dealing with the central questions of the course we adopted no party line. Ideally, the workshops would be places where teachers could work out their own answers to the question "What is human about human beings?" and in their teaching of the course we expected them to express the same respect for the individual point of view of their students. In our summer workshops and training programs we had hoped to generate a spirit of collegiality and mutual inquiry that would carry over into the classrooms and seminars that were to be planned and taught by others, but teaching by example was not always as effective as we thought. To achieve these objectives, we began to realize, would require a course of its own.

The Parallel Curriculum

Following the summer of 1967 we evaluated the teacher-training program by visiting the schools and attending the workshops run by the summer school participants. These visits revealed the weaknesses of our program for teacher-trainers. It was one thing to introduce the course to a selected group of highly skilled teachers and administrators as we had done at EDC. These people had been preselected for their willingness to innovate and for their track record as unusually skilled professional educators. It was quite another thing to construct a program for the average or inexperienced teacher who might easily be threatened by the kinds of issues MACOS raised. Anita Mishler later commented on the magnitude of the teacher education problem:

> When I started that first year to suggest that we ought to do something about teachers, I began to read some of the research on teachers, and was very shocked to find that [elementary school

teachers] were at the bottom in terms of college ability . . . Then I began to find out what went on in teacher colleges and that was very shocking. And I wrote a piece at that time on how [the education of teachers] was . . . counter to anything we thought was needed for teachers; it recruited the least able people who had the greatest interest in security and not taking risks, provided [them] with the poorest education, . . . and put them into work situations that discouraged any change. It was out of this group that we were going to try to introduce this plan—this revolution![9]

Undaunted by these discoveries, Mishler set about designing a course to help teachers overcome their anxieties about unfamiliar content and teaching methods and to relate classroom experiences to larger questions of educational theory and practice. She wanted the workshops to be places where teachers felt free to share their teaching problems and openly discuss the difficulties that they were having with the course. She believed that a successful workshop must recreate the same participatory spirit that had characterized the course development, and that the teacher-training program must be specifically designed to meet the needs of teachers, which were different from the needs of children. The idea of calling the course for teachers a "parallel curriculum," she pointed out, came from the notion that it was parallel to the children's course but not identical.[10]

In her design for the teacher seminar series Mishler established several broad objectives. She wanted the seminar to be a place where teachers could examine the link between the conceptual framework of the course and the process of teaching and learning. Knowing that many teachers only became interested in the content of MACOS after seeing children respond enthusiastically to it, she used the seminar to explore the teaching power of those materials. She believed the course could help teachers think about the social context of learning, about the differences between intuitive and analytic thinking, and about the role of comparison and contrast in learning. These were topics of general value that went far beyond the specific content of MACOS.

She also saw the seminar as an opportunity for teachers to use their classrooms as sources of data for examining the learning process in a systematic way. Since the seminar participants shared a common experience, the teaching of MACOS, the reactions of their students to a common set of materials could provide the raw material for discussions of teaching and learning issues. She hoped, in time, to have teachers engaging in simple, controlled experiments, in observations of each other's classrooms, in generating and trying out their own pre- and posttests, and in implementing other research techniques that would turn their classrooms into learning laboratories. She wanted to help teachers become more self-conscious about what was working and not working in their classrooms, and to gain confidence in their own intellectual powers as teaching professionals able to employ the scientific method to improve instruction.

Still another goal of the teacher seminars was to foster a spirit of professional colleagueship among teachers. By providing an opportunity for teachers to come together regularly to discuss professional issues and to collaborate on shared problems, the seminar could help to overcome the isolation from other adults that characterizes the life of most elementary school teachers. This association with colleagues on a professional basis, Mishler believed, would help teachers develop a deepened self-respect and thereby make them better teachers. The overriding purpose of the teacher program was to empower teachers, to give them confidence in the power of their own minds and in their skills as instructors of the young, just as the course was designed to empower children.

The selection of topics for the seminars precipitated a prolonged in-house debate. On the one hand, we wanted the teacher workshops to be a place where teachers could bring particular problems with content, methods, and value issues, and any other difficulties they were having with the daily lessons. On the other, we also hoped that they could become a place where the collective experience of teachers could be brought to bear in discussing more general issues of educational theory and practice. The former was especially necessary for beginning teachers; the latter made sense for experienced teachers and for ensuring the continuing vitality of the course over the long haul. We expected that in time, the materials and lessons of MACOS would be substantially revised and enriched with new examples and new data but that the underlying pedagogical and philosophical assumptions that had inspired the course could be kept alive through a continuing dialogue about learning among the seminar participants. Although we began by focusing on the specific lessons of the course, when finally published the seminar series reflected the extent to which the parallel curriculum had evolved from a series of training sessions for the teaching of

MACOS to a course in issues of teaching and learning. The list is illustrative:

Seminar 1: On Learning, or, What is School for?
Seminar 2: The Power of an Organizing Idea.
Seminar 3: How Does Contrast Promote Learning?
Seminar 4: The Will to Learn.
Seminar 5: Learning by Observing.
Seminar 6: Learning in Animals, and How It Differs from Human Learning.
Seminar 7: Learning by Comparison: The Values and Dangers.
Seminar 8: Exploring Significant Questions.
Seminar 9: Models as Ways of Knowing and Learning.
Seminar 10: Learning by Doing: The Value of Experience.
Seminar 11: Intuitive and Analytic Thinking.
Seminar 12: Finding Out What Students Have Learned.
Seminar 13: What Kinds of Learning Take Place in a Group?
Seminar 14: The Role of Fantasy and Feeling in Learning.
Seminar 15: Education as Social Invention: The Teaching of Values.
Seminar 16: Education as Social Invention: The Teaching of World View.
Seminar 17: Action/Image/Symbol: Three Ways of Representing Reality.
Seminar 18: Are Variations among Children a Problem or a Resource?
Seminar 19: Why Bother with Conceptual Structure?
Seminar 20: Education as a Continuing Human Invention.[11]

We constructed the seminar series in this way in order to use the specific materials and lessons of the course to address more general issues of teaching and learning. While studying the details of the life cycle of the salmon, for example, teachers examined the power of contrast as a tool for learning. Or when discussing Eskimo seal-hunting practices, they also talked about the kind of learning that occurs through interaction within the group. Our hope was that by combining both practical and theoretical issues we could provide teachers with an experience of generalizable value, which they could relate to their other teaching responsibilities. Discussing theoretical issues with teachers, we found, had little value unless these issues were embodied in specific materials that had been proven to work with children. At the same time, the rote teaching of materials that had the power to engage the intellect and emotions of children was also meaningless unless teachers had the opportunity to explore with sympathetic colleagues the pedagogical power of what was going on in their classrooms. Ultimately, we expected that teachers, having understood what we were trying to do, would cast aside MACOS for courses of their own design.

Experimenting with Film

In designing a course for teachers we came to believe that film could be as powerful a medium for teaching them as it was for teaching children. What we needed was good ethnographic films of the classroom. A grant from the Ford Foundation gave us the first opportunity to experiment with films for teaching, although for technical reasons these films had to be made in a studio setting rather than in the field. We hoped to create an archive of films for teacher-training as rich as the course films themselves, but our funding permitted only limited experimentation. We wanted these films to illustrate a variety of teaching styles and methods and permit teachers to critique the lessons they observed. Mishler set forth the goals in a brief working paper:

1. The films should give teachers an opportunity to watch children on children's terms.
2. They should raise issues pertinent to the course and to the lives of children that may be difficult to handle in class (reproduction is an example).
3. Some films should illustrate ways of making connections between the course and children's lives (the life cycle, the handling of aggression, and the dependency period are a few examples).
4. Each of the films should illustrate a way of working with materials to gain the kind of involvement we hope for (this could be an informal small group activity centered around a project or a question, or it might be an activity or discussion involving the entire class).
5. A general philosophy should shine through: that it is important to listen to kids and respect what they have to say—and that this influences methods of teaching.

6. The films should be no longer than ten to fifteen minutes, preferably ten.[12]

Our first teacher-training film effort produced four films, two taken from the animal studies and two dealing with controversial issues in the Netsilik materials. Although these films were crude first efforts and suffered from the artificial constraints imposed by the studio setting, we used them in many early workshops and discovered, as we had suspected, that film was a powerful teaching tool. It didn't matter that the teaching was awkward at times or that the children sometimes responded in an unexpected way. Teachers could identify with what they saw on the screen, and this opened up some lively discussions of what we were trying to accomplish in the classroom. The success of this effort caused us to press the NSF for funding to continue the project, but this proposal was turned down. The course went to publication without the benefit of our proposed films.

Publish or Perish

Our search for a publisher had begun in the fall of 1966. Elting Morison had anticipated difficulties in our publishing negotiations, and he persuaded Carroll Bowen, the director of the M.I.T. Press, to work with us to develop a publishing strategy for all EDC Social Studies materials. Bowen was well known in the publishing world, and he invited the president of Macmillan, Jeremiah Kaplan, and the head of Houghton-Mifflin, William Spaulding, to meet with members of the executive committee to review our projects and to advise us on the best strategy for approaching publishers. The meeting took place in the basement conference room at 15 Mifflin Place.

These two experienced and widely respected publishing executives listened politely while Bruner described our lofty educational aspirations with characteristic eloquence, but the discussion soon turned to practical matters such as the procedures of state adoption committees, "tumbling test" requirements, per-pupil expenditures, readability formulas, and other restrictions that govern the basal textbook market. Spaulding and Kaplan tried valiantly to instruct us about the realities of the educational publishing world, but we dismissed their remarks as the musings of men who had been corrupted by commercialism. Did they not understand that our mission was to change education, not submit to the strictures that had made much of instruction so meaningless? Could not men so powerful in the publishing world commit some of their resources to support curriculum innovation? Had they no appreciation of the intellectual poverty of most social studies classrooms? I remember leaving that room depressed by the monumental conservatism of our visitors and more determined than ever to prove that there were ways to reach the schools with good materials.

Our arrogance and naïveté were not easily cured. In preparation for further publishing discussions Bowen drafted a tightly worded three-page document summarizing our publishing objectives. He made it clear that we expected to maintain control over both content and design of our materials, and pointed out that, given the complexity of our objectives, it might take several firms, working cooperatively, to satisfy our needs. He even had the nerve to suggest that a non-exclusive agreement might be the answer: "We recognize that few publishers may be in a position to earn exclusive distribution rights by giving us the 'wide-band' capability we seek. Therefore we encourage you to think of the unique contribution which you may be able to make to part of the publishing endeavor, as a partner to a multiple, non-exclusive distribution effort."[13]

Bowen stressed our commitment to continued revision of the materials, to teacher training, and to an ongoing program of evaluation, and he noted three unresolved issues that needed to be addressed by both developer and publisher: making the materials accessible to poor school systems; providing the appropriate level of teacher training to achieve maximum effectiveness; and devising a way to perpetuate through constant revision the dynamic process that produced the materials. He even suggested that EDC and the publishing community band together to form a new kind of "Materials Development and Teacher Training Center." "A partnership in such an enterprise," he suggested, "holds potential excitement and achievement equaled only by the publication challenge itself."[14]

Publishing discussions for MACOS began in earnest in the spring of 1967. By this time the course had been twice tested in summer schools and trial taught in numerous sites around the country. A nationwide evaluation was planned for the following year. The implementation of Anita Mishler's teacher-training program was well under way, the course was generating considerable enthusiasm among teachers and students, and a growing number of school systems wanted to purchase the materials. As the demand grew, we recognized that we had given little thought to the logistical, fiscal, and managerial problems that must be addressed if we were to make the course available on a large scale. A publishing plan was urgent.

In June we made our first formal presentation to publishers. We had invited fifty-four publishers to an all-day bidders' conference to review the materials, to hear presentations from the staff, and to discuss possible publishing arrangements. The day included a speech by Bruner, selected film showings, an overview of the course, small-group examination of several units, a presentation on teacher training, and a discussion of various alternative licensing arrangements. We distributed a list of the proposed materials and Bowen's paper on publishing objectives to all participants. Twenty-eight publishers attended the conference.

Next, we invited publishers to visit trial classrooms at the Heath School in Brookline during July. Twelve came. In September, those publishers that had expressed interest in the course were invited to one of two film showings that took place in October. A dozen firms accepted this invitation and in November these publishers were formally invited to submit publishing bids. The invitation to bid stressed our desire to reach the largest number of classrooms, our willingness to accept modification of the materials to meet the requirements of commercial publication, and our recognition of the publisher's need to realize a fair return on investment. In stating our requirements we asked for commercial publication of the two basic units by September 1969, production of the existing edition for limited national distribution during 1968–69, a commitment to teacher training, multiple distribution arrangements for film, and a willingness to support the development of additional units to be used in other elementary grades. We requested a letter of intent and proposed contract by 1 February 1968, and agreed to make a publisher selection by 1 March 1968.

None of the "interested" publishers chose to submit a bid by the appointed date. Many wrote letters expressing admiration for the program, but none was willing to invest in MACOS. In retrospect, the reasons for the lack of publisher interest were plain. The content was new and unfamiliar to most teachers. By long established convention, American history was the subject of choice for fifth grade, not anthropology. Furthermore, it did not fit comfortably into the conventional "scope and sequence," wherein as children progress from grade to grade they move through an integrated series of courses that build one upon the next. MACOS was a course for one grade with no plan for what should precede or follow it. Equally troubling for publishers was the pedagogical design. Inductive methods, small-group instruction, the teacher as participant rather than authority, and multiple sources of information rather than a single text all presented what seemed insurmountable obstacles to easy implementation. How could a salesman describe the program adequately in a brief sales presentation? What teachers would be skilled enough to teach it or interested enough to try? Teachers want simple programs, publishers told us, programs that are easy to teach and require a minimum of preparation. MACOS, they predicted, would appeal only to the most advanced and innovative teachers, a tiny segment of the educational marketplace.

Another barrier to publication, we were told, was the multimedia format. While there had been a brief flurry of interest in media-based programs following the passage of the Elementary and Secondary Education Act of 1965, which provided federal funds for the purchase of films and audio-visual equipment, and even some mergers between film distributors and publishers during this period, by 1967 the promise of a media revolution in education was beginning to fade, and traditional textbook publishers were fearful of the large-scale investments required for film distribution. Moreover, schools purchased films and textbooks out of separate budgets administered by different departments, which made the prospects for selling a film-based course as a single package extremely difficult. Neither the publisher nor the school system, we were told, were structured in a way that permitted easy distribution of a multimedia program.

Beyond this, publishers were faced with a massive teacher education cost. They agreed that MACOS required extensive teacher training, but they were wary of the financial and logistic burden that a proper teacher education program would impose. Most publishers did their best to avoid teacher training, agreeing to it only with their basal reading programs, which enjoyed massive distribution. Even then, this commitment was limited to a few days of paid consulting for a local university professor or school reading specialist. Yet MACOS required an in-service program amounting to forty hours of classroom instruction, not to mention the additional training required for teacher trainers.

Perhaps most disturbing from the publishers' point of view was the fear of controversy. Educational publishers learn early to purge their products of material that could be deemed threatening to the values or religious beliefs of some segment of the community, such as the John Birch Society or the creationists. Nothing seems to stir the juices of a religious fundamentalist or an ultraconservative more than a textbook fight, and publishers who are dependent on statewide school book adoption strive to avoid offending any vocal constituency. MACOS touched on a number of potentially inflammatory subjects, such as reproduction, evolution by natural selection, wife-sharing, and senilicide, and it was hardly surprising that our potential publishers chose not to expose themselves to possible attacks from the textbook watchers.

And to top it off there was the issue of cost. In 1968 the average per-pupil expenditure for social studies materials was approximately $1 per year, or $5 for a hardbound text with an expected life of five years. Publishers typically mark up their texts at least 400 percent over manufacturing cost, so printing costs would have to be cut to about four cents per booklet if we were to be competitive with other courses. Add to this the cost of the games, filmstrips, and film, and the entire course package would have to be sold to the schools for $1,250, or over $8 per student per year—eight times what the schools normally paid. We had created a course that appeared to be unmarketable from a commercial point of view.

To compound the problem, 1968 saw a new conservatism in the educational publishing business. The much talked about "media revolution" that was supposed to usher in the "new technology of the knowledge industry" had failed to materialize. Peter Goldmark's widely heralded "video record" was a commercial failure, dial access instructional systems proved to be little more than a media buff's toy, cable television for instructional purposes was still a distant dream, and the many recent mergers of high technology firms with textbook companies (Raytheon and D. C. Heath, Random House and RCA, Xerox and Ginn, and so on) were turning out to be uneasy marriages with poor communication between the partners. Our timing for the introduction of an expensive, multimedia course was far from ideal.

Further exploration of the publishing industry did not improve our spirits. From February 1968 to March 1969 we redoubled our efforts to find a publisher willing to distribute MACOS commercially. During this period we wrote and visited forty-three publishers and film distributors. It was a painful and instructive exercise. The larger publishers repeated the same litany of objections we had now learned by heart: no scope and sequence, unacceptable in adoption states, requires too much from teachers, difficult for salespeople to explain and sell, too small a market, possibly controversial. Smaller publishers that cater to the demand for specialized materials were frightened by the need for a substantial inventory investment and by the massive distribution effort required. Textbook houses saw no way to handle the films, and film distributors were ill-equipped to deal with the written materials. All were put off by the logistical complexity of the total package: six hours of film, thirty booklets, nine teacher's guides, three games, and four records, as well as filmstrips, wall charts, photomurals, artifact cards, and a "take-apart" seal. Few publishers, large or small, felt adequate to handle the complex organizational and planning effort required to achieve effective commercial distribution.

Our warmest reception came from firms that had little to lose— new companies like General Learning, which were trying to break into the educational marketplace, or older firms, like A. B. Dick and Simon and Schuster, which had experience with education and books but were entering the textbook business for the first time. Yet none of the publishers we approached during this period was willing to expose itself to the marketing risks presented by MACOS. One well-established firm was candid enough to share with us an internal memorandum that summarized the reservations of all publishers:

> This program is a departure from current courses of study. Since most of the experimental instructors classified this material as anthropology, a sizeable market for the series is unlikely. To our knowledge, no school system has a defined curriculum at the elementary level calling for instruction in anthropology. In state-adoption states the format of this program prohibits adoption consideration and also no state makes an adoption call for this type of material.
>
> The teachers who are using this experimental material are sophisticated and highly motivated. Most of the teachers have masters degrees and are considered innovators in their schools. Here again the school systems that are using this material are basically the better school districts in the nation. This is not true in every instance, but by and large, the experimental centers are affluent, white, suburban school districts.

The content of this program can be considered controversial. Such topics as infanticide, cannibalism, wife exchanging, and senilicide are presented to the fifth-grade student. Most teachers would not consider teaching this type of content at this level, and religious groups would not endorse the teaching of this type of material. [We] must evaluate carefully the impact this controversial material might make on adoption possibilities. Our competitors and others would make issues of the concepts.[15]

Getting to Wichita

Lacking a publisher, we had to devise our own plan for meeting the growing demand among teachers and school systems for participation in MACOS. As teachers and administrators passed the word from school system to school system, increasing pressure from the field to join the project forced us to develop new ways to meet the rapidly expanding teacher-training and implementation requirement. We conceived the idea of setting up a national network of university-based regional centers to inform interested educators about the course, and to handle teacher training, evaluation, and materials distribution (see Figure 4.2). To ensure continuing intellectual vitality we proposed to staff these centers with the same mix of talents that had participated in our early training efforts: class-

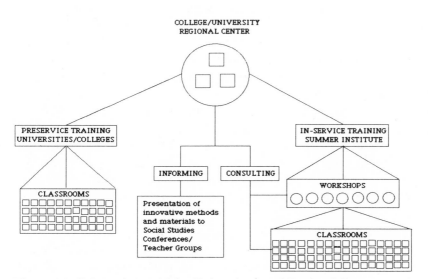

Figure 4.2. Schematic Model for University-based Regional Center.

room teachers, professors of education, and scholars in the social and behavioral sciences. As there appeared to be considerable interest around the country in setting up such centers, we approached the NSF for a grant to launch the program.

During the summer of 1968 we conducted our first summer training sessions away from Cambridge at institutes in Jefferson County, Colorado; Marin County, California; Philadelphia, Pennsylvania; Washington, D.C.; and Watertown, Massachusetts. Only two, those in Watertown and Washington, were run by EDC staff members. Graduates of our 1967 summer training workshop ran the others. The division of responsibility between content specialists, teacher training experts, and school teachers served to keep the seminars from becoming the private domain of any of the participants, and the partnership between scholars and teachers, which had been central to the design of the course, was now extended into the implementation phase. In this way we hoped to keep alive a continuing process of teacher growth and curriculum innovation. Judged by the enthusiasm of the participants, at least, this first effort at regionalization of MACOS appeared to be a significant success.

The popularity of the regional institutes led a number of the university professors, under the guidance and encouragement of EDC, to seek "Resource Personnel Workshop" grants from the NSF to expand their programs. EDC, in turn, applied for a grant to train the new regional center directors and their staffs. The centers were to train workshop leaders during the summer and provide preservice training in the winter, besides offering consulting services to participating school systems. The director was to serve as a full-time "innovation coordinator," mailing out information about the course, running informational workshops, working with school systems, and generally promoting the course. Several of the directors had previously attended EDC teacher-training workshops, and, building on that experience, we were able to design a training-based program of dissemination and implementation. In June 1969 we ran our first workshop to train regional center innovation teams. Faculty members from eleven colleges and universities, who had received fifteen-month grants from the NSF, participated in this week-long conference.

A typical center was located at Central Connecticut State College. Its director, Dennen Reilley, had been a classroom teacher in West Hartford who first learned about MACOS at Themis House and had subsequently run the teacher training program for the West Hartford Schools. Reilley's team included a professor of education, an anthropologist, and two experienced MACOS teachers. Following the June session at EDC he ran a five-week workshop for nineteen educators from fifteen school districts ranging from Maryland to Massachusetts. During the subsequent school year he adapted the course for use as a graduate teacher education program. Reilley saw MACOS as a generic course in teacher education that was particularly valuable for illustrating a wide variety of teaching techniques. As he wrote in a report prepared for the NSF, "The wealth of course materials, teacher-training tapes, and films is a welcome thing to both the beleaguered professor, previously having only his notes and basic text, and the students who have been exposed to innumerable lectures decrying the lecture as a teaching tool."[16]

Reilley's activities during the school year illustrate the diverse responsibilities of the "innovation coordinator." He visited each of the school systems using the course at least twice and in many instances five or more times depending on the needs of the workshop leaders. He attended workshops, conferred with administrators, and spoke at PTA meetings, turning up wherever he was needed to provide implementation support. His own account reveals the range of his responsibilities: "In one community anti-evolutionists attacked the introduction of *Man: A Course of Study* and several meetings were scheduled . . . with this small but vocal group. In another I gave a presentation to teachers contemplating the use of the course in their classrooms the following year. In yet another I conducted in-service workshops monthly for the teachers introducing *Man: A Course of Study*."[17]

Reilley worked with the Model Cities program in Baltimore to implement the project in inner-city schools, and he assisted Roger Landrum in making the course part of the program of Teachers, Incorporated in the Two Bridges Model School District on Manhattan's Lower East Side. He presented the course at professional meetings, and he set about informing every school district in his eleven-state area about the work of the regional center. He mailed letters and brochures to every superintendent and set up five area meetings to which he invited all interested school personnel. And he wrote to each state department of education, state social studies council, elementary school principals' association, and teachers union to tell them about the course and enlist their support in distributing information about *MACOS* to teachers and administrators.

The most effective recruitment device turned out to be the area meetings. Reilley made presentations in Boston, Hartford, New York City, Philadelphia, and Baltimore from January through April 1970, and representatives from 230 school districts and parochial and independent schools attended. These presentations led to invitations to make additional presentations in school districts and on college campuses. Reilley was especially impressed by the role played by teachers at these meetings. "Perhaps our most effective dissemination tool," he wrote, "was the enthusiasm generated wherever the course is being used and our best disseminators were teachers actually teaching *Man: A Course of Study*. We will have to devise ways to utilize this tremendous potential for professional dissemination."[18]

Because of the demand generated by Reilley's dissemination efforts, he examined how he could increase the capacity and efficiency of his summer training program. He reduced the EDC five-week program to an intensive two-week model, thereby doubling the number of trainees he could handle at the center. By the end of his second summer he had trained fifty-nine new workshop leaders representing forty-two school districts. By the fall of 1970, as a result of Reilley's efforts, there were 918 teachers using MACOS with 22,163 pupils. This was strong proof that an energetic and imaginative educational leader could take the teacher-training and implementation program we had developed at EDC and modify it appropriately to meet the demands of a growing constituency.

Reilley's efforts, together with the work of others like Thomas Fitzgerald, who mounted a similarly successful dissemination program in Colorado, suggested that there might be alternative routes for the implementation of innovative curricula than the methods used by commercial publishers. What these energetic men proved was that it was possible to create a network of like-minded educational professionals willing to provide conceptual and administrative direction for the distribution of complex materials and training and support to the people using them. Interestingly enough, both Reilley and Fitzgerald had first encountered the course as teachers, and Fitzgerald continued to teach the course throughout the many years he served as an "innovation coordinator" and regional center director. These dedicated individuals were living proof of Reilley's assertion that "our best disseminators were teachers."

New Angles on Publishing

Having failed to attract a conventional publisher, we began pursuing film distributors. There was some logic to this approach since the most expensive part of the course was the films. Also, because we already had a competent staff of editors and designers in place and were working with several printers, we did not need many of the services normally provided by a publisher. Furthermore, a number of film distributors were exploring new ways to make film more central to learning, so a collaboration with EDC might open up some new commercial opportunities. The national sales manager of one large film distributor corroborated this view: "Man: A Course of Study, in our opinion, represents the finest potential model to test the feasibility and realization of building level purchase of sound films. To my knowledge this is the first classroom course that has been written with films playing the most important role. To describe the films as 'an integral part of the course' is to minimize their role. If ever it has been important to have easy access to film, it is doubly important with this particular course."[19]

During the summer of 1968 we had initiated discussions with Films, Incorporated (FI) and its nonprofit affiliate, the Fund for Media Research, to explore the feasibility of a publishing partnership between EDC and FI for distribution of MACOS. The course at that time was in the hands of over six thousand students in two hundred classrooms, which had been reached largely by "word of mouth" distribution and a modest brochure. Information about MACOS had been spreading through the professional education community, through the activities of our regional workshops, and through the growing cadre of participating teachers. We were beginning to wonder if we could achieve effective distribution without commercial selling methods by simply taking the course directly to the potential user through our expanding network of participants. Perhaps all we needed was a good film distributor to handle the logistics of an expanding program.

Wayne Howell, the vice president of the Fund for Media Research, was especially taken with this idea. Howell believed that we could solve our distribution problems and retain high quality training at a reasonable cost by building on EDC's already established relationship with the education community. He envisioned a national faculty of professional educators who would assume responsibility for training and implementation of the course. By retaining control of the course in the hands of educators he hoped to build credibility for the program and expanded participation, while eliminating the expensive direct-selling methods employed by text-book houses. He envisioned some intriguing new possibilities for widespread educational innovation that did not depend on the private sector:

> There will be no traditional commercial marketing practices for this course of study. Teacher training must precede the materials' distribution and sale even at the college level. The teacher of teachers will have to be trained . . . The teacher-training institutions with their pre-service and in-service courses will, in fact, control the spread of practice. The schools will share in the savings of materials' cost by not having to pay the traditional marketing markup expenses . . . The concept places new curriculum practices back in the hands of educational institutions where quality control in use can be built-in at all levels. The textbook and film salesmen in this case are removed from the pedagogical process.[20]

Howell was so excited by this idea that he immediately began to try to implement it. He contacted a number of education professors he knew and questioned them about their willingness to help us develop a professional dissemination system for MACOS. Response was strongly favorable, and by spring twelve colleges and universities had made a commitment to work with EDC and FI. Eleven applied to the NSF for Resource Personnel Workshop grants to train teacher-trainers for the course.[21] Howell's interest enabled us to expand our growing teacher-training network and to explore further the feasibility of professional dissemination as an alternative to conventional commercial distribution. Just as these plans were taking shape, however, we were informed by FI that they were unwilling at that time to advance the risk capital necessary to support the manufacture of materials, creation of promotional literature, travel, and other costs associated with setting up the proposed professional distribution network. Howell, who was deeply committed to the experiment, left the Fund for Media Research to join EDC to develop the plan.

Noncommercial Distribution

Although discussions with FI continued, EDC faced a new academic year without a publisher. Lacking other sources, we sought funding from the NSF to cover the manufacturing and distribution costs required to meet the needs of the expanding network of universities and participating schools. Because we anticipated at least five hundred new classrooms in the fall of 1969, we were confident that these costs would be defrayed by the anticipated sales income, but we needed a line of credit to pay printers' bills and other expenses, which we estimated could reach approximately $250,000 before cash from our anticipated sales became available. A key feature of our proposed marketing plan was the creation of a single package containing Super-8mm sound film and course materials, which was designed for storage in the elementary school building rather than in the central film library, thereby providing easy access for students and teachers as well as substantially reducing the film cost. We secured an agreement from our film distributors to withhold marketing of Super-8 films, thereby allowing us to become the sole source for the completed course in the Super-8 format. We also acquired distribution rights for Technicolor's cartridge-loaded Super-8 projector, a device that any ten-year-old could operate. By combining the materials into one multimedia package, introducing the Super-8 format, and eliminating commission-based selling, we were able to price the course at $3,000 for a five-classroom set, enough materials for 150 students. At $20 per student this was still more than a conventional textbook, but we had cut our price to 50 percent of what a commercial publisher would have to charge. In May 1979 the NSF agreed to extend EDC a line of credit of $270,000 to cover our in-house publishing investment. Fortunately, our financial projections proved correct and eighteen months later we were able to release NSF's credit line. Through the sale of course materials we were able to meet all our manufacturing and distribution expenses.

Even the addition of five hundred new classrooms to our users list, however, did not persuade Charles Benton, the president of Films, Incorporated, that MACOS was a feasible publishing enterprise. He was genuinely intrigued by the course, but on 26 November he wrote a long, apologetic letter saying that he was terminating our publishing discussions "with heavy heart." In explaining his decision Benton listed the remaining obstacles to commercial success as he saw them: teacher training, cost of revision for use at other grade levels, film royalty problems, manufacturing costs, evaluation, and "EDC's staying power beyond the experimental phase." Would EDC, asked Benton, "remain as committed to it in the application and dissemination phase as they would be to their new programs under development? Where this becomes especially critical is in EDC's diversion and commitment of personnel to service the continuing teacher training course and revision needs."[22] Although the negotiations with Benton had been far friendlier and far more encouraging than any of our prior commercial contacts, in his final response we saw the same fear of innovation that had influenced the reaction of the textbook publishers.

Toward a New Partnership

The collapse of the Films, Incorporated negotiations set up the final phase of EDC's quest for a publisher. By the terms of our funding from the NSF, transfer of ownership of MACOS was a contractual requirement. Consequently, no matter how successful our own distribution program became, it was essential that we find a commercial distributor. By the fall of 1969 the course was being used in over a thousand classrooms, and our regional center directors were predicting a thousand more by the fall of 1970. The plan seemed to be working, so we decided to devise a publishing contract that would return to EDC the funds required to sustain the professional network and ensure its growth. What we needed, so it seemed, was neither the skills of a textbook house nor the experience of a film distributor but rather, an organization that could design and implement a profitable alternative to the NSF-supported regional center dissemination system.

With our growing visibility in the educational marketplace, two new potential publishers began to show signs of serious interest in MACOS: Westinghouse Learning Corporation and Curriculum Development Associates (CDA). The choice between them was to prove difficult. CDA was a brand new firm with few assets, but it had a dedicated senior staff of nationally recognized leaders in education, including Robert Wirtz, Morton Botel, and Max Beberman, and a president of distinguished national reputation, former Secretary of Labor Willard Wirtz. Westinghouse Learning, on the other hand, had substantial financial assets but a mixed track record in education, having lost a good deal of money on an expensive, computer-based instructional system called Project Plan. Philosophically, EDC had much more in common with CDA, for the Westinghouse group had been heavily involved in programmed instruction, a far cry from EDC's open-style approach. The choice was between a large, financially strong organization with a questionable commitment to our educational objectives and a small, new firm with limited resources that shared with us a common point of view about teachers and children.

During the fall and winter of 1969–70 we met frequently with personnel from both CDA and Westinghouse Learning. We made it clear to both firms that we wanted a contract that would provide, in addition to the royalties that must flow back to the NSF, funds for sustaining the delivery of professional services to MACOS users. Prior discussions with NSF had led us to believe that if we could get a publisher committed to providing continued support for the regional center network, or some similar professionally based dissemination system, NSF might consider reducing its usual royalty. With this encouragement from our sponsors, we asked both publishers to include in their publishing proposals a provision for the delivery of professional services to school systems and universities using the course.

CDA strongly shared our view of the efficacy of a professional approach to distribution. Although they were a new organization, Beberman, Botel, and Robert Wirtz had been working for many years on curriculum innovation in a manner similar to ours, and in 1969 they had demonstrated the success of such an approach by achieving state adoption of Wirtz's mathematics material in California. In a letter written in January, 1970, CDA Executive Director Jack Gentry expressed the commitment of CDA to supporting EDC's continuing involvement in dissemination, teacher education, and course revision: "My associates and I at CDA would be interested in *Man: A Course of Study* only if there is a commitment on the part of EDC . . . to do the things that you identified as components of the 'service' . . . contract we have discussed on previous occasions. The concept of teacher training and periodic revision or adjustment of course materials goes to the heart of what we are attempting to promote in connection with our other programs."[23] Gentry made it clear that CDA was strongly committed to preserving the integrity of the training and distribution network we had already established.

Westinghouse Learning, on the other hand, was taken with the commercial marketing potential of the professionally based dissemination system. Less interested in the integrity of the product, they saw in the growing participation of professional educators the possibilities for significant sales growth. They contacted several of our regional centers, visited classrooms, and made tentative job offers to some of our most successful center directors. Although they did not tell us at the time, we later learned that they were preparing to invest substantial funds in the development of a commercial alternative to the NSF-funded centers and that they contemplated a television documentary on the course to bring national visibility to the program.

We requested both publishing candidates to submit proposals that provided for standard publishing arrangements and for EDC's continued participation in training and distribution on a fee-for-services basis. During our negotiations we had suggested as a guideline that they consider allocating 50 percent of their normal distribution budget, or approximately 15 percent of gross receipts, to be paid to EDC in return for support services to be rendered in behalf of the publication of the course. We discussed such activities as liaison with school systems, development of teacher training materials and programs, establishment of communication networks, and continued evaluation, revision, and creation of new materials. In some ways we were proposing a partnership between developer and publisher that was similar to the "Materials Development and Teacher Training Center" originally conceived by Carroll Bowen in 1966.

On 30 January 1970, Verne Atwater, president of Westinghouse Learning, formally requested the selection of Westinghouse as the commercial publisher of MACOS. In his letter he stated a firm commitment to EDC's objectives:

> Westinghouse Learning is in full agreement with your organization that teacher training is an integral component of *Man,* and we would anticipate close collaboration with EDC to ensure the most effective means of strengthening this aspect of the course.
>
> Continuing and highly professional liaison with the educational community is indispensable if *Man* is to gain wide dissemination. Westinghouse Learning, if selected to publish *Man,* would turn over fifteen percent of the gross sales of course materials to EDC in return for professional services rendered by EDC aimed at maintaining this liaison.
>
> Similarly, we fully appreciate the necessity of systematic and continuing research and evaluation focused upon the actual performance of *Man* in the classroom. We are, therefore, if selected

as publisher, prepared to respond to validated results of the evaluation program.

If selected, Westinghouse Learning would be desirous of seriously discussing with EDC the possibility of the expansion of *Man: A Course of Study* into a multi-year elementary social studies curriculum.[24]

After three years of rejection letters Atwater's letter seemed hard to believe. Here was a commercial publisher who was willing to accept all of our terms.

On 23 February Willard Wirtz committed CDA to similar arrangements. He endorsed the professional services contract and pledged CDA's resources to develop a professional dissemination network that was not dependent on the NSF-funded centers. Wrote Wirtz, "*Associates* will assume full responsibility for developing, during the twelve-month period following the effectuation of an agreement, an independent and effective dissemination program. Full use will be made . . . of the Regional Center facilities and personnel; but it will be recognized that this is to be on a phase-out basis."[25] In setting forth CDA's commitment to support EDC's continued participation in the dissemination effort, Wirtz offered EDC the choice of two financial options: either monthly payments equivalent to 15 percent of gross sales or equal division with EDC of revenues above costs. Wirtz went on to suggest even a third possibility:

> *Associates* will consider favorably any suggestion by the *Center* of a contractual arrangement which will assure joint participation in and shared control over the dissemination and staff development policies to be pursued by *Associates*. We think that the mutuality of our objectives is so complete that this can be adequately provided for in comparatively simple terms. It occurs to us as an alternative possibility, however, that an arrangement could be worked out which would involve the establishment of a subsidiary corporation through which *Associates* would disseminate the *Course* and over which *Associates* and the *Center* would have shared control.[26]

This last proposal echoed Carroll Bowen's original idea of a new entity that would be a joint venture between EDC and a publisher.

Incredibly, after a three-year search and innumerable disappointments and dashed hopes, we received two publishing proposals that exceeded our wildest expectations of a few months before. NSF's gamble on professional dissemination had clearly paid off. Not only were both CDA and Westinghouse prepared to share generously from their sales revenues to support such a network, but they were also willing to depart from conventional publishing practice to work closely with us in creating a new way of generating and implementing innovative educational materials. At long last we had come upon some risk-takers in the private sector who, having seen that we had been able to reach a large number of users with our unconventional methods, were willing to take a gamble on our approach.

The choice between CDA and Westinghouse Learning was far from easy. Westinghouse had money, organizational strength, marketing expertise, and a need for success in the educational marketplace. Furthermore, they wanted to make MACOS the centerpiece of a new venture in media-based instruction in the social sciences. The staff was young, but skilled in the uses of instructional film, and Atwater, who had served on the Steering Committee for EDC's Social Studies Program, was very familiar with EDC's mission. Willard Wirtz, on the other hand, had committed his personal resources to the development of an organization devoted to putting professionalism in education ahead of commercial gain. While Wirtz could muster only a fraction of the funds that Westinghouse was prepared to commit, the educational experience represented by the CDA group far exceeded the knowledge of schools that Atwater could provide. An extended face-to-face meeting with Wirtz, in which I questioned him closely about CDA's commitment, convinced me that he was prepared to put his personal prestige behind the success of MACOS. He was a man of enormous eloquence and persuasiveness, and his impeccable reputation in academic circles, together with his political savvy, might be just what we needed to gain the support of the educational establishment. On the other hand, the Westinghouse proposal was clearly superior from a business point of view. Wirtz's academic and political clout were hardly a match for the economic power of the Westinghouse organization if they were really prepared to commit substantial resources to the program. For days we debated the two offers, but in the end the lure of an educator's collaborative outweighed hard-headed business considerations, and we signed with CDA.

In retrospect, I have often wondered if we made the right decision. In 1970 we were still riding the crest of a wave of educational reform, and it seemed logical to progress from curriculum innovation to the invention of new methods of training and dissemination that could provide an alternative to conventional textbook publishing. We expected to be able to raise new funds for these implementation efforts that would rival the funds already invested in the development of materials. Under pressure from Congress to gain visibility for its curriculum work, the NSF was allocating a growing percentage of its precollege educational funding to support teacher training activities, and we questioned the wisdom of "selling out" to the commercial marketplace when the public sector appeared to be so deeply committed to educational reform. Research on the diffusion of innovation was pointing the way to just the sort of involvement of the profession that Wirtz was proposing.[27]

What we did not anticipate, however, was that public support of education would be short-lived. The massive public commitment to the improvement of curriculum brought on by the Cold War, the baby boom, and the space race had run its course by 1970, and the coming decline in school enrollments, together with space successes that made foreign academic competition seem less formidable, brought about a new mood of fiscal conservatism where educational reform was concerned. Federally sponsored programs that had once been hailed as the harbingers of a new era of intellectual vitality in the schools now came to be seen as the pipe dreams of wooly-headed academics, or worse, the schemes of "career curriculum innovators" whose aim was to spend the taxpayer's money to create courses that were in competition with the textbook industry. In such an environment, both EDC and CDA would find it increasingly difficult to compete.

Beyond this, there were other compelling reasons why we should have chosen a bona fide commercial partner for the widespread distribution of MACOS. Government funding was entirely appropriate during the research and development phase, and even during the early stages of teacher training and installation. The establishment of the regional center network demonstrated to the publishing industry that a new kind of marketing program for a new kind of product might make sense. Having done so, however, it was now time to invent the commercial alternative to the NSF-sponsored network that would facilitate implementation on a scale that was beyond the resources of the NSF. This required the skills and financial resources of an organization experienced in dealing with the commercial marketplace. Neither EDC nor CDA had that experience. The ultimate test of an educational innovation like MACOS is its ability to survive in the profit-making sector. To achieve this we needed the marketing experience and fiscal guidance of an organization skilled in these matters. Match those skills to EDC's experience in development, teacher training, and evaluation and we might have created a winning collaboration between two corporations, one public and one private, both dedicated to the improvement of teaching and learning.

It is easy to dream about things that did not happen. What did happen was that the partnership between EDC and CDA proved to be an imperfect marriage. Ironically, we were too much alike, too similar in our goals, to be able to help each other very much. As it turned out we ended up competing for the attention of the schools rather than collaborating to enhance the success of MACOS. Most of EDC's proposals to remain involved with the course after publication were rejected by CDA, and we ended up spending the professional services revenues on the development of other programs. Perhaps understandably, as a new company that was struggling to establish its own reputation with the schools, CDA devoted much effort to establishing the identity of MACOS as a course published and disseminated by them, and the participation of EDC might confuse that identity. CDA felt perfectly qualified to train teachers on their own, and EDC's desire for continuing involvement in the training program threatened to detract from CDA's visibility. Even successful promoters of the course, like Reilley and Fitzgerald, were shunned as CDA set out to construct its own dissemination network of educational professionals. In the end, MACOS suffered from this growing conflict of interest, for we were never able to mobilize the full dissemination potential of our already developed training model and successful reputation with the schools. Unhappily, the full partnership between EDC and CDA, which Willard Wirtz had so eloquently described and which exemplified Carroll Bowen's vision of a publishing partnership between public and private enterprise, was not to be.

Unfortunately, the competing priorities of EDC and CDA brought about the termination of the regional center system before it was able to become self-supporting. Our plans for a national teacher education and dissemination network, based on the regional center model, were never fully realized. In retrospect, perhaps, our aspirations for an alternative to conventional educational publishing were too ambitious—the dreams of a youthful staff unaware of the hard realities of the marketplace. Yet the spirit of the times made believers of us. In the 1960s anything seemed possible if you had the will and the energy to bring it off. When I asked Anita Mishler many years later if she would design our teacher training and implementation model differently if she were doing it again, she replied: "We really thought we could change the world with this course . . . We might all have been more modest. But in a sense I don't think we could have . . . We simply couldn't be modest at that time . . . because we all believed in education. It must seem now like a hundred years ago . . . but everyone believed in education and in the schools."[28]

· 5 ·

The Perils of Innovation

Our struggle for the acceptance of MACOS did not end with the signing of a publishing contract. Other barriers soon blocked the path to widespread distribution. The 1970s brought a new mood to the American educational scene. It was reflected in a distrust of federally sponsored curriculum innovation, an increased involvement of parents in curriculum choices, and a demand for a return to the "basics" of reading, writing, mathematics, history, and "Judeo-Christian values." One sign of the times was a new set of curriculum guidelines issued by the California State Board of Education in 1969. Asserting that the book of Genesis offered an explanation of human origins equivalent to the theory of evolution, the Board mandated that creationism be taught in biology courses side by side with the theories of Charles Darwin. Another reflection of change was a lawsuit brought against the National Science Foundation in 1972 by the religious editor of the *Washington Evening Star,* allegedly on behalf of forty million evangelist Christians, claiming that the agency was using tax revenues to promote antireligious teaching practices in the public schools.[1] This rise of educational conservatism, coupled with renewed concern about federal control of the schools, meant that MACOS still faced a tough battle.

Fundamentalists in Florida

The first sign of impending trouble appeared in Lake City, a small market town in northern Florida (population 10,000), in the fall of 1970. Shortly after school opened in September, Reverend Don Glenn, a Baptist minister who had recently moved to Lake City, visited his daughter's sixth-grade class at the Minnie J. Niblack Elementary School and asked her teacher for copies of the MACOS materials. Lake City was in the process of integrating its schools under a federal court order, and the course was being taught to all

178

of Lake City's sixth graders by three teachers who had been trained the previous summer at a workshop sponsored by the National Science Foundation at Florida State University in Tallahassee. The teachers—one of whom was black, one of American Indian extraction, and the third a white Baptist minister—had been attracted to MACOS because they thought its concern with cross-cultural understanding might help ease racial tensions in Lake City's newly integrated classrooms. Under the integration plan, the sixth grades had been placed in a single school, and approximately 360 students were enrolled in the program. The course materials had been purchased with state funds given to the school system to encourage the introduction of locally selected, innovative programs.

Reverend Glenn did not like what he saw. After determining that the materials did not appear on the list of state-adopted texts, he formed a study group called Citizens for Moral Education and set about examining the materials in detail. Glenn claimed that the course advocated sex education, evolution, a "hippie-yippie philosophy," pornography, gun control, and communism, and he excerpted passages from the teacher's manuals and student booklets to support his views, quoting them in a leaflet he circulated throughout the community to invite participation in his organization. With sponsorship from a local hardware store he purchased air time on a local radio station and presented four hour-long programs criticizing MACOS. He read passages from the teacher's guides and other materials, and warned his listeners that threats to democracy, Christianity, and parental discipline were contained in the teachings of MACOS. Noting our suggestion that teachers might want to keep live animals such as grasshoppers, mealworms, crickets, gerbils, or mice in the classroom so that pupils could observe life cycle stages, including the birth of offspring, Glenn linked the course to Mary Calderone's sex education program (SIECUS), which had recently received national press coverage for the controversy it had caused in some Florida public schools.

At the school's first parent-teacher meeting on 4 November, Glenn rose to attack MACOS as godless, humanistic, evolution-based, socialistic, and "sensual in philosophy." The three teachers, Joyce Tunsil, Quintilla Lynch, and John Millis, vigorously refuted Glenn's charges, claiming that deliberate lies had been spread about the program. Millis, who was well known to the community as the pastor of a small Baptist church and who had an impeccable reputation in the town, disputed Glenn's assertion that the course had no moral guidelines. He stated that he was a person of deep religious convictions, and that he could not teach something that went against his moral principles. Millis then read from comments that children in his class had written in response to the controversy. According to one observer, these comments provided "the most powerful rebuttal of Glenn's charges."[2] One child wrote, "All the course is trying to teach us is how proud we should be that we can do things we want to do, and animals can't. We can build, and animals can't. We can talk and animals can't."[3]

At the Columbia County School Board Meeting on 12 November, the Citizens for Moral Education made an appeal for the removal of MACOS from the Niblack School. The meeting was heavily attended. Glenn spoke for fifteen minutes, and he was followed by six parents, all of whom spoke in defense of the course. The board then appointed an investigatory panel of four educators and four laypeople, including Glenn himself, to examine the program and report back by 24 November with its recommendations. They designated the evening of Thursday, 17 November, for a closed-door hearing during which the proponents and opponents would each have two hours to present their case to the committee. Neither group was to be allowed to hear or to rebut the other's presentation.

Jack Gentry, executive director of Curriculum Development Associates, called and asked me to appear with him before the committee, so I flew to Jacksonville and drove to Lake City on the day of the hearing. It was a tense occasion. I had spoken about MACOS innumerable times but always before friendly audiences, and I was unprepared for the hostility that pervaded the hearing room. I began by recounting the intellectual history that had inspired the course design and then discussed each unit and its intended purpose in some detail. I stressed our commitment to the development of cross-cultural understanding and pointed out that we had done very little with the concept of evolution because it had proved very difficult to teach to ten-year-olds, but that we had included the booklet on natural selection in response to children's questions about why animals were so different. Our purpose in teaching about animals, I pointed out, was to use cross-species comparisons to give children perspective on what it means to be a human being. To stress the point I quoted Jerrold Zacharias's observation that "without contrast you can't see." In discussing the Netsilik unit, I explained that one of its objectives was to make children more aware of human diversity and more accepting of cultural and ethnic differences.

When I had finished, Reverend Glenn looked me hard in the eye, thrust his open palm in my direction, and inquired, "Mr. Dow, do you believe that the human hand is a product of evolution?" I was startled, at first, by the question, suddenly realizing that Glenn was far more concerned about how the developers of the course thought than about what the materials said. However attractive our films and booklets might appear on the surface, he wanted his fellow panel members to believe that the course had been put together by atheists and communists who were out to undermine the religious faith of the young. Whatever the intent of the course, he wanted me to admit, to a room full of Southern Baptists, that I was a committed evolutionist and thus an enemy of fundamentalist Christianity. I had never been faced with such an interrogation before, and I struggled for a response. I spoke of the "fossil record," which suggests, I said, although the evidence is by no means complete, that the human hand, like other parts of the human body, has passed through stages of development. Taking refuge in the "scientific data," I stuck to the known biological facts and avoided being drawn into a discussion of my beliefs. After all, I thought, the course was on trial here, not me. Glenn was visibly exasperated.

The defense of MACOS continued. Jack Gentry talked glowingly about the positive experiences of other school systems, and the assistant dean for instruction at Florida State University spoke about the wide endorsement the program had received within the academic community. Perhaps the most persuasive testimony of the evening came from five parents who spoke about the important influence the course was having on their children's lives, particularly in helping them to adjust to the new relationships they were forming as a consequence of the federally mandated school integration order. The hearing closed with a ringing endorsement from Reverend Phillip Lykes, pastor of the First Baptist Church in Lake City, who directly challenged Reverend Glenn's interpretation of the passages quoted from the teacher's guides. I left town impressed by the depth of commitment that MACOS had evoked in its supporters as well as in its critics.

The behavior of the school administrators in the Lake City controversy was a study in political and bureaucratic maneuvering. The principal of the Niblack School took no position, never spoke in a public meeting, made no statement to the press, and was not even named in the school system's written report of the case. The superintendent, Silas Pittman, a personal friend of Reverend Glenn, privately supported the course but made no public defense of the program. When interviewed by the press, he commented, "The people are divided on the course. Some say children find this their most exciting course. Others want it removed."[4] On the question of evolution, he remarked: "In all the materials for the course, I haven't seen any place where it says man comes from monkeys, apes, or lower animals . . . I don't believe I evolved from a lower form of animal."[5] The State Superintendent of Public Instruction, who had just been reelected to his final term and presumably had little to lose by speaking his mind, refused to comment on the course publicly even though his department was providing funding to support its use in twenty-six schools in the state. He told the state social studies coordinator to stay out of the case, but she chose to defy his instructions and wrote a letter of endorsement to Robert Harrison, the director of our Regional Center at Florida State.

At a special session of the Columbia County School Board on 24 November the review committee presented its report. The crowd was large and emotions ran high. The board chairman opened the meeting by asking Reverend Glenn to lead the group in prayer. Glenn was conciliatory, praying for trust and understanding, and for a spirit of cooperation whatever the decision. Frank King, chair of the review committee and pastor of the First Presbyterian Church, summarized the committee's conclusions and recommendations: "We believe that the primary responsibility for moral and religious education rests more on the home than on the school . . . We recommend that *Man: A Course of Study,* as it is now presented, be continued, and that after the end of this school year . . . the course be made elective and a state-adopted course be offered."[6] An eyewitness recounted what followed:

No one on the board spoke. The burden of responsibility had been transferred and these men sat alone, contemplating, avoiding each other's eyes, temporarily immobilized by their ambivalence. A motion, finally, was made: accept the committee recommendation.

It died for lack of a second. A question: how can children whose parents objected to the course be expected to learn in such a situation? Another motion: Keep the course as it is, but make it elective as of tomorrow, and proceed with both MACOS and the traditional course. Seconded, voted on, and passed. Resolved. A decision.[7]

But the issue was not resolved. The faculty at the Niblack School saw the decision as an invasion of their academic freedom. Twenty-one teachers, two thirds of the Niblack faculty, drafted and signed a letter of protest, which they presented at the next school board meeting on 3 December. They interpreted the school board decision as an invasion of their rights and a challenge to their competency, and they saw it as establishing a dangerous precedent that could lead to further intrusions upon the autonomy of the curriculum. The letter set forth these views in bold language:

> The objections raised in opposition to this course are categorically unfounded. The precedent set by this decision opens the way to further disruptions in the curriculum of this and/or other schools in the county. Such disruptions may endanger the educational atmosphere for both students and faculty. The faction represented by Mr. (Don) Glenn has in fact called into question the competency of teachers in the county. The approval by the board of the recommendation that this course be made elective immediately is a tacit approval of the questioned competency of teachers in our school system . . . We, therefore, wish to go on record as being diametrically opposed to the decision rendered by the board. We believe that "Man: A Course of Study" should be maintained in our school system as a required course for all students for the sixth grade level.[8]

This was a remarkably daring statement on the part of Niblack School faculty in defense of the course and the work of their colleagues. What motivated these teachers to chastise their school board when they had no visible backing from their superintendent or from the principal of their school? Why would two thirds of the Niblack faculty risk their jobs in a public protest when only three of the protesters were teaching the course? What was it about MACOS that could elicit such strong support after just a few months of teaching? This case deserves further study by those who would question the courage of teachers. Yet, the Niblack teacher protest had little impact. Provisions for making the course elective proceeded apace, and in the following year, MACOS was dropped entirely from the curriculum of the Niblack School.

Montgomery County, Maryland

Before long, objections to MACOS began to surface in other places, including some of our most supportive school systems. One of the largest early users of the program was Montgomery County, Maryland, a densely populated suburban community situated between Washington, D.C. and Baltimore. The Montgomery County school system had a reputation for excellence and a commitment to innovation. In 1970 MACOS was pilot-tested in a number of the system's elementary classrooms, and after a favorable evaluation, the county planned to expand the course to several more elementary schools in the fall of 1971. The administrators responsible for implementing the program had been trained by EDC, the teachers using the program were uniformly enthusiastic about it, and from all appearances a very successful adaption was under way.

Then, on 14 August, an article entitled "What Educators Are Doing with Your Federal Tax Dollars," by Dr. Onalee S. McGraw, a Montgomery County resident, appeared in *Human Events,* a periodical distributed by the John Birch Society. McGraw signed the article as curriculum director for an organization called Citizens United for Responsible Education (CURE). The article accused the developers of MACOS of using public funds to teach their own private philosophies and value systems. Quoting extensively from my introduction to the course, which appeared in one of the teacher's guides, McGraw charged that it had eliminated "man's spiritual and moral dimension" from a consideration of what is human about human beings. "Is it the prerogative of the social scientist," she asked, "to impart his own philosophy or that of a particular school as an inherent part of a curriculum developed with federal funds? We believe you will search in vain for a federal grant to a social scientist to develop a humanities curriculum which describes in rich detail with expensive films and booklets the 'development of Christian culture,' let alone additional funds to disseminate the underlying philosophy of such a culture in the school systems throughout the nation."[9]

Following the appearance of the McGraw article, which was circulated throughout the county, the school board asked Superintendent James M. Reusswig to investigate the course. Reusswig prepared a letter with a return postcard soliciting opinions from the superintendents of 167 school systems using MACOS nationwide. The questionnaire was brief and to the point:

In my judgment MACOS is:	☐ Excellent	☐ Good
	☐ Fair	☐ Poor
We had complaints about MACOS	☐ Yes	☐ No
from parents of the community.		
If yes, the major complaint was: _____		

Reusswig received replies from 134 districts in thirty-six states. One hundred districts evaluated the course as "excellent," twenty-eight described it as "good," and the remaining six respondents were not using the program. None of those polled listed the course as "fair" or "poor." One hundred and fourteen districts had received no complaints; 14 districts reported some complaints. The major objections listed were the switch from American history, sex education, teaching of evolution, too much depth, and "too explicit about Eskimo life." After ascertaining that CURE had a membership of approximately twelve to fifteen in Montgomery County, Reusswig and his board approved the continued implementation of MACOS.[10]

Phoenix, Arizona

Similar conservative objections were not so easily quelled in Phoenix. In May 1971 the city's Madison Park School District decided to introduce MACOS for a two-year trial and sent two teachers to an NSF-sponsored summer workshop at Arizona State University. The following fall the course was introduced to 106 sixth- and seventh-grade students. The Madison Park School Board had planned to hold informational meetings with parents to explain the new program, but before these meetings could take place the system became embroiled in controversy.

A new parent, Mrs. Phyllis Musselman, who did not have a child in the course but had recently enrolled her son in kindergarten, led the attack with an article that appeared on 1 September in Arizona's *Weekly American News,* a conservative journal devoted to rightist causes. Musselman had an acid wit and the ability to arouse an audience with a deft turn of phrase. She accused MACOS of teaching antisocial behavior: "While high school sophomores supposedly can't survive without sex education, elementary students will be learning this fall that violence, youth, and power are necessary for survival . . . Teachers are instructed to concentrate on examples of cannibalism, infanticide, genocide, and senilicide until these acts of violence are acceptable and understandable to the children."[11] Musselman alleged that Jerome Bruner had invented the idea of having children "play-act" leaving grandmothers to die to accustom themselves to the idea that old people are no longer useful, and charged that MACOS gave children a choice between whether they wanted to live in human society with laws and regulations, or join a baboon "group-gang, 'where you can see and do everything.'"[12] Her article produced such a flood of telephone calls that the newspaper asked her to do a series on the course. She quickly complied, quoting liberally from the materials, especially the Eskimo myths, alleging that MACOS was an atheistic program designed to teach children to practice sex and violence.

School Superintendent M. E. Hatter reacted sympathetically to Musselman's foray. On 10 September he sent a memorandum to his assistant superintendent, Dow Rhoton, and school principal Marvin Cornell, requesting more information about the program:

> I am attaching a copy of an article in the September 1 *Weekly American News*. If some of the innuendoes and statements are true, I would join with our conservative friends' viewpoints about the dangers of such a program . . . I would like to know what the program actually does relative to some of the references indicated, and I definitely would like to know if it is true that children are not led to the development of values based upon Judeo-Christian ethics. To be forewarned is to be forearmed. We need to be able to answer charges such as those made in the *Weekly American News*.[13]

Rhoton and Cornell responded with a series of hastily called parents' meetings at which the teachers attempted to explain the course. Musselman used the meetings as an opportunity to continue her campaign. At one such gathering, she rose to address the assembled parents: "I am Phyllis Rae Musselman and I speak on behalf of Madison Park parents who love their children enough to have read the MACOS material. We are amazed at the way this board expects us to placidly accept such dull, useless, violent material for our children. We are stunned that you would overestimate our apathy as taxpayers, underestimate our concern as parents, and insult our intelligence in this way . . . This course is an insult to any homo-sapiens, that is, man-who-thinks."[14]

Following one of these meetings, parents returned to their cars to find an unsigned handbill affixed to their windshields that raised the attack to a more vicious level. The opening paragraph set the tone:

WHO DO WE EAT?
Kill useless old grandma, eat the wife's flesh and save the bones. Murder baby girls, exchange wives, learn to think like a baboon, and study animal mating. Simulated hunts and role playing are included which condition children to accept a primitive culture as normal. Children decide the best way to dispose of grandma plus other gruesome customs and then act it out. Lasting impressions are made on children's minds as they pretend. Attitudes form as children begin to think and feel like the extinct Netsilink [sic] Eskimo. This is MACOS (Man: A Course of Study), being taught to Madison District students . . .

Musselman's newspaper articles and their attendant publicity soon captured the attention of the state education department, and in an unusual move, the Commissioner of Education, Weldon Shofstall, banned all future purchases of the materials in Arizona until the controversy was resolved. Shofstall wrote to Superintendent Hatter, with a copy to the governor, suggesting that he urge the opponents of MACOS to file a lawsuit against the school board charging that the teaching of the course was unconstitutional because "teaching that man is an animal and nothing more is teaching about the existence of God and religion."[15]

Few people with children in the course shared Mrs. Musselman's views. One parent, Charlene Patty, who suspected that much of the opposition was coming from outside the parent group, conducted her own telephone survey of 137 parents with 159 children in the sixth and seventh grades. Her poll revealed that 71 parents definitely wanted their children to take the course, 51 parents expressed no opinion because they had little knowledge of the program, 5 parents were not happy with the program but did not request optional study, and 10 parents were against the program and wanted an optional course. Mrs. Patty reported her findings to the president of the Board of Education and urged the board to listen only to parents who had children in the program.[16]

Dow Rhoton took charge of the school system's investigation. On 13 October he sent me several of the newspaper articles and other materials critical of the course and asked if I would appear at a special public meeting of the school board, which had been arranged to permit those who opposed to the program to express their views. I shared the materials with Jerome Bruner, and on the evening before I left, I visited Bruner at his house and asked him how he viewed the accusation that MACOS promoted violence and anti-Christian attitudes. He replied with heated concern:

> I was particularly troubled by the statement in one of the papers . . . that when you talk about this kind of thing you are teaching violence. Quite to the contrary. If one knows about human beings, knows about the fact that there is violence amongst us, and that we have to cope with it and have to find some way of containing it, this starts us on the way toward having a realistic sense of what the human problem is wherever human beings are . . .
>
> I find myself shocked and taken aback by one statement that this was somehow an un-Christian way of going about the study of man. If one can't appreciate the manifestation of humanity in some other culture, then comes the question, "Does Christianity go beyond the edges of the town, or the island, or the country?"[17]

Fortified by my discussion with Bruner, I flew to Phoenix to face Mrs. Musselman and the other parents who opposed the course.

The public meeting was scheduled for 8:00 PM on 28 October. By 7:30 the auditorium, the largest available in town, was filled to overflowing with over seven hundred people in attendance, together with representatives of the local press and television. The five school board members sat on the stage, and a rostrum and microphone had been provided to accommodate the participants. The evening began soberly with dispassionate statements from course supporters. Marvin Cornell spoke briefly about the voluntary nature of the program, stressing that arrangements had been made for an alternative course for the children of any parent who requested it. David Housel, who was teaching the course, strongly endorsed MACOS and suggested that it had hardly been given a fair trial in just twenty-seven teaching days. Another teacher, Kathy Olsen, described her use of the materials in class and read from student responses to an evaluation survey. Cornell reported the results of a questionnaire sent to the parents of the 106 children in the program. Of the 73 parents who responded, 61 were favorable, 5 gave no reaction, and 7 were negative. Fifty-nine reported that they definitely wanted their children to complete the program. Cornell proposed that his school be allowed to continue with the course.

In my presentation I briefly described the origins of the course and discussed the evaluation results. I pointed out that MACOS had recently been cited by the American Educational Research Association (AERA) as an example of the sort of curriculum development the nation should be doing and that Jerome Bruner had been given a special award by the AERA and the American Educational Publishers Institute for leading the effort to create this curriculum. I urged that parents be given freedom of choice and closed with a short film illustrating how the course encourages children to think for themselves. Tom Fitzgerald, the director of our regional center in Denver, spoke about the widespread use of MACOS in the western states and quoted from some of the many letters of commendation he had received from users. Fred Greene, head of the local teachers' association, warmly praised the program, and Al Boyd of the Arizona Education Association stressed the importance of local decision making but took no stand on the course itself.

Then Earl Zarbin, a newly appointed conservative member of the school board who had been invited to fill an unexpected vacancy, took the floor. Zarbin described the course as a deliberate effort by psychologists to mold the behavior of children. He alluded to B. F. Skinner's new book, *Beyond Freedom and Dignity,* published only a few weeks before, which argued the case for improving schooling through techniques of behavior modification. Knowing that both Bruner and Skinner were psychologists at Harvard, Zarbin suggested that Bruner, like Skinner, wanted to mold children's behavior and that MACOS was designed to shape children in the image of the developers. Zarbin quoted from my description of the course in the teacher's guide accusing us of perpetrating a godless philosophy of "humanism." Then he said, "I came away from the Dow article with the thought that the authors of MACOS believed that the schoolteacher in the classroom should be the director in the development of more human, human beings—whatever that means . . . There are some of us who believe some of our fellow men could become more human if they would simply learn to control themselves and if they would abandon their ceaseless efforts of trying to control or reshape others."[18]

Following Zarbin, a parent named Thomas Doeller presented a list of signatures from fifty-two parents who wished their children to continue with the course, and another parent named Virginia Cornell (no relation to the principal) urged that MACOS be continued, noting that a second program, based upon a textbook entitled *The Free and the Brave,* had already been provided for those parents who had requested it. Phyllis Musselman proposed the formation of a parent-initiated textbook committee as a way of heading off a rumored legislative investigation by the state. The committee, she suggested, would be charged with selecting a basal social studies text and thereby eliminate the need for interference from the state board of education. The final scheduled speaker was Frank Lewis, another parent, who presented a statement signed by 350 members of the community that supported the board in its decision to introduce innovative programs like MACOS and urged the members not to yield to pressure from a small group.

The meeting was then given over to two-minute speeches by members of the audience who had requested a chance to express their views, with equal time allotted to those for and against the course. This was by far the most spirited part of the evening. A Boy Scout troop leader charged that his wife was home sick "because of this program" and that parents had lost control of their children because their upbringing had now been taken over by educators like "Skinner, Bruner, and the rest of these jokers from out of state." A man who described himself as a "born-again believer" spoke in favor of the course, arguing that moral values are "caught" at home not taught at school, and therefore there was no way that the program could hurt his child. A mother who was a former school teacher read with dramatic flair a passage from one of the teachers' guides in which anthropologist Alan Beals suggests the close kinship between Eskimos and seals: "Neither the eye of the camera nor the knife of the surgeon can distinguish the man from the seal." Then, brandishing the manual in the air, she exclaimed, "This is MACOS. The man indistinguishable from the seal . . . With a view to human overpopulation and a reminder that the seal is in a diminishing existence, let's be glib. Let's keep our humor. Listen to the expert, Jerome Bruner, and take a seal to bed!"[19]

When the allotted time for public statements had elapsed, Shirley Chisholm, the board chair, upon a motion of the board, brought the session to a close. Following a five-minute recess, the board reconvened and heard a motion to continue the program on a voluntary basis. Zarbin abstained from the vote on the ground that he had joined the board with a preformed opinion. Another member proposed tabling the issue to allow the evening's expression of views more time to influence the board's decision. But there was little support for postponement and the motion carried. Mrs. Chisholm voted with the majority. As in Lake City, the Madison Park School Board passed the responsibility for choosing to the parents themselves.

The following day the manager of KRUX, a Phoenix radio station, asked me to appear on a talk show hosted by Logan Stuart, a well-known local radio personality, to debate the merits of MACOS with Phyllis Musselman and another parent, Mrs. Anna Day. I was wary of squaring off against this mistress of half-truth and innuendo, but I accepted in the hope of bringing an alternative view to a public discussion that had been dominated almost exclusively by Mrs. Musselman. Stuart's program was an hour-long, loosely structured inquiry called "Paragon or Paradox?" In a brief exchange shortly before we went on the air but too late to make a change, I learned that Stuart shared Mrs. Musselman's views on MACOS and that he had no intention of conducting an unbiased exchange.

Stuart's radio show brought me face to face with Phyllis Musselman for the first time. She and Anna Day sat opposite me across a table piled high with books and course materials, which they had obviously studied in great detail. Scraps of paper protruded from each volume, presumably marking passages that I was supposed to explain and defend. Various books by Bruner and Richard Jones were in evidence, and many other works besides. Clearly Musselman and Day had done their homework, and in a brief moment of panic it crossed my mind that they might know some things about the course that I didn't know myself. I was about to experience a challenging hour.

The debate with Musselman and Day and Stuart proved to be more thought-provoking and less painful than I had feared. Although serious dialogue was impossible, since my opponents were close-minded and fanatically rigid in their views, I admired their perseverance and their devotion to what they believed. Their objections to exposing children to the darker side of Netsilik life—birth control through infanticide, the vulnerability of old people, or the necessity of killing to survive—made me pause to wonder why we had chosen to include so many of the harsh realities of Arctic life, and, in particular, what purpose we had served by dwelling on one Netsilik's decision to abandon his aging mother-in-law. Was the inclusion of this rare instance of Eskimo hard-heartedness really so central to our aims? Such "honesty" in our presentation went over well in Cambridge, but was it really so necessary to expose the world to these painful truths? Why had we left ourselves open to such easy criticism?

Logan Stuart had his own agenda, which weakened his effectiveness as a moderator. At one point Mrs. Day was steering the discussion in a direction that would soon force me to discuss my views on evolution. Both Day and Musselman wanted to know more about the rationale for including the study of animals in a course on "Man," and they were particularly interested in finding out the basis of our animal-human comparisons. Were we saying that human beings were just "evolved" animals? Fortunately Stuart was too preoccupied with his own concerns about the cultural materials to pick up on my discomfort. Interrupting Mrs. Day's penetrating line of questioning, he abandoned the moderator's role altogether to press his own view that schooling should support the prevailing value system. By introducing children to the values of another culture, he charged, the course was undermining the very moral foundations of our society. When I protested, he vented his exasperation by blurting out his view of the role of the school: "What I am trying to extract from you, Mr. Dow, is an admission that the most important thing to teach a child is faith!" "Not in the public schools," I replied. "In Sunday School, of course we teach children what we want them to believe; but as for the rest of the week, the proper purpose of schooling is to cultivate doubt, to raise questions, to help our children see the world from another point of view." Schools, I contended, should concern themselves with the growth of the mind, not with the transmission of belief.

The exchange with Logan Stuart crystallized for me one of the fundamental issues that separated the developers of MACOS from its detractors. For us, the goal of the course was to help teachers and children think about human behavior in a new way. We wanted them to question and explore their own preconceptions about what it means to be human in a spirit of inquiry that would permit a diversity of views and invite children to think for themselves. At the core of our approach was a respect for the intelligence of children, and the belief that exposure to new knowledge would strengthen their ability to think about behavior in a systematic way and draw their own conclusions. We did not believe that such knowledge would undermine their values, although we expected that it would call into question certain prejudices. Why should respect for the humanity of others be a threat to our value system?

Such a stance toward children's learning was anathema to our opponents in Phoenix. They saw the course as a violation of the accepted ways of schooling children and a repudiation of social studies materials that promoted American values. Children should not be encouraged to question; they should be taught what to believe. A social studies course that deliberately set out to cultivate in children a questioning attitude about human behavior and human values was dangerous to people like Earl Zarbin and Phyllis Musselman precisely because it did not deal in absolutes, in cultural imperatives. It did not cultivate unquestioning acceptance of a particular set of values, and that is what made it unacceptable. Between these two points of view there was an unbridgeable gulf, and I packed my bags knowing that MACOS would not survive long in Madison Park.

Reaction from the Right

The Phoenix controversy was a foretaste of the growing conservatism that was beginning to pervade the public attitude toward schooling in the early 1970s. In part the new mood reflected a reaction to the heavy spending programs of the 1960s; in part it expressed a resistance to the growing power of the federal bureaucracy; and in part it sprang from an increasing distrust of large-scale, centrally administered educational innovations. Typical of this reactionary spirit was a full-page editorial by publisher Gene Pulliam entitled "Will the Federal Bureaucracy Destroy Individual Freedom in America?," which appeared in the *Arizona Republic* during the height of the MACOS controversy. Pulliam argued that the federal establishment had grown so large it now functioned as a "third political party," stronger than the other two and capable of imposing its own programs on the country irrespective of the party in power. Speaking of this new political force in America, he wrote: "As their control over our economic life has grown, the bureaucrats and regulators have shown their intentions more and more openly. In a wide variety of cases they are advancing the idea of 'social engineering'— the notion that government 'experts' should take children away from their parents, break the ties of family life, and mold American youngsters into the image of the bureaucrats themselves."[20] Pulliam was referring to busing programs, but his words have a familiar ring. The critics of MACOS shared the same point of view.

The immediate outcome of the Madison Park incident was a modest victory for the proponents of the course. While 22 of the 110 students in the program were eventually removed, the course remained in the school with little further disruption. Phyllis Musselman, however, continued her campaign against the program, and despite the efforts of the superintendent to silence her, was warmly received at a parents meeting on 13 December. She called and wrote to me several times to report on her progress, but by January she had tired of the battle and withdrew her son from the Madison Park kindergarten, saying that he was too young to keep up with the work. Musselman then turned her attention to other crusades like the abortion fight in the state legislature. In her last letter to me she was candid about her role as a professional agitator. "Please don't feel that you are alone in your problems regarding Mrs. Musselman," she remarked. "I'm a pain in the neck to the Arizona chapter of Planned Parenthood."[21]

In June 1973 Edward Martin, director of teacher training at EDC, visited Madison Park to find out what had ultimately happened with MACOS. Dow Rhoton informed him that the course had run through its two-year trial period and then had been quietly removed from the school system. Rhoton said that the composition of the school board had become more conservative, and that the board was now questioning everything the schools were doing and demanding measurable proof that each program was worthwhile. The new measures included the introduction of "performance objectives" and "minimal grade standards," the freezing of administrative salaries, increased pressure from state authorities, and a demand that the schools provide a "basic general education" that stressed reading, writing, and mathematics. While the concept of providing alternative programs within a school district had been explored, Rhoton spoke of the practical difficulties in an era of declining enrollments. Even Marvin Cornell, he said, had recommended dropping the course. While he did not regret the controversy, Rhoton wondered about the effect of the debate on children's feelings and attitudes, and he felt that, given the current political climate, it did not make sense to attempt innovation: "We felt that right now the proponents of the three 'Rs' are so strongly in the saddle as far as the Madison District is concerned, and so far as the State of Arizona is concerned, that people ought to be well warned ahead of time before they take on a program such as MACOS."[22]

Nationwide Resistance

When the trouble first began, it seemed that both the Lake City and Phoenix controversies were isolated local affairs uninfluenced by outside forces. Although Reverend Glenn was a newcomer to Lake City and Phyllis Musselman had enrolled her child at Madison Park only during the few months she was agitating against the course, there was little reason to think that these efforts had organizational support beyond the local community. On the day of the committee hearings in Lake City, the president of the School Board, John Dees, had received a telegram signed by a woman who identified herself as the "coordinator of the National Coalition on the Crisis in Education," which warned that "parents across the country are watching the Columbia County School Board," but Dees interpreted the wire as a local scare tactic. At that time it was hard for us to believe that there was any systematic, national opposition to the course.

But within a few months that impression began to change. In April 1972 I received a letter from Art Ware, the social studies coordinator for the Bellevue, Washington, public schools reporting that MACOS was being challenged in Bellevue's twenty-four elementary schools. Bellevue was an innovation-minded school system that had implemented the course with great enthusiasm a few years before, and this sudden surge of opposition after several successful years of teaching was difficult to explain. The charges, presented by Mrs. Rosanne McCaughey and Mrs. Richard O'Hara, read like a legal brief and included many of the same quotations from both the teacher's manuals and the student books that had appeared in the Lake City and Phoenix discussions. The ten objections read like excerpts from Phyllis Musselman's newspaper articles, and to these were added a new complaint: "The booklet form of the course material does not allow a direct point of reference for the total concept of the course, as a complete and whole text would."[23] The document concluded with the following statement: "We maintain: Parent-taxpayers do not wish to see their monies supporting a 'Social Studies' course so remote from the common understanding of what 'Social Studies' are supposed to consist of and so much at variance with commonly accepted beliefs and values in America."[24]

I wrote to Ware offering some thoughts on how he could respond to the charges and suggested that he seek help from Bill Harris, the regional center director at the University of Oregon. Ware soon discovered that opposition was quite limited and that the course was enthusiastically supported in this basically liberal, middle-class community. There were no emotion-charged public meetings, and Bellevue kept the program, but the Bellevue incident was worrisome, for this was the first time a parent group had attacked the course in a progressively minded school system. Was there evidence of outside influence in the carefully worded document that appeared in a community which had strongly endorsed the course only two years before? If a school system like Bellevue could come under attack for using MACOS, we would certainly face trouble in many other systems as the program grew nationwide.

The accounting records of Curriculum Development Associates indicate that sales of the course achieved a modest growth from 1971 to 1974. CDA deliberately avoided rapid expansion in an effort to ensure proper training for teachers and the use of the materials in ways that reflected the intent of the developers. Frances Link, who had been instrumental in introducing the course to the Cheltenham Township schools near Philadelphia, directed CDA's implementation effort, and she was scrupulous about seeing that teachers, administrators, and parents were thoroughly informed about the content and purposes of MACOS. The National Science Foundation made some support for this effort available through its Resource Personnel Workshop Program, providing grant money for teacher training and implementation. For a time it appeared as if CDA's modest commercial objectives, careful implementation efforts, and focus on intensive teacher training were the key to the course's success and to the management of controversy.

But despite CDA's cautious approach, renewed opposition surfaced in 1973 when Mrs. Norma Gabler of Longview, Texas, went to Burlington, Vermont, where MACOS had been peacefully taught for several years, to proclaim the course guilty of teaching "moral corruption and anti-Americanism."[25] Mrs. Gabler, who was well-known for her efforts to monitor the Texas textbook adoption process, had been invited to Vermont by a group called Citizens for Quality Textbooks, an organization headed by Donald Davie, a South Burlington engineer. Mrs. Gabler and her husband had been examining textbooks since 1963, leading a personal crusade against what they believed to be the erosion of Judeo-Christian values in the nation's schools. With MACOS she disapproved of the "immoral content" of the Netsilik materials, and she called for the participation of private citizens in the textbook decision-making process to defend children from immorality in the social studies. "Unless local people take an active voice in assisting the authorized units of government in . . . selecting textbooks," she argued, "the selection will continue to deteriorate."[26]

Following Gabler's visit the Vermont group brought in John Steinbacher, a former newspaperman and educator from California, who had written two books, *The Child Seducers* and *The Conspirators: Man against God*. Steinbacher accused MACOS of teaching Deweyism, pragmatism, behaviorism, psychic manipulation, and humanism, and argued that such programs were paving the way for a communist takeover and the destruction of the religious faith of the younger generation. Charged Steinbacher: "The tax-supported school system in the United States has become the leading vehicle for transporting Marxist revolution to the streets and into other institutions of this society. It is doubtful if the Humanist revolt against God could succeed without the public schools—yet millions of Americans still place their trust and confidence in a system that is destroying the souls of an entire generation of America's young and that will, unless abated, destroy the human civilization con-structed with loving labor in the United States over the past two centuries."[27]

Steinbacher envisioned the school system as a "vast mental hospital for the psychic manipulation of the young," an institution manned by behavioral scientists armed with techniques of brain-washing developed in mental hospitals, who were bent on taking over children's minds, separating them from the values of their parents, and preparing them to accept without protest "the concept of a socialized One World totalitarian state."[28] MACOS exemplified for Steinbacher the kind of program he feared, for it replaced the study of American history at an impressionable age with the study of a culture and life-style that he saw as "diametrically opposed" to our own.[29]

Steinbacher's warnings touched a chord. The problem for MACOS now ran deeper than a few fundamentalists in Florida or John Birchers in Phoenix. The national mood, influenced, perhaps, by the Vietnam War and our disillusionment with Watergate, was moving rapidly toward a more conservative and self-protective view of schooling. A course that proposed to introduce children to "the common humanity that all people share" was increasingly seen by people like Donald Davie and his associates as a program conceived by "humanists who do not believe in God and who feel America's love of family, of God, and of country must be erased in children before they can accept the humanist idea of one world in which all are 'world citizens.'"[30] Courses that promote cross-cultural understanding, he argued, must be replaced by courses that teach commitment to God and country.

In January 1974, a group of parents disrupted classes at the Springbrook School in Corinth, New York, where 112 children were studying MACOS for the first time. The course had been successfully introduced years before at the Lakeview School a mile away, where most of the students were children of university faculty, but Springbrook was a working-class community. A classroom discussion of evolution had turned into an argument, and some children had come to school brandishing religious tracts that denounced evolutionary theory. Several children had taken MACOS booklets home, and soon the principal was embroiled in a confrontation with parents, who demanded that the school give equal time to the teaching of traditional religious beliefs if it was going to "preach" evolution. "If we cannot sing Christmas carols," they argued, "then we are not going to let you teach other kinds of religion."[31] The principal attempted to solve the problem by offering an alternative program for the children of the objecting parents, but the controversy continued, and in April Springbrook dropped the course.

During 1974 the opposition continued to spread. The Gablers traveled to many of the communities that were using the course, voicing their criticisms and pushing their crusade against anti-Americanism and the teaching of evolution. In 1969 they had succeeded in getting the Biological Sciences Curriculum Study removed from the Texas state adoption list, and now MACOS was their principal target. Unwittingly, Curriculum Development Associates had aided the critics by publishing a directory listing every school system in the country using the program, so the targeted schools were easy to find. The Gablers were joined by Onalee McGraw's National Coalition for Children, and other conservative organizations, such as the Heritage Foundation and the Council for Basic Education, took up the fight against MACOS. The opposition of the Council was ironic, for it was the writings of men like its founder, Arthur Bestor, that had helped to bring about the curriculum reform movement twenty years before.

The Controversy Comes to Congress

The dispute over MACOS reached the national level in the spring of 1975 when Congressman John B. Conlan of Arizona took the debate to the floor of the House of Representatives. A Fulbright scholar and graduate of Harvard Law School, Conlan had been elected to Congress from a conservative district in Phoenix in 1972. He had first learned about the course as a state senator through complaints he had received from constituents during the Madison Park incident in 1971. George Archibald, a staff aide for Conlan and a former writer for the *Arizona Republic,* had made textbook watching something of a personal mission, and he had followed the implementation of MACOS with considerable interest for several years. Archibald had served on a commission to develop guidelines for social studies texts for the Arizona State Board of Education, and he had set himself a personal goal "to get schools out of the business of social engineering and indoctrination."[32] Archibald knew that Conlan faced a tough fight for reelection, and he must have seen MACOS as the perfect issue to give his congressman some much-needed national visibility.

Conlan's Attack

Conlan was a member of the House Committee on Science and Technology, the committee that reviews and submits to Congress the National Science Foundation's budget. The proposed NSF appropriation of $755 million contained a line item under the Education Directorate of $110,000 for "information workshops" for MACOS. Conlan had not mentioned MACOS during the subcommittee hearings, but when the bill came to the full committee's "mark-up" session, normally a routine review prior to floor action, he rose to attack the course, objecting to the MACOS appropriation on the grounds that federal subsidies for educational materials put the government in direct competition with the commercial textbook industry. Besides, charged Conlan, the controversial aspects of MACOS were giving the NSF "an unnecessary black eye." Drawing upon his considerable rhetorical skills, he mounted a blistering attack on the course:

> MACOS is designed to mold children's social attitudes and beliefs along lines that are almost always at variance with the beliefs and moral values of their parents and local communities . . . Recurring themes of the sixty lessons include communal living, elimination of the weak and elderly in society, sexual permissiveness and promiscuity, violence, and primitive behavior. This is for ten-year-olds.
>
> Many psychological devices are used throughout the course, including role-playing, group discussions, and encounter sessions, in which students are required to openly discuss intimate aspects of their personal lives and those of their families and friends . . . Teacher's guides and course materials inculcate in children an abandonment of love and help and concern for the weak and elderly in society.[33]

Conlan went on to charge that MACOS taught children to spy on each other and their parents and to bring their observations to class, where they were encouraged to "bare every emotion." He hinted at "lurid examples of violence and sexual promiscuity," and cited two cases in which psychologists had testified that children had experienced insomnia, school phobia, severe anxiety, and "sexually obsessive thoughts" as a result of the course. He spoke about the "uproar" in his own community over the program, suggested that thousands of parents were campaigning to get MACOS removed from their schools, and proposed an amendment to the appropriation bill that will deny further federal funding for implementation of the course.[34]

Conlan's assault took the committee totally by surprise. Most members were unfamiliar with MACOS, and Conlan cleverly exploited this ignorance to discredit both the course and the NSF. He not only criticized the course, he called into question the credibility of the agency itself. Recalling the specter of Watergate, he sharply attacked Lowell Paige, the head of the Education Directorate, suggesting that Paige had lied when he indicated, in an exchange of the previous day, that the contracts for dissemination activities had already been committed for the current year. Paige had apparently failed to produce the documents at Conlan's request, and the Congressman rejoined: "I strongly suspect that this type of contempt of the concern of this committee is such that he is likely to go and backdate the contracts like some of the boys in the White House did."[35]

The attack on MACOS disguised a deeper congressional concern: the competition between government-funded programs and commercially produced materials. A few years earlier, Congress had criticized the National Science Foundation for failing to disseminate educational programs that had been created with large investments of federal money and had appropriated special funds to do so. Many of NSF's current curriculum dissemination and training activities were an outgrowth of that earlier congressional mandate. Now Congress, in an apparent turnaround, began to challenge NSF's promotional activities under pressure from the publishing industry. Congressman Barry Goldwater, Jr., who spoke following Conlan, expressed no opinions on the substance of the course but questioned the need for continuing federal support for government-created programs after the initial development period. He quoted from a letter he had received from one of his constituents in the publishing business: "There are 20 or 30 competing programs available in the private sector. My editorial staff is convinced that a large number of these programs provide a more beneficial and satisfying educational experience for children than is available through the use of *Man: A Course of Study*. If *Man: A Course of Study* is of any value, by now, after many years of federal support, it ought to be able to stand on its own feet. If it is of no value, then artificial support is unwarranted. Let the program die a natural death."[36]

The implementation issue produced a lively debate. Congressman Dale Milford of Texas backed the amendment on the grounds that the schools are "exclusively the product of the local community" and federal intervention should be avoided.[37] Congressman Charles Mosher of Ohio, the ranking Republican on the committee, vigorously opposed the amendment, arguing that it was wrong to "cave in" to pressure from a small, organized group. This could open the way, he said, to attacks on all NSF programs and expose the committee to charges of censorship.[38] During the lengthy exchange that followed, the issue of censorship versus preferential treatment for federal programs surfaced repeatedly. While few favored denying the schools access to worthy materials, the notion of providing support for the distributor of federally sponsored programs upset a number of the members. Representative Philip Hayes of Indiana raised the question of "sweetheart contracts," while others worried that the length of time the government had funded the program gave the publisher of courses like MACOS an unfair advantage in the marketplace.

Congressman James Symington of Missouri, chair of the subcommittee sponsoring the appropriation bill, sought to fend off Conlan's amendment by stating that his committee report would direct the NSF to cease all further support for MACOS until an impartial review of the program, together with its publishing arrangements, had been carried out. Symington suggested that members of the full committee be given access to the course materials and that the NSF appoint an ad hoc review group of distinguished citizens and academics to examine the course. After considerable debate, Conlan's amendment failed by three votes and Symington's more moderate suggestion, which avoided the taint of censorship, prevailed, with the proviso, suggested by Conlan, that the review group be appointed by committee chair Olin Teague, not the NSF director.

So ended the matter—for the moment. On the following day I received a call from the NSF asking me to come to Washington to present the materials to the members of the Committee on Science and Technology. George Archibald was in the room during the presentation, making notes on my remarks and often interrupting to take issue with what I said. Archibald was well-informed about the program, and it was obvious from our first encounter that he was fervently dedicated to seeing it removed from the schools. If Archibald's behavior was indicative of Conlan's commitment, the NSF was in for a prolonged and determined fight. And the NSF had a lot more at stake than MACOS. Conlan's campaign against federally sponsored educational programs threatened to destroy the NSF's entire science curriculum reform effort, a program that had enjoyed generous congressional support for twenty years.

My talks with the committee members proved relatively uneventful. Most of the representatives, if they had bothered to examine the course at all, were mainly interested in viewing the "gory" film sequences they had heard about. Only a few took time to read the materials and inform themselves about the goals and specific content of the various units. An exception was the only woman on the committee, Representative Marilyn Lloyd of Tennessee, who was finishing out her recently deceased husband's term of office. Mrs. Lloyd questioned me in detail regarding our objectives, voiced her deep concern about the moral and ethical education of children, and expressed her worries about the many emotionally unhealthy influences that young people increasingly face. She spoke movingly about her own daughters and how she hoped to protect them from exposure to the decadence she observed in contemporary society. She was shocked by the amount of bloodshed in the MACOS films, and no amount of persuasion could convince her that the course should be used in her children's school.

Congressman Symington, on the other hand, was genuinely enthusiastic about MACOS. He had obviously studied the materials, was looking for additional ammunition that he could use to fend off Conlan's attack, and appeared to be quite prepared to carry his defense of the program to the floor of the House if necessary. He had hoped to work with members of the NSF staff to develop an appropriate case in support of the NSF's work in the improvement of science education, and he was upset when the director of the NSF, Guyford Stever, failed to strengthen his hand in the struggle with Conlan. Stever, perhaps understandably, seemed more concerned with preserving the reputation of his well-funded agency than with fighting to protect an educational program that was of small consequence in the context of the Foundation's total budget. Funding for NSF's total education effort at that time amounted to only about sixteen million of an appropriation of three quarters of a billion dollars.

On 17 March Stever sent committee chair Olin Teague a five-page letter announcing his decision to conduct an in-house investigation of NSF curriculum activities with particular attention to MACOS. Wrote Stever:

Because of the concerns expressed on all sides of several issues, I have decided that, regardless of what action is taken by Congress, no further 1975 funds will be obligated for MACOS and no 1976 funds, if authorized and appropriated, will be obligated either for MACOS or any other pre-college science course development and implementation until we have conducted a thorough review of the NSF effort in these areas and reported to the National Science Board and Congress with recommendations. I will assign a top-level group of staff from the Foundation with some members outside the Education Directorate, together with some carefully chosen outsiders, to make this report to me.[39]

Apparently Stever reasoned that by initiating an investigation of his Education Directorate he could placate Conlan, and he wrote this letter of appeasement in the hope that it would speed the passage of the NSF's budget. Symington was angry with Stever for capitulating in this way, for he feared that the letter would be interpreted as an admission of guilt and only feed Conlan's determination to press his case against the Foundation.

Margaret Mead

Symington turned out to be right. Stever's letter notwithstanding, Conlan pressed his attack on the NSF and reintroduced his amendment at a committee meeting on 19 March. The committee's staff director, John Holmfeld, invited me to Washington to attend this meeting on the outside chance that an opportunity might arise for me to give informal testimony. Shortly after my arrival I encountered Margaret Mead, surrounded by an entourage of admirers, making her way purposefully, forked staff in hand, to a luncheon where she was scheduled to address the National Women's Caucus. Her presence in the Rayburn Building on the day of this important committee meeting seemed remarkably fortuitous, and Holmfeld and I both wondered if we could enlist her support in defending the teaching of anthropology to the young. I told Holmfeld that she was not particularly familiar with MACOS, but that she had visited EDC as a consultant on our NSF-funded high school program, Exploring Human Nature, and that she knew about the work upon which the course was based. With a little preparation, I thought, she could certainly be helpful.

Holmfeld set up a meeting with Mead following her luncheon talk and a hearing with Chairman Teague prior to the committee session. Time was tight, for the committee was scheduled to convene at 2:00 PM, but Mead's willingness to take part lifted my spirits and I prepared to brief her as best I could in the few minutes we would have together before Teague's arrival. At exactly 1:30 PM I entered a small vestibule next to the committee room where Mead was waiting. I introduced myself, showed her the materials, and began to describe the course when she cut me off. Glancing at the title page, she said, "Who wrote this? DeVore? I know him. Balikci? Fine work. But who are you? And what is EDC? Aren't you the people who misused my Arapesh material in one of your high school courses?" As I began to answer she interrupted again. "What are the Congressmen so upset about?" As I started to reply her eyes fell on the "Old Kigtak" lesson. "What's this about?" she asked. With a sinking heart I carefully explained that the Netsilik material included a story that Knud Rasmussen told about an old woman named Kigtak who had been left behind on the sea ice by her son-in-law, Arfek, a poor hunter who feared for the survival of his wife and children.

Mead's exasperation grew. "What do you tell the children that for? Haven't you read Carpenter? Don't you know that Eskimos are famous in the anthropological literature for their kind treatment of old people?" I replied that I did know that and pointed out that the materials strongly emphasize the importance of close family ties and mutual support between families among the Netsilik. I told her that the Kigtak story had been included as a way of reinforcing the centrality of these communal values, because we presented it as an Eskimo moral dilemma. Like us, we tried to show, they too struggle with questions of right and wrong. What better way to illustrate their humanity? With this explanation Mead appeared to soften a little, but she remained upset that the MACOS debate had apparently given her profession a bad name. "I have been teaching anthropology for forty years," she remarked, "and I have never had a controversy like this over what I have written. But that won't help us now. What do you think we should say to the congressmen? Why did you develop this course anyway?"

Sensing that Mead was beginning to warm to the challenge of defending MACOS after all, I remarked that, as she probably knew, in the public schools we have a very ethnocentric curriculum. I told her that American history is typically taught at least three times—in the fifth, eighth, and eleventh grades—and that most other courses in history and the social sciences focus heavily on American society. It was with this in mind, I said, that we had developed a course that would expose students to the way others live, would introduce them to the concept of culture, and would enable them to observe and think about human behavior in a more general way. Such a course, we believed, could contribute to the appreciation of cultural diversity by helping American children to comprehend the common humanity of all people, including some who live very differently, such as the Netsilik Eskimos. But Mead's anger quickly returned. "No, no, you can't tell the senators that! Don't preach to them! You and I may believe that sort of thing, but that's not what you say to these men. The trouble with you Cambridge intellectuals is that you have no political sense!"

Chastened once more by Mead's criticism, I quietly asked, "Dr. Mead, how would you explain Man: A Course of Study to the members of Congress?" Her answer was quick: "You tell them what they want to hear. You point out that the reason we teach about Eskimos is to help children understand the differences between our culture and theirs, that we have choices they don't have. You tell them that we have the wheat fields of Kansas and the oil fields of Texas, that we are a culture of abundance, not scarcity, and we don't have to leave our old people behind to die on the ice like the Eskimos—if we choose not to."[40]

At that moment Congressman Teague arrived. He appeared red-faced and impatient, and he was obviously annoyed at being summoned to this impromptu audience. Mead rose to face Teague and delivered a brilliant and intensely patriotic speech in defense of MACOS. All traces of irritation toward EDC and contempt for my political naïveté had vanished from her voice as she spoke eloquently about the power of cross-cultural studies to deepen children's appreciation of the American way of life. She was forceful and persuasive, but Teague was unmoved. He said a few words about the angry reactions of his Texas constituents—letters he had received, phone calls, visits—and then turned away to begin his meeting, leaving our eagerly awaited invitation to speak to his committee unissued. Mead turned to me ruefully. "Too late," she said. "He has made up his mind. You've lost."

Mead was now fascinated by the controversy, and she postponed her flight to hear the debate. The committee was more informed than at the previous session, and two Democratic congressmen, who had voted with Conlan on 6 March, now appeared to support the course. According to one observer, who took detailed notes of the proceedings, there appeared to be a noticeable shift toward increased support for the course since the previous session. "Much of the support," he later wrote, "was, quite properly I think, directed at the question of whether the committee should get into such detailed supervision of an agency's program as indicated by the Conlan proposal."[41] Even the opponents of the course seemed to be moving to the position that congressional oversight should not be directed at a particular curriculum but rather, that some greater degree of supervision should be provided over NSF's curriculum efforts. The committee took no vote on the Conlan amendment, but it seemed likely that Conlan would reintroduce his proposal when the appropriation bill reached the floor of the House.

Attempted Defense

By this time the MACOS debate was becoming increasingly visible in the public press. Late in March nationally syndicated columnist James J. Kilpatrick began a series of highly critical articles on MACOS under such provocative headlines as "Is Eskimo Sex Life a School Subject?" Kilpatrick clearly had not taken the time to study the course himself, for his charges were full of inaccuracies, but his attack reflected the growing public reaction to federally sponsored educational reform. He labeled the NSF's education effort "an ominous echo of the Soviet Union's promulgation of official scientific theory" and brooded about the Orwellian implications of federal support for curriculum making: "For my own part, I am repelled by the manipulative theories of such behavioral scientists as Brunner [sic] and B. F. Skinner . . . But even if they were propounding sound doctrine, they would have no right to pursue academic freedom with the people's money. Once the notion is accepted that government has power to commission and to subsidize textbooks in social science, we move a significant step down the road to 1984."[42]

In an effort to respond to this spreading campaign against the course, I prepared a letter that went out to all MACOS users explaining the congressional debate, stating the case for academic freedom, and providing support materials to help school systems defend the course against the public reaction that would inevitably arise from the growing national publicity. I wrote in part:

> Attacks such as Congressman Conlan's, if not properly resisted, can seriously damage the federal effort in pre-college education—a commitment that has exceeded $500 million on the part of the National Science Foundation alone, and has made an enormous

contribution to the improvement of instruction in all areas of the curriculum. Teaching in mathematics, the basic sciences, and more recently in the social sciences has been greatly enriched by this investment. This is a time, we believe, when educators must stand up for their right to carry out significant research and development in areas that are too risky to be undertaken by the commercial marketplace, and to protect their access to programs that offer significant alternatives to the products created by textbook publishers . . .

The NSF authorization bill is still pending and is scheduled to reach the House floor within the next few days. As it is possible that Congressman Conlan may reintroduce his amendment at that time, other articles may appear in the press and you may receive queries from parents and members of your community interested in the *Man: A Course of Study* controversy. In the event that you get such inquiries, the most effective response, in our view, is to provide the public swiftly and openly with full information about the content and purposes of the *Man: A Course of Study* program . . . We urge you to contact your congressman to explain the experience you have had with *Man: A Course of Study* in your school system and to voice your own views on the value of materials of this kind.[43]

Conlan saw my letter as further ammunition. He sent a copy of it to Guyford Stever with a cover letter accusing EDC of using the NSF "curriculum promotion network" as a "political weapon" to manipulate MACOS users. Once again Conlan pulled out the stops:

The enclosed Education Development Center "Dear Friend of MACOS" letter is a political call to arms to malign and intimidate parents and citizens on the local level who oppose EDC's imposing a uniform national social studies curriculum with NSF funding, aimed at changing children's social values and behavior and questioning their religious upbringing . . .

EDC's letter went to a large mailing list of educators promoting and using Education Development Center curriculum programs with NSF funds throughout the country. It urges members of the NSF-funded network to start a propaganda campaign in their communities against anyone who does not share EDC's view that children should be used as guinea pigs in the classroom. The letter carries the clear implication that NSF had endorsed EDC's views, as well as its political appeal . . . This latest attempt to turn your NSF-funded curriculum promotion network into a political force to intimidate and misrepresent local citizens disagreeing with the NSF/EDC party line strikes at the very heart of our cherished free institutions. It is a highly dangerous assault on academic freedom in local communities throughout America.

Hopefully you and the National Science Board will publicly disavow and condemn these activities by Education Development Center, as well as reaffirm your stated intention to thoroughly investigate abuses and irregularities in NSF/EDC curriculum activities.[44]

As the controversy grew I wrote to Jerome Bruner, who was now teaching at Oxford, and sent him some of the articles that had appeared in the press describing the congressional debate. I asked him how he viewed his role in the federal curriculum effort, and he replied with characteristic commitment:

Several columnists and Congressmen have raised the question whether NSF should be in the business of trying to improve course content in the schools. I'm afraid that they have forgotten recent history. In the 1950s and 1960s there was a desperate call to upgrade instruction in our schools, and the NSF did a tremendous job in recruiting the efforts of university-based mathematicians, physicists, chemists, biologists, geographers, and behavioral scientists in projects that brought America into leadership in the world in the teaching of these subjects in our schools. Please note again, this was all done in dedication to better education, for all of the projects were nonprofit. Did this throttle freedom of speech, as some seem to be claiming? Nonsense. Publishers were as free as ever to go about producing their textbooks by their old formulae, and did so. The effect of the new materials was to improve in general the quality of publishing by setting higher standards. The educational publishers, I think, welcomed the challenge. Why else would they have given me a prize for improving the state of the art by leading the MACOS team?[45]

He then went on to discuss his view of the role of the behavioral scientist in curriculum reform and the educational philosophy that lay behind the development of MACOS:

I have always had the conviction that the academic student of human development should take an active part in trying to improve the state of public education, much in the same spirit as the student of other aspects of human growth seeks to improve the practice of pediatrics. Unfortunately, the criteria for good health and for being well educated are not equally plain. I have tried to resolve the lack of clarity about what constitutes a well-educated man by favoring diversity and openness, not trying to shape minds to one pattern, but to make it possible for a growing mind to develop according to its own interests and values and for people to find their own ways of contributing to the society. That, it seems to me, is the essence of democratic education. But I am well aware of the fact that helping young people develop a broad sense of the alternatives open to man does not always meet with favor among those who think that they know the truth as it really is. And because these are anxious times, there are probably more frightened and angry reactions to innovations in school curricula than before.[46]

Was Bruner right that fear motivated the reaction against MACOS? Perhaps. But we can also see in Conlan's opposition the resurgence of an attitude toward schooling that was far more characteristic of the average American's view of what was appropriate for the young to study than the notions of Harvard professors. The participation of behavioral scientists in school reform was a product of a unique period of American history, when fear of Soviet scientific and technological prowess led to the involvement of large numbers of university academics in school reform. Now that the immediate threat of Soviet space dominance had passed, the urgency to change the schools soon evaporated, and we returned to the historic pattern of local control. Congressman Conlan spoke for a new political constituency that was intolerant of academia, suspicious of federal reform initiatives, and fiercely protective of the autonomy of the local school district.

Debate in the House

The NSF authorization bill came to the floor of the House on 9 April. As expected, Conlan reintroduced his amendment, but this time he had broadened the proposed prohibition to require a thorough review by Congress of all NSF curriculum projects prior to implementation. The consequence of such a restriction would be to establish the right of congressional censorship of any educational program generated with public money, as well as to impose on Congress an enormously time-consuming administrative function. In effect, passage would mean a vote of no-confidence in the NSF's ability to select and implement appropriate educational initiatives in science and mathematics education without congressional review. Citing EDC's dissemination activities as "a dangerous plan for a federally-backed takeover of American education," Conlan declared, "We must reassert effective congressional authority over all NSF activities in the area of developing and promoting school materials."[47]

Conlan's amendment provided the occasion for a vigorous debate on the purposes of schooling and the role of the federal government in helping to meet the nation's educational needs. Many of the members knew little about MACOS other than what they might have read in one of Kilpatrick's articles in the *Washington Post,* but all felt competent to comment on the education of children. The Conlan proposal gave them an opportunity to talk about their own educational experiences and the extent to which the federal government should be involved with the public schools. Following Conlan's lengthy attack on the course, EDC, CDA, and the NSF, Congressman Frank Annunzio of Illinois rose to speak: "As a former teacher in the Chicago public school system, and as a parent and grandparent, it is my firm conviction that our schools should be seen as an extension of the family function which instills moral standards in children. The exposure of children in their formative years to these vagaries of other civilizations and cultures without appropriate perspective constitutes a condemnation of the moral standards of the Judeo-Christian culture which have made this nation so great."[48] Annunzio praised the investigation that was under way and pointed out that the government should get out of the educational implementation business because there was "plenty of capital available" to support distribution of worthwhile programs without federal subsidies.

Congressman Symington, on the other hand, argued that the Conlan amendment was a form of censorship, and that local school boards, not Congress, should determine the value of educational materials. He pointed out that he had "testimonials as thick as the gentleman from Arizona" from school systems that strongly believed in the value of the program. Then, taking issue with Annunzio, he pointed out that children today need to be exposed to foreign cultures: "The time for know-nothingism has long since passed. I cannot think that we will cross the threshold into our Bicentennial year with the idea that America is turning inward intellectually, academically, trade-wise, and in every other way."[49]

Warming to a defense of MACOS, Symington began describing

some of the Eskimo films he had seen, including a scene from a caribou hunt showing two families driving their prey into a lake, spearing them from kayaks, and dragging the dead creatures ashore for skinning and butchering, while a small child watches. Of all the hunting sequences in the films, this is perhaps the most difficult to look at for someone who has never killed and prepared an animal for food. Symington, who had known rural life as a child, saw educational value in the material: "There is no evil in it. We try to pull a cosmetic shade over the violence we are required to commit in order to eat and live. They do not do that. Mr. Chairman, I think it is useful for citizens, even at the age of ten, to see how it is that a great people live, struggle, and survive in another part of the world . . . When I was a boy working on my grandfather's farm, I used to see how they dispatched hogs before the bacon could be made available. Nothing I saw in that film exceeded the severity of that operation."[50]

Congressman Mosher followed Symington, adding his support to Symington's defense of the course content. The committee had reviewed the MACOS materials for two days, he said, and he believed that the majority of those who had actually seen them would thoroughly disagree with Conlan's assessment of the program:

> The materials to which the gentleman from Arizona particularly refers have to do with the customs and the mythology of the Eskimo tribes. These are in every respect very similar to some of our own traditional myths and fables. There is, in my opinion, absolutely nothing in these materials that cannot equally be found similarly in Grimm's Fairy Tales and in Aesop's Fables, scattered throughout the Bible, in the Odyssey, and in many other traditional stories that are so familiar to us, and as the gentleman from Missouri, Jim Symington, has said, in the lives of the pioneer farmers, the basic civilization in which we are rooted.
>
> Mr. Chairman, the principal impact of these Eskimo fables, as I have read them, is to impress upon youngsters . . . the fact that members of a family must hang together and must be interdependent. That seems to me to be a lesson that our society today could well learn.[51]

As the floor debate developed it became clear that the central issue before the Congress was not so much the content of a particular social science course but the question of freedom of choice within the educational community. Were local school districts to be allowed to choose between a variety of available course materials, including government-sponsored programs, or was it appropriate for Congress to pass judgment on any program funded by taxpayers dollars before it was released for public consumption? On this point Mosher remarked, "Mr. Chairman, I am shocked, really, that the gentleman from Arizona, whom I think of as responsibly and philosophically in the conservative tradition, would propose what is essentially thought control . . . These matters should be determined strictly at the local elected school board level."[52]

Representative Robert Krueger of Texas, a member of the Science and Technology Committee who did not particularly approve of the course content of MACOS, agreed with Mosher that the federal government should stay out of the business of judging school books. He argued that a body that could not find more than a few hours to discuss a $22 billion dollar federal budget deficit should hardly be spending its time worrying about matters that were properly the concern of the schools: "Although the values of this particular program . . . may not be mine—and they are not—they are nonetheless values which have the right to be heard and to be judged by local school districts, and therefore, in order to keep the Federal Government from wrongly intruding upon this local decision making power . . . we should oppose this amendment."[53]

Conversely, another member of the committee, Congressman John Wydler of New York, argued in defense of government monitoring of federal school expenditures. Wydler rejected the censorship argument, stating that all Congress was doing was exercising its responsibility to evaluate how the taxpayers' money was being spent. His only objection to the Conlan amendment was the difficulty in administering it, but he asserted the right of Congress to oversee its own expenditures. The federal government, not the school districts, he said, is spending tax revenues to produce certain results and selling them to the school districts, and there are value judgments involved in that process. "I think that we, as Members of the Congress, not only have a right to examine it; I think we have the duty to do so."[54]

And so the debate continued, for more than two hours. The question of the appropriateness of congressional oversight became the key issue, and the discussion returned again and again to the emotionally charged topic of censorship. Congressman Richard Ottinger of New York, who did not feel particularly strongly for or against the course, was vehement in his opposition to turning the Congress into a textbook review group. He said that if Congress were to pursue the full implications of the Conlan amendment, it would have to read all the books in every library that receives federal assistance and look at all books and materials that the federal government finances in the schools. In his view censorship of this sort was "absolutely abhorrent": "I assure the members of this committee that the Holy Bible would never pass muster under the kind of demagoguery in which my friend, the gentleman from Arizona, is engaging, because in the Holy Bible there is murder—indeed murder of brother against brother, Cain against Abel."[55]

Congressman John Rousselot of California challenged Ottinger on his Bible test. He said that Ottinger was unfairly invoking the "gray ghost" of censorship when the real issue was the use of federal funds to promote school books. Would Ottinger care to ask if the Congress would object to the distribution of the Bible with federal dollars? No doubt there would be many in Congress who would object to such use of tax money. On the same grounds Rousselot felt that Conlan had a right to question the expenditure of federal funds for the promotion of what he called "highly questionable and un-provenly sound books."[56]

Before the Conlan amendment came to a vote, Symington rose again to review the issues and to make one last pitch in behalf of the content of MACOS. He recounted the history of Conlan's op-position to the course, describing his various political maneuvers, including the latest amendment, as a strategy for circumventing a solution already agreed to by the National Science Foundation. He then appealed to his congressional colleagues to consider the social value of the course: "My impression is that a misinformed national consciousness concerning other races and other peoples has been in part responsible for our participation in wars and other mistakes simply through want of understanding of how other races and cul-tures live and how other peoples gather themselves together to meet the problems of life. To broaden the perspective of the young citizen in this regard improves the judgments he will make both for his own and the country's benefit."[57]

When the vote finally came, the Conlan amendment was defeated by a slim margin of 215 to 196. But the conservatives were not to be deterred. In a surprising turn of events, Congressman Robert Bauman of Maryland then introduced a far more sweeping amendment that called for congressional review of all NSF grant proposals every thirty days and requiring the agency to submit documentation to show "to the maximum extent practicable the manner in which the national interest will be fostered by the approval of such grants."[58] Bauman's amendment moved the issue of congressional oversight far beyond the debate over classroom materials. It was a challenge to the time-honored peer review system for federal grants and could be construed as an invasion of academic freedom. Inexplicably, after a comparatively brief debate, the Bauman amendment carried by a vote of 212 to 199.

The congressional debate of 9 April alarmed the scientific community. Not only had Congress challenged the freedom of academics to create school materials with federal funds, the legislators had asserted their right to monitor all federally funded scientific research. Philip Handler, the president of the National Academy of Sciences, denounced these actions of the House of Representatives in his annual address before that prestigious assemblage of scholars a few weeks later. He cautioned that the narrow vote on the Conlan amendment had brought the Congress "dangerously close" to an act that was "tantamount to book burning," and he charged that the Bauman amendment has established the House as "censor of the National Science Foundation." Deploring this political intrusion on the awarding of scientific grants, Handler called the behavior of Congress "a giant leap backward by a supposedly egalitarian House which voted to adopt a procedure appropriate only to authoritarian regimes." Handler called upon his scientific colleagues to come to the defense of the social sciences, the particular target of congressional criticism, for, he warned, "if the social sciences are not defended by all of us, it will be our turn next."[59]

The Achilles Heel

The Bauman amendment was later killed in the joint House-Senate conference on the NSF authorization bill, but not before the Senate, too, had debated the merits of MACOS. There was no floor battle over the course, but Senator Edward Kennedy's Special Subcommittee on the National Science Foundation achieved considerable publicity when Dr. Onalee McGraw appeared as a witness to testify against the program. Much of her testimony was a repetition of earlier arguments, but she caught the attention of the press when she presented a chart (see Figure 5.1) that purported to illustrate how EDC, CDA, and NSF had collaborated to impose MACOS on the nation's schools at the expense of the American taxpayer. McGraw's chart provided a provocative reinterpretation of the dissemination network that EDC had established in 1969 and suggested that EDC and NSF had set up CDA under questionable contract arrangements to achieve publication with federal dollars after private industry had rejected the course. The three agencies, claimed McGraw, had then collaborated to set up a lobbying apparatus at the federal, state, and local levels to overcome parent and teacher resistance. Echoing Conlan, McGraw asked, "Why should we taxpayers have to support and subsidize promotion and sale of any school materials, when the best test for their need is the private marketplace?" Charging that the combined pressure of professional educators and government bureaucrats expending federal funds put parents and local decision makers at a disadvantage, she invoked "academic freedom" as an argument to support her own point of view: "The combination of vastly reduced cost because of federal marketing and teacher training activities for the publisher, plus heavy educator pressure to adopt EDC course materials, is enough

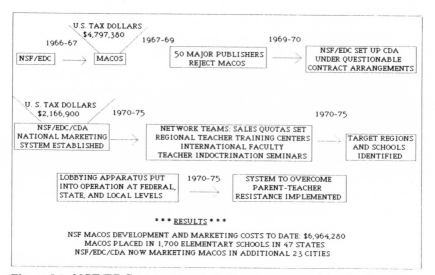

Figure 5.1. NSF/EDC Major Events in Development and Marketing of "Man: A Course of Study" (MACOS), a chart introduced at subcommittee hearings on 21 April 1975 by Dr. Onalee McGraw.

to induce most school boards to adopt these programs before parents know what is coming into the classroom . . . We believe this heavy and aggressive involvement of the National Science Foundation in the promotion and marketing of school materials is unhealthy and a dangerous invasion of academic freedom and choices of taxpayers on the local level."[60]

McGraw's criticisms of the MACOS dissemination network, although vastly overdrawn, had some merit. At what point should federal agencies cut the umbilical cord with the programs they have sponsored? Publishers of government-sponsored curriculum products do have an advantage over their competitors if public money is continuously available to support implementation. While innovative programs require a period of nurturing in the transition from development to widespread use, the time must come when successful programs can be commercially marketed without federal subsidy. Plans for such a transition should be built into the development process from the outset. McGraw's questions about the relationship between EDC, NSF, and CDA were legitimate ones, and they pointed to the need to deal with the issue of training, dissemination, and publication at the beginning of the curriculum development enterprise. The issue of dissemination was the Achilles heel of the MACOS project.

Federal Investigation

While the House and Senate debated the pros and cons of MACOS, the review committees initiated by Congress and the NSF began their work. Three federal investigations of the course took place in the spring and summer of 1975: the evaluation made by the Ad Hoc Review Committee appointed by Chairman Teague, the study carried out by the internal review team appointed by the director of the NSF, and a report prepared by the General Accounting Office at Teague's request. Each of these investigations shed light on NSF's curriculum reform effort.

NSF Internal Review

The first group to complete its work was the National Science Foundation, which, as promised, delivered its final report to the Committee on Science and Technology on 16 May. On 7 April Guyford

Stever had appointed an eleven-person review team consisting of two members of the National Science Board and nine high-ranking NSF officials. No member of the Education Directorate was included on the committee. Stever's charge was fourfold: investigate all NSF education programs to determine whether the content is educationally valuable, the scientific concepts accurate, the developers responsible and competent, and the institutional and contractual arrangements sound. Five programs, including MACOS, were earmarked for in-depth study.

NSF moved swiftly. After a two-day visit to EDC to talk with staff members and examine files, the NSF officials returned to Washington to complete their study and write the report. A few days later EDC learned in the press that the NSF had turned over some documents to the Criminal Division of the Justice Department for examination, but we were not informed of the content of the documents or of the alleged charges. We subsequently learned that Chairman Teague had requested a full substantive and fiscal audit of EDC's government funded activities back to ESI's inception in 1958. Presumably Teague's action was prompted by NSF's referral of documents to the Attorney General's office.

As it turned out, the NSF review group found very little to fault in the substantive, administrative, and fiscal aspects of the development and implementation of MACOS. In response to Stever's first three questions the report stated: "It appears . . . that in the judgment of scientific peer reviewers, representatives of the educational community, staff of the Education Directorate, and the National Science Board . . . the proposed subject matter did fit within reasonable limits or norms with respect to educational value. Further, there appeared to be no questions on accuracy of content nor doubt about competence and experience of the developers."[61] With respect to the institutional and contractual arrangements the report was critical of the way the NSF had managed the program. The reviewers found that the foundation had been somewhat lax in its overview procedures, failing to monitor project development closely and conducting no detailed review of EDC's publication planning. They concluded that the contractual arrangements between EDC and CDA, while somewhat unusual, "appear to be fiscally sound and adequate for the purposes intended."[62] The report recommended that the Foundation establish a needs assessment program, a better system of proposal evaluation, more rigorous oversight of projects, an in-depth summative evaluation, a program of dissemination research, written disclaimers on all materials, and a study designed to develop new ways of administering curriculum implementation while allowing the NSF to stay at arm's length from the process.[63]

Ad Hoc Science Curriculum Review Group

While the NSF investigation focused primarily on the conduct of the agency's Education Directorate and how project administration could be improved, the Ad Hoc Science Curriculum Review Group appointed by Chairman Teague took a broader look at the federal role in curriculum reform. The eight members included two college presidents, James Moudy of Texas Christian University and James Zumberge of the University of Nebraska; two government officials, Elam Hertzler of the Office of Education and Rocco Petrone, head of the National Center for Resource Recovery; two parent representatives, Claire Schweickart (wife of Lowell Schweickart, the astronaut) and Joanne McAuley of Dallas; a former congresswoman, Edith Green of Oregon; and Gerard Piel, the publisher of *Scientific American*. The chair, Chancellor Moudy, was a personal friend and constituent of Teague.

At the outset, the Moudy committee was predominantly negative toward MACOS. Teague was openly hostile to the program, and he saw to it that the membership reflected his views. He charged the group to conduct a study of the science curriculum implementation policy of the National Science Foundation with particular emphasis on MACOS, and he asked for a quick response. The committee members came to Washington in mid-May expecting to complete their work in a few days and to report back to Teague by the end of the month. The schedule provided little opportunity for serious investigation of the complex issues surrounding the selection, development, and implementation of a federally funded curriculum program, and it left no time to examine the experience of those who had actually used the course.

The atmosphere in Washington at the time was hardly conducive to a rational appraisal of MACOS. The congressional controversy had produced a spate of articles in the press, many of them derogatory, and Rachel Scott, a television reporter at NBC's Washington affiliate station WRC-TV, had produced two sensational commentaries on the program for the evening news on 24 and 25 April that were advertised in the *Washington Post* under the banner headline, "HORROR FLICKS. Is Your Ten-year-old Watching 'X-rated' Films at School?" The *Chronicle of Higher Education* had carried a series of articles following the congressional debate, one of which reported the transfer of documents to the Justice Department. Several students and teachers who had participated in the course in the Washington area wrote supportive letters and articles, but these protests were swamped by a well-organized and well-funded critique of the course mounted by Conlan, McGraw, the Heritage Foundation, and the Council for Basic Education. The committee set about its work in an environment highly charged with criticism of the program.

On 13 May Edwin Campbell, the president of EDC, and I appeared before the Moudy committee, at the committee's request, to explain EDC's role in the development and implementation of the course. When we arrived, the atmosphere in the meeting room was somber. Campbell began by describing EDC's long and distinguished record in curriculum development, including PSSC Physics, the Elementary Science Study, and EDC's extensive educational work in foreign countries. I followed with a statement explaining the content and educational purposes of the course, and documenting our extensive experience with the implementation of the program in schools. I discussed many of the issues raised in the congressional debate, explained the role of Jerome Bruner, and concluded by reading a letter from a seventh-grade student in Connecticut who questioned Conlan's charges by describing his own experience with MACOS in the sixth grade. Rejecting claims that the course taught negative values, he commented that the course helped him understand his present social science course, which taught that "wars occur partially because one culture doesn't understand another." "MACOS," he said, "helped me to understand another culture."[64]

Our presentations did little to improve the mood of the gathering. Mrs. McAuley, who sat behind a stack of well-thumbed books, reminded me of my encounter with Phyllis Musselman in Phoenix during our radio talk. When I had finished she gave a short speech to the group describing the content of the course as she saw it and repeating many of Conlan's charges. Edith Green then spoke angrily about the intrusion of the federal bureaucracy on the autonomy of the schools, while Gerard Piel sat in a corner taking voluminous notes but saying little. Mrs. Schweickart expressed guarded interest in the program but appeared to remain skeptical, despite my efforts to convince her of the merits of the course's cross-cultural perspective. We left the meeting feeling that we had stated our case well, and that there was some support for the course in the room, but as a group they would be difficult to persuade. We subsequently learned that the committee was split five to three against the course, but that Piel was working vigorously to put off a final judgment until the investigation had continued for at least another month.

In the midst of the rising emotion surrounding the MACOS controversy, Gerard Piel proved to be a wise and cool head. Piel believed that hasty judgment had benefited the course's critics, and he induced the Moudy committee to abandon its original timetable. He argued that it was important to gather facts from all sources, including the schools using the course, before passing judgment on the program. He called for a thorough assessment of the entire science curriculum reform effort, not just a judgment about MACOS. During the next few weeks Piel gathered as much information as he could find about the course. He asked me to prepare a set of background materials detailing EDC's activities in teacher training, dissemination, implementation, and publication of all its NSF-sponsored programs, and to provide him with a survey of the evaluations of the course that had been carried out by EDC and others. He wrote letters to every school district using the program and requested a candid appraisal of the system's experience with the course. He personally contacted and interviewed many MACOS users, and he studied the history of NSF's involvement in curriculum development back to the funding of PSSC in 1956. Piel's research and letter-writing campaign produced a voluminous response from the school systems using MACOS, most of which was overwhelmingly favorable. Convinced that the committee was misinformed, he set about trying to persuade his colleagues to reconsider their negative stance.

Piel drafted a position paper setting forth the argument that the movement that had produced MACOS, contrary to the charges of Conlan and other critics, was not a government-dominated invasion of local school districts but the product of what he termed "a self-governing democracy of science." Piel's analysis was based on the well-established practice of *peer review,* in which judgments about the quality of government-funded programs are sheltered from political influence by the evaluation of competent professionals within the field. In an address later delivered to the National Science Teacher's Association, Piel explained his position:

> The science curriculum reform movement was never a government enterprise. It was an enterprise of the voluntary initiative of university professors and school teachers. They originated the ad hoc groups that set up the curriculum projects in each field. They had to seek the funding they needed from the National Science Foundation, but that agency had been created by Congress to support education as well as research in the sciences. At every stage in the development of each curriculum, the peer review procedures that have insulated the independence of scientists in our universities from the government granting agencies served to decouple the control of the content of the new courses from the authority of officials in the National Science Foundation. Peer review groups monitored the development of courses, reviewed the classroom tests, and ultimately signed off the curricula for release to the market.[65]

Piel asserted that the National Science Foundation had been scrupulous in its efforts to keep itself removed from questions of content, to delegate to the developers the selection of publishers by competitive bidding, and to maintain a stance of neutrality with regard to the school system's "total responsibility" for determining the substance and content of what is taught in the schools. The Foundation, he pointed out, was supporting a considerable variety of innovative approaches, based upon the initiatives of scholars and teachers, and had funded over fifty reform projects in precollege mathematics, science, and social science curricula. Far from promoting a particular point of view, he said, the Foundation's education initiatives were noted for their diversity.

After two intensive sessions in June and July Piel succeeded in turning the tide. The Teague committee report, submitted on 1 October, recommended that the NSF continue its work in curriculum development and implementation. Two members, however, argued that the NSF should confine its curriculum efforts to natural science and mathematics, and Mrs. McAuley remained unchanged, holding firmly to her position that the agency should get out of curriculum reform altogether. The committee proposed the creation of a continuing "needs assessment" program and the inclusion of "representative" parents in the curriculum review process in order to establish closer monitoring of the quality and content of curriculum projects. They also suggested tighter structuring of the NSF's management and review procedures to ensure timely completion of projects and the elimination of favoritism, the inclusion of disclaimer statements on all materials, and the establishment of a congressional policy on royalty income. With respect to MACOS in particular, the group recommended an early termination of implementation activities and a renegotiation of the publishing agreement.

In a separate addendum Gerard Piel and James Zumberge set forth their view that the federal government's responsibility for the quality and content of curricula should continue to be exercised through the peer review system: "In curriculum reform, peer review has served not only to mobilize the best qualified judgment of content and quality but also to insulate the locally controlled schools from the Federal Government. The authority of the peer group is different from the authority vested in a government agency. It does not carry any coercion to the decision-making of local school authorities; they remain free to accept or reject the curriculum validated by a peer group. Peer review thus fosters the pluralism essential to self-government."[66] Piel and Zumberge were skeptical of the effectiveness of "needs assessments" and parent participation in the development of curriculum priorities. They felt that "peer review" still offered the best guarantee for the preservation of academic freedom and the protection of curriculum reform activities from undue political influence. They held out for the preservation of academic freedom as the best way to ensure intellectually responsible educational innovation.

Joanne McAuley, however, disagreed strongly with the committee's findings and submitted a minority report, a blistering attack on the NSF education effort that recommended immediate cessation of all of the NSF's work in curriculum reform. She charged that the agency had funded a small cadre of "career curriculum innovators," had failed to monitor their activities properly, had conducted no independent outside evaluation, had disseminated the products with no clear congressional mandate, had conducted no needs assessment, and had not involved any parents in setting priorities. She proposed that all responsibility for educational materials development be returned to the publishing industry: "It is time for the Federal Government to acknowledge the vast capabilities of commercial firms in the private sector to do the education curriculum job without Federal interference. I have found in my discussions with parents and taxpayers across America that this is the prevailing view, and I strongly urge Congress to terminate unwanted NSF curriculum activities."[67] McAuley voiced the opinion of a growing body of conservatives that the federal government should get out of education altogether.

General Accounting Office Audit

One more evaluation remained: the substantive and fiscal audit carried out by the General Accounting Office (GAO) at the request of Chairman Teague. This report, submitted to Teague on 14 October, turned out to be the most thorough of all the reviews of MACOS prompted by the congressional inquiry. Two government auditors based themselves at EDC for six months and reviewed every paper and document relating to the funding, development, evaluation, implementation, publication, and proceeds derived from the project. The resulting report, which ran to over sixty single-spaced typewritten pages, exhaustively documented the administrative and fiscal history of MACOS. The GAO report began by examining peer-review procedures, noting that of the thirty-five reviewers of the program during various stages of its history, almost all were university academics and only three were from potential user groups. Pointing out that some reviewers had questioned the potential for controversy and had commented on weaknesses in the evaluation design, they were unable to determine what steps the Foundation had taken to follow up on these criticisms. To correct this, the GAO suggested open competition for NSF moneys through formal requests for proposals and the establishment of clear procedures for selecting peer reviewers and documenting their findings.[68]

The report contained a lengthy critique of the Hanley-Whitla evaluation, an in-house study that had been conducted by EDC, challenging the findings on student learning gains and the performance of students with poor academic backgrounds and suggesting that EDC had misled the public in the way these findings were reported in its promotional literature. The report also recommended that the Foundation take steps to implement Department of Health, Education, and Welfare guidelines regarding the protection of human subjects but admitted that these guidelines are ambiguous in their applicability to curriculum programs. Since the GAO was in the process of studying the evaluation procedures in nine other NSF science education projects, detailed recommendations on evaluation were deferred until that larger study could be completed.

The sharpest criticism of MACOS in the GAO report concerned EDC's publishing arrangements. After reviewing the process by which CDA was selected, the report claimed that the NSF should have monitored the publisher choice much more closely, reviewed all contractual arrangements in detail, and continued to review these arrangements after publication to ensure that the Foundation's interests were protected. The GAO was especially concerned about the conditions that brought about the establishment of unusually low royalty rates, as well as the circumstances surrounding the development of the professional services agreement with CDA. As the report stated,

> The Foundation should be particularly vigilant in monitoring publishing arrangements where low royalty rates and other non-routine arrangements, such as the professional services contract, are permitted, to insure adequate protection of the government's interest. In this respect, the Foundation should have reviewed the professional services contract since it provided for teacher training services considered essential to marketing MACOS. Had the Foundation reviewed and approved the professional services contract, it could have provided for the disposition of the accrued income after services under the contract were deemed no longer necessary.[69]

The GAO was determined to find out if there were irregularities in EDC's decision to publish with CDA. They searched EDC's board minutes and personnel records for any evidence that less than arm's length negotiations had taken place between EDC and CDA. They also requested that we verify all arrangements between present or past EDC staff members and the staff of CDA. Some associations were found. Wayne Howell, it turned out, had done some unpaid consulting for CDA from July 1969 to July 1970 after he left EDC. CDA had offered him stock for these services, but he returned the stock claiming a conflict of interest between any formal involvement with CDA and his employment with the Kettering Foundation. Catherine Motz Peterson, who had worked at EDC between 1965 and 1969, went to work for CDA on a part-time basis in 1973, as did

Jerome Bruner's stepdaughter. None of these individuals could be seriously accused of having arranged the publishing agreement for their own benefit.

In the wake of this investigation, we were belatedly grateful that we had not published the program with Westinghouse Learning because Verne Atwater, the president, had served on the steering committee of the EDC Social Studies Program at the time of the publishing negotiations. Although Atwater had scrupulously removed himself from any active part in the publishing arrangements—which was one of the reasons we knew so little about his plans for investing heavily in a publicity campaign on behalf of the course—one can imagine the charges that would have embroiled EDC if we had signed with his firm. In fact, Atwater had made his proposal more out of a spirit of public service than in any hope of major private gain, for he knew of the considerable obstacles to widespread commercial distribution that a program like MACOS faced. That argument would have been a difficult sell, however, to the Comptroller General and his staff.

The investigation uncovered only one matter that the auditors regarded as a "questionable transaction." As I have pointed out, the intent of the professional services agreement had proved difficult to achieve in practice, since CDA wished to establish its own corporate identification with the course and its own commercially supportable system for training and implementation. As the course expanded, CDA did not want EDC staff members conducting dissemination activities and actually sought to eliminate EDC's continuing association with the course. After several abortive attempts to develop a collaborative marketing program using EDC's contract proceeds, we proposed to Jack Gentry that we invest the professional service funds in the development of another EDC project, People and Technology, a program supported by a grant from the National Endowment for the Humanities (NEH). Gentry agreed and suggested that the funds be donated to NEH under the matching funds provision of our grant, enabling us to double the amount that would otherwise be available from the professional services agreement. We proposed this arrangement to NEH's general counsel in September 1972, and the Endowment agreed, with the proviso that CDA receive no favorable consideration at the time People and Technology was offered for publication.

Examining this transaction, the GAO determined that it was "arguable" that the CDA donation to NEH was not a legal "gift" because it consisted of moneys that belonged to EDC under the terms of the professional services agreement. The report stated that "since the 'gifts' were made by CDA discharging its obligation to EDC under the services contract and in effect the moneys were simply returned to the party to which they would otherwise have been payable, no bonafide gift occurred . . . Alternatively, since EDC had the legal right to these moneys, it could be suggested that EDC actually made the 'gifts' through CDA. However, restricted gifts from grantees conducting the project for which the gift is intended cannot be accepted for matching under the provisions of the Endowment's publication."[70]

EDC and CDA countered this argument by pointing out that full disclosure had been made to NEH about the source of the matching funds in a letter from Jack Gentry on 6 October 1972. Gentry's letter stated clearly the origin of the funds:

Our understanding and agreement provided that in addition to normal royalties on the film and print material . . . we would provide EDC for its use an unspecified sum of money each year for continuing review and development of the MAN program . . .

We are pledging to the National Endowment for the Humanities a contribution in the amount of $100,000 for support of the "People and Technology" unit now under development at EDC. This grant is in lieu of a like amount which would be made under the previously mentioned agreement for EDC services in connection with the MAN program.[71]

Despite this defense, the GAO advised the Endowment to review the transaction to see if the matching funds transferred to EDC should be recovered.

On this final note of criticism the formal investigation of MACOS came to a close. The NEH, as it turned out, made no attempt to recover the matching funds, and, since EDC received subsequent grants from the agency, its credibility with the NEH presumably remained unimpaired.[72] But the consequences of the congressional investigation for the future of the science curriculum reform movement were profound. The NSF eventually terminated several of its science and social science curriculum projects, and support for others was substantially curtailed. As for MACOS, no new funds were forthcoming in any form, save for the completion of a pending evaluation study, and even a three-month extension for work related to the writing of this history was denied. The negative publicity from the investigation, together with the continuing campaign against the course carried out by Congressman Conlan and his staff, brought about a precipitous drop in sales from which the course never recovered.

Those of us who were caught up in the struggle to save MACOS from its detractors received a powerful lesson in educational politics. Indeed, the battle to defend the course before school boards, parent groups, and ultimately the United States Congress forced us to examine the forces that shape American educational practice. How could a program generate so much enthusiasm among students, teachers, scholars, and educational professionals and yet produce so much opposition from some segments of the larger political community? Clearly the way we choose to educate our children has more than intellectual implications. It involves a conscious choice of values. Historically, our greatest educational reformers— Thomas Jefferson, Horace Mann, John Dewey—have known this well, but it was imperfectly understood by the curriculum innovators of the 1950s and 1960s. Reforms that appeared to be purely scholarly in their origins turned out to be profoundly political in their applications. Failure to comprehend this, and to design and implement MACOS in a way that was responsive to these political realities, doomed the course to a premature demise.

· 6 ·

Aftermath at the Foundation

MACOS was not the only casualty of our political naïveté. As the investigation deepened, the controversy threatened to engulf the entire educational program of the National Science Foundation and, in so doing, weakened the agency's credibility with Congress. Arguing that school reform was an inappropriate mission for the federal government, Congressman John B. Conlan expanded his attack to include the whole range of science education activities receiving NSF sponsorship. He charged that the Foundation's educational programs represented an effort on the part of liberal academics to impose their social values on the young, and he redoubled his efforts to expose the weaknesses of the Foundation's procedures for funding educational projects. As it turned out, he was aided in this effort by members of the Foundation staff who shared his views about the inappropriateness of the NSF's involvement in elementary and secondary education.

The NSF under Siege

"It was the worst political crisis in NSF history," commented Harvey Averch, former acting assistant director for science education, as he recalled the MACOS crisis a decade later.[1] An agency that had been submitting its annual budget for twenty-five years without a ripple of debate now came under intense congressional scrutiny. For more than a year the director and his staff did little else but defend the Foundation against the full-scale assault led by Conlan. According to William Wells, the staff member on the House Committee on Science and Technology who was principally responsible for shepherding the NSF budget through Congress, debates on the floor were intense, and votes on the budget were extremely close. Wells was convinced that the public outcry against the Foundation expressed the carefully orchestrated views of a small group. He remembers dealing with thousands of postcards, obviously engineered, that read, "Abolish the National Science Foundation." According to Wells the protesters saw the NSF as a "spawning ground for these evil creations that MACOS represented."[2]

The intensity of the attack took the agency, and the handful of congressmen who were dedicated to its work, totally by surprise. With little warning they found themselves caught up in a series of floor fights that not only jeopardized the education program but threatened the future of the agency itself. James Symington and Charles Mosher in the House, and Ted Kennedy in the Senate, took up the battle to protect the Foundation, but they succeeded only by sacrificing much of the agency's work in education. The psychic energy and staff time this struggle demanded caused many to wonder just what role, if any, the NSF should take in the nation's effort to improve the schools.

The controversy caused Congress to call for a review of the entire history of the National Science Foundation's work in precollege curriculum reform. A study prepared by the Congressional Research Service of the Library of Congress, which ran to over two hundred pages, traced in detail the evolution of NSF's support for science education from its inception in 1950. The report praised the Foundation's effort to improve science education but pointed out that the agency had been remiss in certain areas of project administration. It questioned the confidentiality of NSF's peer-review procedures and its "laissez-faire" style of project management, laxness in monitoring implementation activities, and failure to identify controversial content. Furthermore, the report criticized the National Science Board for not requiring the Foundation staff to exercise more careful oversight in sensitive areas. Pointing out the general lack of discipline and direction in the way the Foundation carried out its curriculum development work, the study concluded that "a greater measure of staff initiative and independent staff judgement might have aided in identifying the problems that arose."[3]

While acknowledging the need to review sensitive projects before disseminating them, the National Science Board issued several policy statements in June 1975 reaffirming its commitment to curriculum development. Many congressmen took this as an indication that the NSF was unwilling to respond aggressively to congressional concerns, and, in order to pressure the NSF to address these matters, the House Committee on Appropriations recommended that no money be made available for curriculum implementation in fiscal 1976. The committee expressed the view that support for implementation gave NSF-funded courses an unfair advantage in the marketplace and called for the Foundation to explain to the Congress, to the education profession, and to the public at large the compelling national need for such material.[4]

The Senate joined the House in expressing its concern about the appropriateness of certain materials for use in the schools, and in particular about monitoring support for the implementation of value-oriented social science material. In a lengthy introduction to its report on the House appropriations bill the Senate Committee on Appropriations urged the Foundation to be more sensitive and responsive to the taxpayers whose children were being exposed to materials that dealt with value questions. The senators stressed that federally sponsored curriculum projects "should rise and fall on their merits" and that the federal government should not take part in influencing the schools to buy such materials. The Senate concurred with the House recommendation to withhold support for the dissemination of NSF-funded curriculum materials in fiscal 1976.[5]

The NSF Responds

Under mounting congressional pressure, the NSF began reviewing and restructuring the work of the Education Directorate. Lowell Paige, the director of NSF's education effort, resigned from the Foundation in the summer of 1975, and Guyford Stever named Harvey Averch, a trusted aide in the director's office, as Acting Assistant Director for Science Education. Averch was a career bureaucrat with a mind for proper procedure, and he immediately initiated a careful, objective review of every education project currently under development and implementation with NSF funds. He set up seven panels to review nineteen projects. He invited seventy-three panelists from forty-two organizations representing science, education, child-development, and publishing to come to Washington during the week of 8 December to review the projects and make recommendations to the Foundation regarding the future of NSF's education effort. The panels were asked to consider such issues as clarity of purpose, scientific and pedagogical soundness, the desirability of objectives, the cost to the schools, and the quality of project management. On the basis of these reviews Averch was prepared to decide whether to terminate a project, wind it down, or recommend it for completion.

Armed with his panel recommendations, Averch appeared before the House Subcommittee on Science, Research, and Technology on 10 February. He presented a four-part program for the Foundation's conduct of curriculum activities in the future:

> No new curriculum projects would be undertaken without a systematic needs assessment.
>
> For new projects the Foundation would adopt a "prototype approach," making several small awards and evaluating the results before proceeding with further funding.
>
> Large projects would be reviewed regularly and terminated if they failed to meet objectives.
>
> Independent evaluation procedures would be established for all projects.

Averch was determined to convince Congress that "we were masters of our own house" and that professionalism reigned in the Education Directorate.[6] He had sought guidance from a broad range of professionals in science, education, and psychology as well as business people and private citizens. He had worked tirelessly to restore credibility to NSF's education activities by clarifying the procedures by which the Directorate carried out its work. And he had made a sincere effort to open a continuous line of communication with the Congress. Averch summarized his views about the proper place of NSF's curriculum efforts in a press release: "There is a selective Federal role in pre-college curriculum development, but certainly not on as large a scale as in the past. The pre-college curricula market by itself may simply be unable to capture new knowledge and transmit it as fast as we would like."[7]

But despite Averch's statesmanlike efforts to respond to congressional concerns, Congressman Conlan would not be deterred. During "peer review" hearings on the Hill, which had taken place during the summer and fall of 1975, Conlan repeatedly claimed that the Foundation had misrepresented the opinions of its curriculum reviewers to the National Science Board and that the recently published NSF self-study, directed by Dr. Robert Hughes, was "seriously flawed." Richard Atkinson, the newly appointed Deputy Director of the NSF who had attended most of the hearings, recalled a heated exchange over the witness table in which Conlan referred to the Hughes study as "a pack of lies."[8] Finally, according to Atkinson, Guyford Stever became so exasperated that he said to Conlan, "We've done our best. We've made a careful study, and as far as I'm concerned it is an honest study, and I can't do any more . . . If you don't like what we have done, you should have a GAO investigation."[9]

Congressman Symington, who remained one of the NSF's staunchest defenders, had picked up on the idea of a GAO investigation as a way of silencing Conlan. Accordingly, in October he had asked the Controller General to examine the Foundation's handling of a program entitled Individualized Science Instruction System (ISIS), a project at Florida State University. For a time Conlan seemed placated by this redoubled effort at agency self-examination. Paige had left, Averch was cleaning house, and the fall passed quietly, despite some unsettling rumors within the Foundation that there could be some problems with the GAO report. As it turned out, however, the GAO study, issued on 12 January, was a body blow to Symington and other NSF supporters in Congress. It confirmed Conlan's charges that there had been some "laundering" of peer reviews in staff reports to the National Science Board. One staff memorandum, the GAO noted, had omitted reference to forty-five comments of nine of the reviewers, and of the thirty-three references that reflected favorably on the proposal, five were deemed to misrepresent the intent of the reviewers. While the memorandum claimed that all reviewers recommended funding, the Controller General found that "this statement was not fully justified for three of the eleven reviewers."[10]

At the budget hearings that began on 10 February Conlan had a field day. He spoke of the "scandal of deceit and corruption" in the NSF grant award process, accused the agency of engaging in a "cover-up," and called for a one-year suspension of funding for all NSF projects. He showed that one of the ISIS reviews, written by Philip Morrison of M.I.T., had been edited to remove all criticisms and make it appear that Morrison endorsed the project without reservation. He charged that Morrison's review had been "clearly manipulated" and "deceitfully edited" by Foundation personnel and that the Hughes study had been laundered by Foundation officials with the full knowledge of Hughes himself. In an obvious reference to Stever and Atkinson, Conlan remarked, "I have reason to believe that higher NSF officials are aware of this cover-up but have not yet acknowledged the full gravity of this matter to members of this committee or the scientific community." Conlan refused to reveal his sources but said he would be happy to help Symington and his staff with their investigations.[11]

Richard Atkinson had come to the NSF in June of 1975, shortly after the completion of the Hughes report. He immediately set out to assist Stever in defending the NSF against Conlan's charges. He had read the Hughes study, which he found to be "a model of . . . considered self-analysis," and he was perplexed by Conlan's repeated accusations in the face of the obviously sincere efforts of senior NSF personnel to uncover any areas of incompetence within the Foundation. He had urged Stever to pursue the GAO investigation of ISIS as a way of removing any cloud of suspicion about how the Foundation conducted its business, and he was dismayed when the report came out. Atkinson suspected that there were "moles" in the Foundation on Stever's own staff who had been feeding Conlan information and who apparently shared Conlan's determination to discredit the Education Directorate. Conlan's assistant, George Archibald, later confirmed that Conlan had a direct pipeline into the Foundation during this period. As Archibald reported, "We knew within hours after one of Stever's top staff meetings exactly what had taken place."[12]

The ISIS report led to further probes of NSF activities by the General Accounting Office. On 19 March, Symington and Mosher asked the Comptroller General to investigate the accuracy of the Hughes study. Once again Conlan's charges proved to have some substance. The GAO found that the work of the Hughes committee had been sloppily done and lacked the quality controls necessary to ensure completeness and accuracy. Many statements in the report were not properly documented, and some management problems went undetected in the hastily prepared self-study of NSF curriculum development activities. Although Stever had called for a study that was distinguished by its "objective and professional analysis," the Controller General chastised the NSF for its failure to uphold proper standards of scholarship in its own self-examination. In a notable departure from the usual government bureaucratese, the report admonished, "The Foundation, as the Nation's 'science agency,' would have been wise to have applied the principles of the scientific method during its review."[13]

The cumulative impact of these investigations, and investigations of investigations, was devastating for the work of the Foundation. As Guyford Stever struggled to restore his agency's credibility with Congress, it became increasingly clear that the spotlight focused on the NSF had brought to light a general lack of discipline and orderly process in the way the Foundation went about its business. As Averch observed, "We are a procedural agency, and proper procedures are what make our decision-making legitimate."[14] The NSF was found guilty of failing to carry out appropriate methods for curriculum making, but in fact, as Averch pointed out, the agency "had never thought of [an] 'optimal' procedure for curriculum projects."[15] The accepted method for ensuring quality control in the curriculum field was the peer-review system that had been used for decades in awarding research grants. Unfortunately, this approach had proved inadequate as a way of selecting and monitoring programs as complex and politically sensitive as some of the large-scale curriculum projects, especially in the social and behavioral sciences. The Foundation would need new methods for making choices about curriculum matters in the future.

On 10 March Averch announced his decision regarding the nineteen projects that had been evaluated in December. Eight, he said, were virtually completed and would need little or no additional funds, five projects would be terminated, three would be continued but with reduced funding, and three others would be scheduled for continued funding. These decisions, he reported, were based on budgetary considerations and the results of the extensive reviews, together with site visits and third-party evaluations. Averch had moved swiftly to involve both the professional education community and the general public in the evaluation and selection of appropriate curriculum materials. No longer would precollege curriculum-making at the NSF, if it continued at all, be the sole province of the research scientists. Projects would be selected with the participation of those who might ultimately use them.

Behind the struggle between NSF and congressional conservatives lay fundamental questions about the appropriate role of the National Science Foundation in curriculum research and development, especially in the social and behavioral sciences. When legislation to establish the National Science Foundation was first introduced after World War II, some members of Congress and the scientific community questioned the appropriateness of a federal science agency supporting social science research. Vannevar Bush, who drafted the first report calling for the establishment of a "National Research Foundation" in response to a request from Franklin Roosevelt, deliberately excluded the social sciences from his proposal, and despite President Truman's strong backing for social science research, the original charter of the Foundation, which was written in 1950, did not include mandatory support for the social sciences. An office of social sciences was established in 1958, but only in 1968 was the Organic Act of the Foundation changed to make the social sciences part of the legislated jurisdiction of the NSF. This reluctance on the part of Congress to support social science research reflected a belief on the part of many conservative congressmen that social science research fosters social change. As Roberta Miller, the current NSF social science chief, puts it, "[They] felt that untrammeled social science research might undo the existing social order."[16]

Such fears motivated John B. Conlan, who saw curriculum-making in the social sciences as a tool in the hands of left-wing professors, who were pushing their own social agenda in the guise of the objective study of social behavior. Although Conlan and others pressed their attack by trying to expose administrative incompetence and by searching for evidence of fiscal irresponsibility, their real target was the cadre of liberal academics who they believed were using the curriculum movement to weaken the patriotism of the young. Programs like MACOS, in Conlan's view, challenged American values by exposing children to the folkways of another culture at an early, impressionable age. He opposed our commitment to the development of critical thought on social questions, contending that such an approach would undermine children's political loyalty and make them vulnerable to alien values and beliefs.

The Atkinson Era

In August 1976 Guyford Stever resigned his post to become science adviser to President Ford, and Richard Atkinson became Acting Director of the NSF. As a veteran of the Conlan wars, Atkinson was determined to restore the credibility of the Foundation in Congress. He was the first social scientist to head the agency, having come to the NSF from Stanford, where he had chaired the psychology department. As a research psychologist Atkinson was particularly sensitive to the potentially controversial nature of social science research, and he took immediate steps to eradicate areas of potential criticism. It was a time when Senator William Proxmire was giving out his "Golden Fleece" awards for frivolous-sounding grant proposals and the *National Inquirer* was offering fifty dollars to any reporter who could find a crazy title, such as the engineering study of metal stretching techniques that was called "A Mathematical Study of Necking Behavior."[17] In his effort to make sure that NSF research grants were immune from such easy criticism, Atkinson was criticized by the scientific community, who saw his censorship efforts as an invasion of academic freedom. But the new head was determined to free the Foundation from needless exposure to congressional scrutiny, and he told potential grant recipients in blunt terms what he thought of their objections: "Screw you guys . . . If we don't like the title we're going to rewrite it, and we'll check with you but we're going to have a title which we think appropriately communicates what should be communicated."[18] During Atkinson's tenure at the NSF there were no Golden Fleece awards from Senator Proxmire.

A skilled negotiator as well as a personal friend of Proxmire and Kennedy, Atkinson quickly gained the respect of Congress, and President Carter appointed him permanent director of the NSF in the spring of 1977. Working closely with Averch, he implemented more effective grant administration procedures in the Education Directorate and named James Rutherford, a science educator from Harvard, as division director. Rutherford had been one of the principal authors of Harvard Project Physics, and he brought to the Foundation a strong background in curriculum research and development.

Rutherford, an able manager, was uncommonly sensitive to Washington power struggles and public opinion. He viewed the MACOS controversy as a symptom of changing political priorities in Washington at a time when a swing to conservative governments was taking place all over the world. He was particularly aware of the emergence of the radical right as a growing force on the political scene. "If it hadn't been MACOS," he reflected a few years ago, "maybe it would have been something else. But [MACOS] certainly dramatized the issue. To this day I think . . . the effects linger, and people are afraid . . . to say we want to do curriculum development again."[19] Rutherford believed that the NSF should remain active in the reform of science education, but he supported the Carter administration's desire to strengthen the federal role in education through the establishment of a cabinet-level education department. Some congressmen were now arguing that education, with its larger budget and its established network of school contacts, would be a more appropriate place to house curriculum reform projects than the NSF, and in this view the NSF's work in education, if it continued at all, would be confined to those projects that required heavy participation by the scientific community.

In this changing and uncertain political climate Rutherford steered NSF's Education Directorate away from controversy and into relatively safe activities that promised a long-term impact regardless of how the debate about where to house science education was resolved. He funded research on preadolescent learning patterns, launched a major national survey of science teaching practices, and helped to shape the design of Carter's proposed Department of Education. When the department was formed he left NSF to join the new agency as head of the Office of Education Research and Improvement, a job that provided him with a much larger budget and an opportunity to design far-reaching research and development projects. But after only eight months in the new department his work was cut short by the election of Ronald Reagan, whose transition team included Dr. Onalee McGraw. McGraw and her colleagues refused to look at Rutherford's files or talk with his staff, and on Inauguration Day he left government service to become Chief Education Officer at the American Association for the Advancement of Science.[20]

Education Policy in the Reagan Administration

The Reagan election brought to power the conservative forces that had attacked MACOS. To aid the new administration in setting priorities for the cabinet departments and the regulatory agencies, the Heritage Foundation had prepared a lengthy document setting forth a blueprint for change. Any thought that the Reaganites might consider continuing the educational initiatives of the Carter presidency was quickly laid to rest by this document. In the section dealing with education policy the report stated: "A new administration must count among its first priorities the revision of the Elementary and Secondary Education Act . . . in order to recommend an incremental reprogramming of money authorities back to the states."[21] The authors called into question the entire federal effort in educational reform that had been under way for a generation. A major focus of their concern was the Education Directorate at the National Science Foundation.

The Heritage Foundation attacked what the Reagan administration saw as a hidden political agenda in the NSF social science projects. "During the past 15 years," stated the report, "there has been a concerted nationwide effort by professional educationists to turn elementary and secondary school classrooms into vehicles for liberal-left social and political change in the United States."[22] Millions of taxpayer's dollars, it charged, have gone to support of "values clarification," "situation ethics," and preaching the philosophy of "secular humanism." The report claimed that students were told that there are "no absolutes, no truths, no certainty with regard to right and wrong," and called for the restoration of moral authority in the upbringing of children. Quoting Dr. Rhoda Lorand, the child psychologist whose views had often been cited in the Conlan debates, the authors asserted that such programs invade the privacy of the home and deny to parents the right to provide moral guidelines for their children. "Whenever a parent is thus demoted," said Lorand, "the child's development suffers."[23]

The report singled out MACOS as the type of program that should be eliminated from the schools. Pointing out that MACOS had been designed by "behavioral psychologist" Jerome Bruner, who was well known as "the principal advocate of the 'inquiry' or 'discovery' approach to education," the report charged that the course allowed ten- and eleven-year-olds to engage in "free-wheeling discussions about Eskimo behavior" and then to compare native customs to value questions and moral issues facing our own society. Teachers, it claimed, were being instructed not to take sides or tell children what is right or wrong but to allow open-ended discussions in which there were no definitive answers. The treatment of old people, the problem of unwanted children, and wife stealing were specifically cited as examples of the types of issues that came up for consideration in MACOS classrooms. George Weber of the Council for Basic Education was quoted as observing that "there is an air of indoctrination about the course," and he charged that the authors had "definite ideas about what conclusions the children should come to."[24]

These conclusions, according to the Heritage Foundation, had been drawn up at a series of conferences held in the 1960s and early 1970s, which were designed to lay the groundwork for the construction of a new worldwide social and political order. The outline for the MACOS plan, said the report, was contained in a 1970 publication of the National Association of Independent Schools entitled *The Wingspread Report on New Dimensions in Teaching of the Social Studies*. Dozens of "liberal-left education activists," charged the Heritage Foundation, who had endorsed the ideological position of the Wingspread report, had been able to mobilize a major effort to create and distribute instructional materials with "hundreds of millions of dollars" provided by the National Science Foundation. The Heritage Foundation identified several "career curriculum innovation centers" that had been established to implement the Wingspread philosophy. These centers, said the Heritage Foundation, were able to draw upon the support of the federal government to bypass the educational publishing industry. At the top of the list was EDC, Education Development Center.

The recommendation on federal support for curriculum innovation submitted to the Reagan administration by the Heritage Foundation stated the position that was to become President Reagan's official policy stance on federal funding for curriculum development: "The Administration should draft and propose legislation to terminate federal support for development and marketing of school course (curriculum) materials, so that full responsibility and control over this important area can be returned to State and local education agencies and private schools, in conjunction with private sector commercial firms."[25] The conservatives now had a president who shared their view that the federal government should get out of the education business.

The scientists in the National Science Foundation who were responsible for administering the agency's education program were in for some rough sledding during the Reagan years. As the NSF celebrated its thirtieth birthday, program officers in the Education Directorate who had survived the congressional battles began updating their vitas in anticipation of what Washington calls a "reduction in force." Although it took a year or two for the full impact of the Reagan education policy to take effect, by 1982 a division that had once employed 125 people was reduced to a staff of a dozen or so. This skeleton crew stayed on to administer the Graduate Fellowship program, a particular favorite of the Congress that was blessed with multiyear funding, but for the rest, the Reaganites, true to their promise, disbanded the agency's Education Directorate. With a conservative in the White House and a tough-minded budget director, who supported the president's program, Congress bowed to the Reagan administration's pressure to eliminate education at the NSF.

The NSF Reacts

But the leadership of the NSF was not easily cowed. Undaunted by this opposition from the Reagan administration, the National Science Board formed a "blue-ribbon" commission of distinguished educators headed by William T. Coleman, Jr., former Secretary of Transportation, and Cecily Cannan Selby, chair of the Board of Advisors of the North Carolina School of Science and Mathematics, to develop a detailed plan of action for addressing the problems facing American elementary and secondary school systems in the teaching of mathematics, science, and technology. The resulting report, *Educating Americans for the 21st Century,* appeared in 1983 and set forth a bold plan for bringing about sweeping changes in the nation's schools. Coleman and Selby called for student achievement in the United States to be "the finest in the world" by 1995, and they outlined a detailed plan of action based on an initial appropriation of $1.5 billion for the first year of implementation. Although the focus of the plan was primarily mathematics and science education, many of the recommendations, as the authors said, "apply equally well to other areas of study—literature, foreign languages, social science, history, art, etc."[26]

Educating Americans was only one of many critiques of the schools that appeared in 1983, the so-called "year of the reports." A decade of declining scores and poor achievement had begun to worry professional educators and the lay public alike, and the Foundation's action plan came at a time when once again concern about the schools was in the forefront of public discussion. Unlike the post-*Sputnik* worries about how to produce more research scientists and mathematicians to compete with the Soviets in the space race, discussions of school improvement in the 1980s turned around how to raise the level of performance of all students. And in place of the earlier obsession with the Russian *Tekhnikum,* attention now centered on an examination of Japanese education. "Japan, like

America" said Coleman and Selby, "pursues the goal of universal education. The top students in both nations score equally well in mathematics and science achievement tests. But the remaining 90 percent of Japanese pupils do far better than their American counterparts."[27]

The Coleman-Selby report cited some impressive facts about Japanese schools. It pointed out that Japanese children attend school 220 days a year compared to 180 days for American children, and that during four years of high school the typical Japanese student spends three times as much time on science instruction as the American science student. In addition, the Japanese provide for more coordination and continuity of instruction between grade levels, spend far more per student on instructional supplies and materials, and invest more in teacher training than we do. And Japanese science teachers are paid more, have a higher social status than American teachers, and have access to two hundred science teaching centers throughout the country where they can continue their professional development. While the report recognized some limitations in the Japanese educational system, particularly its monolithic character and its restrictions on social mobility and opportunities for women, it challenged the United States to find ways of matching Japan's achievement without losing the unique strengths of America's diverse and decentralized educational enterprise.[28]

With this report the National Science Board called upon the president and other national leaders, including members of Congress, the secretary of education, the president's science adviser, the director of the National Science Foundation, as well as governors, mayors and other state and local officials, to help bring to the attention of the nation problems of American mathematics and science education, to encourage all students to learn math and science, and to stress the importance of such knowledge for successful living in the twenty-first century. The report proposed the formation of a National Education Council, representing a cross section of interests, which would meet regularly to monitor the progress of the reform movement and report directly to the president. It called for the establishment of governors' councils that would perform similar functions at the state level. It urged local school boards and school officials to form partnerships with business and industry, labor leaders, and parent groups and to involve the whole community in helping to bring about constructive educational change. And it called for a "national assessment mechanism" to monitor progress toward the commission's goals and to build on the work already under way by the National Assessment of Educational Progress. Recognizing that the achievement of the average American student ranks very low by world standards, the commission sought to develop ways to measure higher level competencies, such as writing for a purpose, problem-solving skills, and analytical ability, and proposed supervision of the assessment program by the National Educational Council.

The Coleman-Selby report carried the full endorsement of the National Science Board behind its recommendations. Never before in the three-decade history of the NSF, not even during height of the *Sputnik* era, had its leadership come out so strongly in support of a federal presence in education at the precollege level. Despite the intense criticism the Foundation had endured at the hands of Congress just a few years before, and the strong opposition of the Reagan administration notwithstanding, the National Science Board was clearly prepared to reestablish as a major priority of the agency the welfare of science and mathematics education in the nation's schools.

The Year of the Reports

In taking a stand for educational reform the NSF was reflecting a growing national concern about the troubled state of American education. In 1983 educators and the general public were treated to the largest outpouring of criticism of the nation's schools in history, eclipsing even the complaints of the early 1950s. Nearly fifty reports totaling more than six thousand pages voiced a new wave of national concern about the troubled state of American education. They spoke of the fragmented state of the school curriculum, the failure to define any coherent, accepted body of learning, the excessive emphasis on teaching isolated facts, and the lack of attention to higher order skills and concepts. They called for more individualization of instruction, the development of a closer relationship between teachers and students, and methods that encourage the active participation of the student in the learning process. They suggested that teachers must become more engaged in bringing about change and that schools should be reorganized into smaller functional units, so that both students and teachers could take a more central part in shaping the learning environment.[29]

Among the most widely read of these reports was a study prepared by the Education Commission of the States entitled *Action for Excellence: A Comprehensive Plan to Improve Our Nation's Schools*. Chaired by James B. Hunt, Jr., the governor of North Carolina, the commission stressed the relationship between education and the country's economic well-being, and it called for a partnership between government, business, labor, and the schools to bring about lasting educational change. The report cited the need for higher levels of competence in reading, writing, mathematics, science, reasoning, and the use of computers in order to support continued economic growth, and pointed out that productivity in manufacturing was growing four times as rapidly in Japan as in the United States. "There are few national efforts that can legitimately be called crucial to our national survival," intoned the report. "Improving education in America—improving it sufficiently and improving it now—is such an effort."[30]

An even more influential and widely quoted critique came from Secretary of Education Terrel H. Bell, who set up the National Commission on Excellence in Education in response to what he saw as "the widespread public perception that something is seriously amiss in our educational system."[31] Chaired by David P. Gardner, the president of the University of California, the Bell Commission, produced a report recalling the fears of the 1950s entitled *A Nation at Risk,* which equated educational strength with national defense. To allow our schools to continue in their present state, warned the report, "is an unthinking act of unilateral disarmament." "Cafeteria-style" curriculum programs that allow students to substitute soft appetizer and dessert courses, such as physical health and personal development, for the main courses of math and science are depriving future American citizens of the shared scientific and technological knowledge upon which a free, democratic society is based. The Bell Commission called for immediate national action to reverse the "rising tide of mediocrity" in the nation's schools.

The overriding message of reports like *Action for Excellence* and *A Nation at Risk* was that the United States could no longer tolerate incompetence in the educational system because the poor quality of schooling was threatening the strength of the national economy, and even the structure of the country's free, democratic institutions. Unlike the school watchers of the 1950s, who were concerned primarily about competition in space, the new critics worried that the United States was losing its competitive edge as the world's leading commercial power to heavily industrialized allies with outstanding educational systems, such as Germany and Japan. The challenge today, they pointed out, was not just to educate a scientific and technological elite who could create sophisticated weapons systems and place a man on the moon. Rather, it was, to undertake the even more complex task of providing a broadly based general education to a culturally and ethnically diverse student population that must learn to compete successfully in an increasingly complex, technologically based, worldwide economy.

Reagan Administration Resistance

Despite the mounting public outcry for educational change, the Reagan administration stood firm in its opposition to a federal role in school reform. When Congress allocated funds to address the deficiencies noted in the growing collection of national reports and studies, the Office of Management and Budget impounded those funds in response to White House directives to withhold federal support for school reform. George Keyworth, Reagan's science adviser, fiercely defended the president's position that responsibility for the improvement of schooling must remain with local communities. Federal agencies, including the NSF, failed even to request the funds that Congress was prepared to appropriate. Although the "year of the reports" brought a growing public demand for bold new initiatives in the field of education, government bureaucrats refused to act without support from the White House.

Harvey Averch was among those who supported the president's position, and he questioned the view that educational reform could contribute significantly to the improvement of the economy. In a book analyzing science and technology policy, Averch scrutinized the rationale behind the new educational reform proposals. The Soviets, he pointed out, have much more rigorous science and mathematics education than we do, but they have never been able to get their economy to work effectively. Even many Western European nations, he said, who significantly surpass us in what they require of their students, have not been noted for their economic success. At the same time, much less developed nations have learned to be highly proficient at turning out high technology products. Would we not be better off, he asked, to pay attention to interest costs, price levels, and exchange rates if we want to make our economy competitive rather than worry about our educational system? "After all," Averch commented, "while the National Commission on Excellence in Education sees the mediocrity of the schools as an outcome sufficient to rebut the presumption of no federal presence, President Reagan sees the mediocrity as caused by twenty years of intrusion into the schools."[32]

Yet public pressure soon overwhelmed the conservatives and, as William Wells observed, "the Reagan administration was brought kicking and screaming back into the science education business."[33] In the wake of the reports, the National Science Foundation turned its attention once again to curriculum development, and in 1985 the newly formed Directorate for Science and Engineering Education published a program announcement seeking proposals for the development of materials for teaching mathematics, science, and technology, with particular emphasis at the elementary and junior high school levels. "A broad understanding of science and technology on the part of the American citizenry," stated the announcement, "is essential to the strength of our scientific enterprise and to the economic security of our nation."[34] This understanding, it said, cannot be achieved unless all schoolchildren are given a broad-based education in science and mathematics throughout the precollege years.

But the new funding for science education represented a small fraction of the NSF's total budget when compared to the early *Sputnik* years. In 1960 the funds available for education represented 42 percent of the entire NSF budget. Even in 1970 educational funding still represented 26 percent of NSF revenues, but by 1982 the amount for education had declined to 2 percent. Although funding began to increase in 1984, by 1987 it still hovered just below 6 percent.[35] Having observed NSF's wavering commitment to education, and its low priority compared to research, Congressman Don Fuqua of Florida, the outgoing chair of the Committee on Science and Technology, proposed that the entire education program of the NSF be scrapped and that responsibility for science and mathematics education be turned over to the Department of Education. In his farewell address to the committee Fuqua voiced his disappointment at NSF's reluctance to seek support for education. He said that he had been a "leading advocate and defender" of NSF's program of science education. But he was concerned that there had been no improvement in the historic pattern of decline in funding for science education, and he feared that, given the NSF's overall

priorities and the competition for limited resources, research would
continue to dominate. "It is time to think the unthinkable," he remarked. "It may well be that the problem of pre-college science
education in the nation is better handled by educators than by research scientists."[36]

Fuqua may have been trying to provoke the NSF to take action.
If so, his comments had the desired effect. The Advisory Committee
of the Education Directorate was alarmed at the turn of events. At
a stormy meeting in November 1986, the committee passed a series
of resolutions urging the director of the Foundation to seek substantially increased funding for science and engineering education in
fiscal year 1988. Referring to the vastly increased education budget
proposed in the National Science Board's 1983 report, the committee argued that the NSF is the appropriate place to support
science education "because of the Foundation's unique and strong
linkage to the science and engineering professional community,"
and it called for a much larger federal investment in science and
engineering education.[37] In a letter to Bassam Shakhashiri, NSF's
assistant director for Science and Engineering Education, the committee chair, Gerald Holton of Harvard, conveyed the group's deep
concern. "There is a strong and widely shared undertone of dismay
in the Committee," he wrote, "about evidences of inadequate commitment within NSF to its unique statutory function—the support
of science and engineering education at all levels."[38]

Shakhashiri responded with a bold program. Appointed to head
the Education Directorate in 1984, when the Foundation's education budget was just recovering from its record low, Shakhashiri
immediately began lobbying Congress for science education funds.
A chemistry professor from the University of Wisconsin who often
sported a "Science is Fun" button on his lapel, Shakhashiri wooed
the Congress with outspoken testimony about the inadequacy of the
nation's investment in science and mathematics education and by
entertaining legislators and their families with Christmastime "Science Shows" at the Smithsonian's Air and Space Museum. Through
such efforts, Shakhashiri managed to increase his budget from a
$55.5 million appropriation in fiscal 1986 to over $200 million in
1990. When asked how he did it, he replied, "Seven days a week,
fourteen hours a day."[39]

In February 1987, the Foundation announced the first major results of Shakhashiri's efforts: three multimillion dollar grants designed to foster the development of a coherent program of science

education in the elementary and secondary schools, the largest NSF grants for science education in a dozen years. The grants required the participation of a publisher who would provide matching funds for testing, teacher training, and marketing. Expenditures on these three projects alone are expected to reach $50 million before completion. In announcing the new grants, Shakhashiri compared them to the original NSF science curriculum projects developed in response to *Sputnik I,* which, he said, had been created to educate "the best and the brightest." "Now we face a different problem," he remarked. "It is not just our 'best and brightest' who are inadequately prepared. We are failing to provide an adequate background, an adequate introduction, and an adequate level of science 'literacy' for the population as a whole."[40] As of fall 1990, the agency had a $285 million budget request pending before Congress with a good chance of approval, largely due to Shakhashiri's persuasiveness and his candid views on the inadequacy of federal funding for education. When asked by Congress in the fall of 1989 what he thought the Foundation's education budget should be by 1993, he boldly told them $600 million.[41]

Such outspoken politicking on behalf of his division, however, did not endear Shakhashiri to his boss, Eric Bloch, the director of the Foundation. In June, following a swiftly implemented reorganization plan that envisioned a transfer of much of the responsibility for educational programs to the research directorates, Shakhashiri found himself out of a job and his division replaced by the newly formed Directorate for Education and Human Resources. Bloch's removal of Shakhashiri raised questions about the depth of the Foundation's educational commitment and was regarded by some on the Hill as a sad day for science education. When he received the news, Doug Walgren, a Democrat from Pennsylvania who sits on the House Science Research Subcommittee, remarked, "I think we will look back on this as a last dismal chapter in the events surrounding science education efforts by NSF."[42]

Thus, after more than a decade of debate, the National Science Foundation is back in the business of educational reform. In retrospect, much of the controversy that was fostered by Conlan and his conservative colleagues seems outdated and overblown. To argue that there is no place for national curriculum projects and that participation by the federal government in educational reform is a dangerous intrusion upon the autonomy of the local school district ignores the fact that in today's technological world most school systems share common objectives. It also repudiates the reality that effective curriculum preparation requires exacting skills and access to academic, creative, and financial resources rarely available to the neighborhood school. To meet the profound national concern about the inadequacy of our educational system, the only agency with the appropriate organizational structure and financial resources is the federal government.

But the design of Shakhashiri's new projects reflects the fact that the Foundation has learned a lesson or two about how to conduct itself in the educational arena. Favorable "peer reviews" are no longer sufficient justification for funding a curriculum project. Before major funds are committed, provisions must be made for effective teacher participation and education, for validating results in the real world of the school, for the involvement of parents and communities in curriculum decision-making, for meeting the special needs of minority and underserved populations, and for private publisher investment to ensure widespread distribution of the resulting materials. The projects of the 1980s and 1990s may be less pedagogically imaginative than some of their counterparts from the *Sputnik* era, but there is greater likelihood that materials prepared with hard-earned tax dollars will reach the schoolchildren for whom they have been designed.

Does some ambivalence remain within the Foundation about its proper role in the current educational reform movement? There must be those who see Shakhashiri's budget success as a pre-emption of funds that would otherwise go to the research directorates, and there are those on the Foundation staff who must still recall the agony of the Conlan wars, when serious research projects were put in jeopardy by educational experimentation. Is educational reform too risky and political a business for those accustomed to focusing on purely scientific matters? Will the Congress really support a growing NSF commitment to large-scale educational intervention? Should this commitment include closer collaboration between the research directorates and the education division, as Bloch's reorganization scheme seems to envision? Or are we seeing a transitory concern that will again disappear when the perceived inadequacy of the educational system begins to fade? The recent debate over the management of education within the Foundation would suggest that these matters remain unresolved.

· 7 ·

Reform Reconsidered

The ascent of the Soviet *Sputnik* in 1957 inspired an era of school reform in the United States and the expenditure of federal funds on an unprecedented scale. Although comedian Bob Hope quipped that their German scientists were just better than our German scientists, *Sputnik* convinced many Americans that the apparent scientific and technological prowess of the Soviets was the product of a better educational system, particularly in the fields of science and mathematics. As long as this public perception of Soviet scientific superiority prevailed, Congress passed legislation providing millions of dollars for curriculum reform through the National Science Foundation and other agencies. Yet once the United States had outpaced the Russians in space by putting a man on the moon, public concern about education began to wane, and in the 1970s federal support for school reform dramatically declined. Historically, Americans have always been wary of the intrusion of the federal government into educational matters, and when the Russian scientific threat receded, there was little popular support for curriculum innovation. "Back to basics" became the educational rallying cry of the post-*Sputnik* era, which meant, among other things, restoring responsibility for schooling to the states and local communities.

As we enter the last decade of the twentieth century we find ourselves in a situation not unlike that which brought about the *Sputnik* reforms. Our technological prowess is being challenged anew, this time by our allies rather than our enemies, most notably our formidable economic rival, Japan. Once again we find ourselves blaming the schools for our weaknesses. A plethora of research studies and reports in the 1980s dramatized the deficiencies of our educational system, and despite significant efforts to correct those weaknesses, we have seen few demonstrable results. By most standardized measures of performance, American students, when compared to their foreign counterparts in other industrialized nations, come out at or near the bottom of the groups tested.[1] By almost any measure our schools are failing. We pride ourselves on opening educational opportunities to the broadest range of students while other nations emphasize specialization at an earlier age, yet too many students are graduating from our high schools without the skills to function successfully in an increasingly complex society.

The poor performance of American students when compared with students from other countries has caused us to worry once again about the adequacy of our schools in preparing the next generation of Americans to compete in an increasingly technological and globally interdependent society. Will our students have the skills they need to function in the kinds of jobs this society will have to offer? Will they have the problem-solving competence, the language facility, and the social sophistication they will need to be productive citizens? Or will the poor performance of our schools eventually erode our historic preeminence as a nation of innovators and entrepreneurs? Will educational weakness threaten our position as a world power? These are questions that increasingly trouble the school watchers, who extol the virtues of foreign educational systems much as the educational critics of the 1950s praised the Russian *Tekhnikum*.

In many respects the education gap we face in the 1990s presents an even greater challenge than that spotlighted by *Sputnik* in 1957. No longer is our concern confined to mathematics and the basic sciences. The performance of American students now lags behind students in most of the developed nations in all areas of the curriculum. They are weak in reading and writing, language skills, historical understanding, and the social science knowledge they will need to communicate effectively with people from other cultures and understand the problems of the modern world. Children growing up in other developed nations know much more about us than we know about them, and this puts us at a competitive disadvantage in the world marketplace. They speak our language, study our history, and strive to understand our cultural values. To recapture our economic leadership our children and grandchildren will need more than the basic skills that sufficed in the past. They will need to become much better trained and more informed global citizens. It will take a revolution in the schools to make this happen.

In contemplating this challenge it may be useful to reflect upon some of the strengths and weaknesses of the *Sputnik*-inspired science curriculum reform movement. With all of its imperfections, this effort marked the most productive period of educational innovation in our time. Never had such a concentration of money and talent been assembled to examine how we could more effectively educate our children, and to develop and implement specific reforms in all areas of the curriculum. Yet its full potential was never realized, in part because of the political naïveté of its founders and in part because it fell victim to the attacks of a small number of activists, who took advantage of growing national indifference to the problems of the schools. Cut short by declining funding and changing national priorities, hampered by a poor understanding of the problems of implementation, and weakened by its limited grasp of the politics of educational reform, the movement lost the support of the public it had hoped to serve.

In looking back at the MACOS experience and other *Sputnik*-inspired programs of the time, we confront important questions that still need resolution. Do the disadvantages of large-scale, federally funded educational projects outweigh their potential benefits, given our historic national commitment to the decentralization of schooling? In education there are compelling reasons why Americans cling to the doctrine of local control. The neighborhood school board is the first rung on the ladder of political participation, and there are important symbolic reasons for retaining power at the local level when it comes to the education of our children. As M.I.T. president James Killian pointed out at the White House conference of 1955, centralized educational planning is the hallmark of totalitarian regimes, and we pass responsibility for improving our schools to the federal government at our peril. Yet it would also be a mistake to disregard the reforms of the *Sputnik* era merely because they sprang largely from federal sponsorship and involved the participation of a rather limited academic elite. We need to look beneath the surface of those objections to consider what we learned in this endeavor, if only to do it better the next time around.

Scholars in the Schools

Perhaps the most unusual feature of the American educational reform movement of the late 1950s and 1960s was the widespread participation of university research professors. For a brief period some of the nation's most distinguished academics left their laboratories to spend time in schoolrooms. Nobel laureates labored to find ways to teach the very young how mathematicians think, and scientists who had worked in the Manhattan Project invented "kitchen physics" courses for the elementary schools. Scholars from every major discipline took part in the enterprise; in the process they advanced the science of pedagogy and redefined the parameters of curriculum design. During the *Sputnik*-inspired curriculum movement hundreds of research scholars worked on improving the schools, an allocation of brain power unique in the annals of educational reform.

While this partnership between scholars and school people did not come easily in a society that tends to distrust "eggheads," the participation of research professors brought fresh insights to the problems of instruction. They clarified the central concepts, organizing conjectures, and compelling examples of the disciplines and worked to close the gap between the frontier of research and the practical world of the school. In a time of rapid expansion and obsolescence of knowledge, this involvement of people who were working at the forefront of their fields helped to define the content of instruction, and provided assistance to teachers in working out the most appropriate ways of structuring the presentation of these ideas to the young. This collaboration not only strengthened the professional development of teachers, it also focused attention at the university level on the quality of teaching.

One of the most important contributions of the science curriculum reform movement was the new insights it generated about the teaching process itself. By getting involved with the schools, scholars became immersed in the creation of new materials and methods that were dedicated to engaging young minds in the processes of scholarly inquiry. Participation of university academics in the schooling process helped to bring about a transition to an emphasis on the cultivation of thinking skills rather than the transmission of content, the sorts of skills that may be particularly relevant in an increasingly complex society. By relating children's learning to the work of scientists on the frontier of research, the *Sputnik*-driven reformers challenged conventional assumptions about how children should be taught and helped to redefine what effective instruction is. If they sometimes overrated children's intellectual capacities in their effort to push the limits of what children can be taught, as David Page did at Woods Hole, they greatly expanded our knowledge of the range of issues and problems that children can grapple with and understand.

This questioning of the prevailing wisdom about children's learning capacities opened a new field, one that needs to be more fully developed. An oft-stated refrain at EDC was, "We need a theory of instruction on which to base our work." One of the contributions of the curriculum reform movement was to create a context for the pursuit of such a theory. Jerome Bruner was a pioneer in setting up just such an intelligence function, and his Instructional Research Group, staffed by people like Howard Gardner, Judy Krieger, and Marilyn Clayton, among many others, made significant contributions to our knowledge about children's thinking processes in a school setting. This new knowledge was invaluable for the design of materials, but it would have been even more valuable for teacher training and for the continuous restructuring of the schooling experience. Unfortunately, the pressure to publish and "complete the project" sometimes made it difficult to respond adequately to what we discovered, but the process of development that provided for continuous observation, feedback, and revision was an invention that offered promise for learning more about learning itself.

If we had been successful in implementing our professional services agreement, we might have been able to put in place a permanent model for learning more about what goes on in a classroom and for applying the results of this research to the development of new and more effective instructional materials, much as research and development to improve health care is a continuing process in the medical profession. Such procedures are part of the increasing professionalism of many aspects of our society, including the commercial sector. When the Japanese introduce a new car into the American automobile market today, they immediately place an evaluation team in the field to ask their customers what is wrong with it so they can make it better. To create more effective educational materials and teaching strategies, we must learn how to respond in a similar way. A collaboration between developers, the university, the schools, and the educational publishing community could make this happen.

Bruner epitomized the importance of the role scholars can play in helping to redefine schooling, and how that participation can in turn have an impact on scholarship, when he took leave from Harvard's Center for Cognitive Studies in 1964 to devote full time to the development of MACOS. As he commented many years later, the time he spent in the elementary classrooms was among the most intellectually rewarding periods of his academic life. He found that attending to the problems of learning in real classrooms kept his research honest, because it focused his attention on how young minds grow, or fail to grow, in the real-world setting of the school. His experiences in elementary classrooms caused him to think more deeply about the practical application of his laboratory research and changing educational priorities. This influence was reflected in *The Relevance of Education,* a book of essays he published in 1971, which spanned the period of his work on MACOS. The book began with a piece entitled "The Perfectibility of Intellect" written in 1964 and concluded with a 1970 essay called "Poverty and Childhood."

Bruner's interest in education went beyond the transmission of new knowledge in the social sciences. He came to the curriculum movement as a psychologist looking for ways to strengthen the overall process of learning in school. He captured the attention of a generation of educators by questioning accepted assumptions about the limits of children's intelligence and by enunciating his premise that "any subject can be taught effectively in some intellectually honest form to any child at any stage of development." As a noneducator he asked fresh questions about children's intellectual capacities, and he brought to the work a scholarly skepticism about the established way of doing things. He had a passion to know more about the inner workings of young minds, and he inspired his collaborators to push what schools could do to the limits.

Jerrold Zacharias and his colleagues in the natural sciences brought a similar commitment to school reform. As academics who had thought deeply about complex problems like atomic energy and radar, they turned their minds to the problem of educating the young with a freshness of view untrammeled by conventional wisdom about children's intelligence. If children could not understand something they were trying to teach, they assumed that it was they who were not clever enough, not the children. This effort to push back the boundaries of learning and to devise new and more imaginative ways to engage the intelligence of the young set new standards for schooling, and opened up new pedagogical frontiers. And it focused new attention on the crucially important issue of how children's minds grow. It is unfortunate that the work was only just getting under way when changing national priorities led to the withdrawal of financial support.

We need to reengage the commitment of scholars like Bruner and Zacharias in the current educational reform effort. Research professors are particularly helpful in dealing with the young because they tend to identify with the child's curiosity about the unknown and have a deep commitment to the cultivation of thinking processes. Beyond this, they are in touch with what is happening at the "cutting edge" of their disciplines and can help teachers close the gap between knowledge as it is developing in the university and the work-a-day world of the school. This is especially important in the scientific disciplines, where new knowledge is rapidly generated and can swiftly become obsolete. At the same time, engagement with the schools may help to focus the attention of scholars on matters of social concern.

The Importance of Teachers

The *Sputnik*-driven reformers also discovered the centrality of teachers in the educational reform process. Early talk about creating "teacher-proof" materials was quickly discarded when the curriculum innovators found that the insights and contributions of teachers were essential to the achievement of effective curriculum reform. While the participation of scholars provided intellectual stimulation and conceptual clarity, it took the classroom expertise of good teachers to translate new ideas and materials into productive classroom experiences. One of the most gratifying aspects of the experience at EDC was the collaboration between teachers and scholars and the mutual respect that developed as they worked together to create lessons and materials for children.

Catherine Motz's vivid recollections of the excitement of working with Bruner in a fifth-grade classroom exemplify the power of the scholar-teacher partnership. This experience was duplicated many times as MACOS moved from the curriculum laboratory to the educational marketplace, and it was the key to its continuing success following commercial publication. During the period when we were struggling to find a publisher, it was largely the collaboration between university professors and classroom teachers that carried the course and allowed for its expansion. As Tom Fitzgerald and

Dennen Reilley demonstrated, it was often teachers who turned out to be the most effective organizers of the training program and the most persuasive promoters of the course. Fitzgerald and Reilley were particularly credible in their presentations because both had experienced firsthand the power of the course with children.

Unfortunately, the way we usually market educational innovation leaves little room for enlisting the power of teachers or providing for a continuing relationship between schools and universities. Teachers are typically confined to their classrooms with schedules that preclude significant interaction with other educational professionals. When this partnership disintegrated or ran into resistance from the authority structure of the school, much of the power of the course to bring about positive change in the classroom began to disappear. As John Goodlad and his colleagues pointed out in *Looking behind the Classroom Door,* the decline of the scholar-teacher partnership was one of the major reasons for the demise of the science curriculum reform movement. Goodlad found that when teachers are treated as passive recipients of innovation rather than as vital participants in the educational reform process, reforms lose their power to stimulate change.[2]

Most teachers, I believe, would welcome continuing contact with the university community. When asked about the impact of the *Sputnik* curriculum reforms on their lives, many teachers who had participated in the movement recalled the association with scholars, and the opportunity to be active players in the development and implementation of new materials and teaching methods, as the most stimulating intellectual experience they had ever known, including their college years. But working with new materials was only part of the impact of the science curriculum reform movement. Equally important was the sense of collegiality that developed between scholars and teachers who worked together as collaborators in hundreds of government-sponsored development centers and training institutes across the country. This scholar-teacher partnership in curriculum innovation was the cornerstone of post-*Sputnik* educational reforms.

The Medium Shapes the Message

Although Marshall McLuhan may have overstated the case when he said "the medium is the message," he was right in pointing out that the method of delivery affects the way people learn. ESI began as a film studio because Jerrold Zacharias wanted to expose students to the excitement of the research laboratory. Film may not have been as effective as direct participation, but it was a vast improvement over the textbook. For the first time, thousands of high school physics students could be exposed to an M.I.T. research professor plying his trade, and it brought them far closer to "doing science" than reading a textbook. One of the major contributions of the *Sputnik* reforms was their extensive experimentation with a variety of instructional media, including film, still photographs, physical materials, games, original documents, construction activities, laboratory experiments, and fieldwork as well as a multiplicity of written materials, rather than a single text, in order to find the optimal match between the medium, the message, and the student. At the time, what we jokingly called "the new technology of the knowledge industry" was in its infancy. Today, with computers, videodiscs, and CD-ROM players at our disposal, we should be even more committed to understanding how the learning medium influences both who learns and what is learned. As Peter Drucker has recently observed, "Just as the printed book became the new 'high tech' of education in the fifteenth century, so computer, television, and video cassettes are becoming the high tech of education in the twentieth century . . . The new technology is bound to have a profound impact on the schools."[3]

MACOS was an early example of the potential of the multimedia course. The best way to introduce children to anthropological research would have been to take them into the field to study baboons with DeVore and Washburn, or to accompany Balikci to the Arctic. The next best thing was film. Films far surpassed a text in giving children "firsthand" knowledge about the animals and people they were studying. All students had access to the same information, regardless of reading ability, and through repeated viewings they were able to learn from direct observation rather than only the unchallengeable authority of the text. The power of this direct approach to learning led us to the introduction of many of the fresh sources of information I have described—still photographs, artifact cards, kinship charts, environment boards, sound recordings, and hunting games. Although it stirred the ire of conservatives, we even encouraged children to study behavior directly using Marilyn Clayton's *Observer's Handbook*. This diversity of media conveyed to children the idea that there are many ways of perceiving and interpreting information and invited them to commit themselves to explanations of their own. The notion that there could be more than one right answer or one way of explaining a body of data was a direct consequence of our multimedia approach. A gratifying side benefit was the discovery that a diversity of media stimulated the curiosity and engaged the intellect of those children who are often nonperformers in school because they do not learn easily from the printed page. Teachers were surprised to find that they could no longer predict who might be the star performer on a given day.

This experimentation with educational media confirmed the inadequacy of the conventional textbook. Although educators have come to regard the textbook as an efficient way of delivering information, it fails to respond to much of what the curriculum reformers learned about children's learning. The textbook is a limited learning tool for many reasons:

It covers a lot of material briefly, although we know that facts and concepts have staying power only when children study them in depth.

It reduces written communication to "readability formulas," although we know that the writing children relate to best is writing that has literary quality.

It forces children to carry around a heavy volume full of information they do not use, although the kind of book they like is one they can read in one or two sittings.

It treats learning as if everyone is supposed to come away with the same result, although we know that children respond best when they are treated as individuals with different interests and different ways of learning.

It focuses on the transmission of facts, although we know that children relate to interesting questions and provocative ideas.

In short, it is an educational technology from an earlier era that has outlived its value. As Jerrold Zacharias said about Leften Stavrianos's A Global History of Man at Endicott House, "You turn that loose in a school and you've got nothing."

The Power of the Case Study

One reason the textbook turns out to be such a poor teaching tool is that it short-changes the learning process. Although there was much debate at the Endicott House meeting about what to teach, everyone agreed that the only way to get any idea across to children is to pursue a subject in depth. The idea of "post-holing" received unanimous endorsement as the only sensible way to get students to make an intellectual commitment. Every attempt to shortcut the process, including Bruner's valiant efforts to get "maximum travel from a minimum array of information," failed us. We found that if you want children to commit their minds to a subject, you must give them time to immerse themselves in the data so that they become emotionally engaged in the material at hand. They must identify with the subject and care about it, and assimilate it at whatever intuitive level captures their curiosity, before they can begin to impose upon it the formalities of conceptualization. When we tried to rush their learning, they became bored and disengaged.

In developing MACOS, we decided to expose children to a small number of well-researched animal studies followed by a detailed look at the seasonal migration cycle of a subsistence society as a way of exploring a few central issues and questions about what it means to be a human being. By introducing children to large amounts of data of gradually increasing levels of conceptual complexity and abstraction throughout a whole school year, we were able to achieve strong emotional identification with the materials and at least some beginning levels of conceptual understanding. But even with this approach, children discovered the abstractions we wanted to teach slowly. The process could not be forced. This approach assumes that children have deep reservoirs of intuitive understanding, but if their learning is to acquire abstract levels of meaning, or general relevance, they must participate in the process of constructing that understanding for themselves. Pursuing a subject in depth increases the likelihood that children will achieve such meaning in what they learn, and this is the kind of learning that has staying power long after specific facts have been forgotten.

Elting Morison was our most eloquent spokesman for the "post-holing" argument. He once suggested that we could teach a good bit about the culture of Renaissance Italy by having students investigate how Benvenuto Cellini got the commission to make the Pope's buttons.[4] With this approach, he said, you can bring in all there is to say about art and religion and ecclesiastical administration, letting the general idea of Renaissance culture arise from a close examination of one intriguing episode. He elaborated further with an example from American history:

Take a thing like . . . Jackson's war on the Bank, the Second National Bank, and . . . get, not bound up into a book of readings, but . . . have in photostated form . . . so that they looked like what they were at the time—pieces of evidence: the Presidential veto as it was, all written out, a speech from the Congressional Record, Nicholas Biddle's Bank account, newspaper clippings, all kinds of . . . private correspondence at the time . . . A bale of loose data— all loose—and then say to the kid, "Make your own statement about what you would have done if you were Jackson, or what happened here, or who was the writer"—ask him any question, but give him the data to organize in any way he wants. . . . At Endicott House [we] propounded [the] notion of putting in irrelevant data also. In this way, we would deal with the problem, you see, of getting him to feel the thing itself.[5]

Morison's proposed approach makes the inadequacy of the textbook self-evident. Today, with the advent of the computer in education, his vision seems increasingly possible. Indeed, this approach is now close to a reality in Harvard's Perseus Project, a multi-million-dollar effort to provide teachers with quantities of original source material on archaic and classical Greece, including multiple views of seldom-seen pottery, fragments from ancient texts, and photographs of the Parthenon and other buildings that permit students to construct their own guided tour of the Acropolis. These resources are made available through the use of Apple Computer's Hypercard system coupled to a television monitor and a CD-ROM player. Devices of this kind may finally replace the lock-step tyranny of the textbook with a process of learning that draws upon the individual curiosity and imagination of a much broader range of students, in which the pursuit of the interesting question becomes more important than knowing the "correct" answer.[6]

Getting to Wichita

Few of the academics who directed curriculum research and development projects gave much thought at the outset to how the products of their work would reach the schools. They assumed that the educational publishing industry would welcome the new programs and that private funds would be readily available to convert laboratory prototypes to commercially successful products. They were poorly informed about the economics of publishing, school book purchasing restrictions, and the textbook adoption procedures in places like Texas and California, and they failed to appreciate the inherent conservatism of most school boards. Although they were imaginative about how to convert the products of academic research into classroom materials, they knew little about how to engineer the process of educational reform, and they failed to cultivate the support of the educational establishment in pursuing their reform objectives.

One exception to this rule was Jerrold Zacharias. Zacharias realized early on that if PSSC was to succeed, he would have to devise a way to cultivate widespread support within the physics teaching establishment. He tried to reach as many physics teachers as possible by training teacher-trainers and trainers of teacher-trainers, (T_2s and T_3s as he called them), thereby establishing a national network of physicists and physics educators committed to the PSSC program. Fortunately, the physics market was fairly small compared to the potential market for MACOS, only about 12,000 teachers in all, and with his carefully orchestrated approach, he eventually succeeded in reaching over 50 percent of the physics classrooms in the country.

The regional center system we designed for MACOS was based on the Zacharias model. As the course expanded, we created a national network of scholar-teacher teams who trained teachers and teacher-trainers. This system worked well as long as EDC was able to keep in touch with what was going on and respond to new experiences with the course. When the controversy erupted at Madison Park, for example, we flew to Phoenix to support the school system and took along a film crew to record events so we could use the Phoenix experience for training purposes with future groups of teachers and administrators. We intended to include the films, together with related readings, in our teacher seminar series because we felt that curriculum innovation was a continuously changing enterprise that had to respond to our field experience at every stage. When our publisher disagreed, we withheld the Phoenix film from distribution at their request, but we were convinced that avoiding controversy would not prevent future controversy and that it was a mistake not to use what we had learned in Phoenix to alert other teachers and administrators to what they might encounter in their own communities.

But controversy was not the only barrier to successful implementation. In a penetrating study of the fate of MACOS in Oregon, Lynda Falkenstein examined the conditions that caused the course to be removed from a number of Oregon schools. She concluded that innovations that lacked the commitment of administrators able to provide long-term support and continuing teacher training beyond the initial implementation phase were bound to falter regardless of their quality. Even more than controversy, she found, the greatest barrier to successful innovation was the lack of continuity of support from the internal structure of the school system itself. In summarizing her findings she emphasized that effective educational reform requires an integration of the processes of development and implementation: "For the kinds of institutional changes to occur that will permit innovative curricula such as MACOS to be developed and maintained over time in local school districts, the curriculum development and implementation processes will need to be thoroughly reconceptualized. It may be that when redefined, these processes will be viewed so inextricably combined as to be inseparable."[7]

Falkenstein's study pointed up the need for a new kind of implementation structure to support curriculum innovation. For curriculum reform to be successful, there must be a close and continuing relationship between those who create and distribute the new curriculum and those who use it. Long-term implementation strategies must be designed to take into account the need for this continuing support, and developers must devise a way to respond appropriately to what is learned in the implementation process. Curriculum innovation is not a static enterprise. It must provide for a dynamic interaction between developers and users so that materials and strategies can be updated and revised to meet the changing needs of the participating schools.

Falkenstein's findings in Oregon reflected EDC's experience across the country. Whenever we worked closely with a committed administrator, whether it was a building principal, curriculum supervisor, or deputy superintendent for instruction, the implementation of the course went well. Teachers felt supported, parents were well informed, and the appropriate resources, including time for proper training and preparation, were provided. But when these relationships did not exist, or when they began to break down after a few years of implementation, we could expect trouble. The lesson from MACOS was clear: for the process of innovation to be successful, it must be institutionalized within the school system so that when the initiating administrator-innovator moves on to other responsibilities, as he or she often does, the new program will continue to receive on-going support. School systems are by nature conservative institutions, and no innovation will last long unless it has strong administrative backing and unless provisions are made for continuing assistance at every stage of the implementation process. Innovators must learn how to design permanent networking systems that provide for perpetual interaction between developers and users, encourage the professional growth of classroom teachers, and ensure regular communication with the local community. Without such support, it will be difficult to progress much beyond the textbook.

The Challenge for Publishers

Fixing the schools will also require new approaches and attitudes on the part of educational publishers. Even more than in the *Sputnik* era, we live in an age of educational publishing giants—eight or ten companies at most—which are increasingly driven less by the desire to meet the particular needs of individual school systems than by the desire to win larger pieces of the textbook adoption pie. To do so requires the development of a product that will not only satisfy the largest number of users but be devoid of material that might alienate potential purchasers. Winning a major state adoption means financial success for a textbook publisher, while failing to compete successfully in the adoption sweepstakes can create serious financial problems. Thus, the larger publishers are organized to produce lavish, hardbound textbooks with attractive covers and innocuous content, which will offend no special interest group or political constituency at the state adoption hearings and which can be introduced with a minimum of investment in teacher training. It is this sort of educational product, expensive to produce and dull to use, that stands in the way of significant educational innovation. Such textbooks consume enormous development and distribution resources that could otherwise be devoted to the creation of more intellectually demanding and pedagogically exciting materials.

A publishing strategy that avoids educational risk may be counterproductive in an era of rising educational expectations. There is hope, for example, in the recent stand taking by Bill Honig, California State Superintendent of Public Instruction, and the California Board of Education. In 1985, California rejected all of the junior high school biology textbooks submitted for adoption and insisted that the publishers improve their coverage of evolution and human reproduction. The following year, the state rejected the elementary mathematics texts, charging that they placed too much emphasis on rote memorization and not enough on the teaching of problem-solving.[8] And in 1990, the California Curriculum Commission rejected the books of all but two publishers of history and social studies texts for their simplistic presentation and their failure to give proper exposure to cultural and ethnic differences.[9] Pressure of this kind from the nation's largest textbook purchaser is bound to improve textbook quality, but we are still a long way from introducing the kinds of learning materials that can provide the most effective instruction. Educational publishers need to be in close and continuing communication with the schools if they are to learn how to create diversified educational materials designed to meet individual learning needs. Perhaps we need new forms of collaboration between developers, publishers, and the schools if we are to reallocate some of the countless millions of dollars that are spent each year to develop the pedagogically unsound textbooks that continue to trivialize the learning process. The courageous stand taken by California is an important first step.

To some extent, the "new technologies of the knowledge industry," much touted in the sixties but now finally at hand, may come to the rescue of both the publishers and the schools. It is at last becoming practical to individualize materials. One major publisher, McGraw-Hill, is now collaborating with Eastman Kodak in an experiment designed to tailor textbooks to an instructor's requirements. While practically speaking this will find more application in college courses than at the primary and secondary level, the technology now exists to personalize a textbook if the schools require it. We have known for years that to bring about significant change in the classroom we need a variety of products that promote flexibility in teaching and respect diversity among students. We know that students have different interests, that they respond to different media, and that they learn at different rates of speed, but until now we have lacked either the will or the technological capability to create and market materials that make response to that diversity possible.

In developing MACOS we tried to accommodate diversity. We deliberately created materials in a variety of media that would offer children alternative approaches to the subject and designed the course so that teachers could structure the program to fit their individual student's needs and their personal teaching preferences. This instructional flexibility was not immediately accepted by teachers, who were accustomed to the simplicity and uniformity of the textbook. Many were initially uncomfortable with the range of choices these nontext materials introduced and uncertain about how to conduct a class in which children were working with different materials at the same time. We expected these reactions, and dealing with these objections was one of the goals of our teacher-training seminars. Our purpose was not to provide teachers with the comfortably familiar. We wanted to stretch their imaginations and expose them to new educational possibilities. Most teachers responded to this challenge, and the result was the intellectual growth of both teachers and students.

Publishers must find a way to collaborate with the schools in this development process. They possess the technology to provide every child in the country with exciting, diverse, personally challenging educational materials in print, visual, audio, digital, and other forms. In this kind of rich communications environment we must reject the limitations of the conventional textbook and work to replace it with educational tools that are more responsive to diversified educational needs and objectives. We must find enlightened publishing executives who are willing to collaborate with developers and school people to reach these goals. This may already be taking place in the new development programs designed around publisher-developer collaborations, such as NSF's "Triad" projects, in which the Foundation helps to finance publishers who demonstrate a willingness to work with developers in designing new programs that reflect the best pedagogical research and are responsive to the needs of individual school systems. This will only succeed if publishers are willing to risk an investment in products that may have a longer term payback than their present educational materials.

Changing Educational Values

There have been times in our history when politicians would have considered it political suicide to affiliate themselves with school reform. Prior to World War II, people with too much learning were often regarded as social misfits or distrusted as purveyors of subversive ideas. The absent-minded professor and the "egghead" who inhabits the scientific laboratory have seldom been revered as national heroes; indeed, some of our most distinguished scientists, including many who worked on the development of the atomic bomb, later became politically suspect during the McCarthy era. Even today, Americans remain ambivalent about the value of a formal education, and it is the rare politician who is willing to take up the cultivation of the intellect as a personal crusade. Yet once again we are worried about our schools, and it will be instructive to see how far our politicians are willing to go in promoting serious educational change. For the first time since Jefferson we have a chief executive who would like to think of himself as "the education president." We shall follow with interest the recent agenda established by the state governors for making American schools first in the world in math and science achievement by the year 2000, a set of goals described as "breathtaking" by some observers.[10] So far, the Bush administration has given us far more rhetoric than results.

One of the interesting revelations of the science curriculum reform movement, and of the MACOS experience in particular, is the degree to which educational policy-making in America is driven by political considerations. Our discussions of what we want to teach our children are seldom separated from our image of who we are as a people and what we want to become as a nation. This was true of the *Sputnik* reforms, and the success of the current effort to change the schools will also be measured against this vision. Does it further our goals as a nation and contribute to our sense of national identity? Does it strengthen our position with respect to those who are perceived to be our competitors or our adversaries? Is it liberating for all people, not just a privileged elite? Is it morally defensible? These questions are too important to be left to the professional educators alone. The discussion of our national educational goals requires the participation of our political leaders, who reflect the will of the people and thus can chart the course of educational reform in directions that are politically acceptable. They must articulate the nature of our current educational crisis and craft solutions that will attract long-term public support.

In recent years the public discussion over the purpose and content of schooling has taken place mainly in the courts, where parents have challenged what their children are being taught. During the past decade this dialogue has been enlivened by the creationism versus evolution debate and the controversy over how much control parents should be able to exercise over what their children read in school. Conservatives have attacked the teaching of materials on the Holocaust, charging that they "disturb the stability" of classrooms, and as recently as October 1986, a U.S. District Court judge ruled in favor of seven Tennessee families, who claimed that their religious beliefs were offended by *The Wizard of Oz* and *The Diary of Anne Frank*.[11] In March 1987, U.S. District Judge Brevard Hand ruled in favor of 624 Protestant and Catholic parents and teachers who filed a class action suit for the removal of forty-six social studies and economics textbooks from the schools of Mobile, Alabama, claiming that the books unconstitutionally promoted "secular humanism" as a religion.[12] If the school system would not permit "equal time" for teaching their religious beliefs, then no "religion" should be taught, they argued. But later that year the Supreme Court, in a decisive seven to two vote, put to rest the "equal time" argument by declaring a 1981 Louisiana law mandating equal treatment for creationism and evolution unconstitutional on the grounds that the law violated the First Amendment prohibition against the establishment of religion. Speaking for the majority, Justice William Brennan wrote, "The Act's primary purpose was to change the science curriculum of public schools in order to provide an advantage to a particular religious doctrine that rejects the factual basis of evolution in its entirety."[13] This decision was applauded by the academic community and praised by the Harvard biologist Stephen J. Gould as a victory for those thousands of teachers "who uphold, often at personal peril, . . . the ideal that truth . . . shall make us free."[14]

But is the majority of American citizens ready to allow unfettered science education in the schools? The authors of MACOS, like most of the science curriculum reformers, were insufficiently aware of the extent to which political considerations shape the content of instruction. We saw ourselves engaged in the task of closing the gap between the research laboratory and the classroom, and we assumed that the social value of this enterprise was self-evident. We did not foresee that in devising an anthropologically based program for elementary students we were challenging beliefs, deeply held in some parts of the country, about what children should learn. When our motives were called into question in these communities, we were unprepared: Was the course designed to displace the teaching of American history and the transmission of American values? Were we cultivating cross-cultural sensitivity at the expense of patriotism and national loyalty? Was there something subversive in the unusual nature of the course design, in which the familiar textbook was replaced by a variety of books, games, and films and diversity of instruction replaced conformity? Was sending children into the schoolyard to observe behavior a form of surveillance training? Was talking about the problems of growing up an invasion of parental prerogatives? Was discussing the problems of the elderly an inappropriate subject for the young? These were some of the values issues the course raised, and we were ill-prepared to address them. We naively assumed that what we were proposing to teach was within the mainstream of political acceptability and did not need to be explicitly defended. We were dead wrong.

Doubtless the debate over curriculum content and the pressure to include or exclude materials that reflect the value positions of particular interest groups will continue, and the result will be the intimidation of teachers and administrators—to the detriment of children's education—unless our political leaders join the fray and help to articulate and support the educational values that are acceptable in their communities. The matter is too important to be left to professional educators who, as we have seen, almost always take the line of least resistance in the face of community opposition. We need politicians who are unafraid to speak their minds on the subject of educational reform, since publicly elected officials are most qualified to explain new programs in value terms the general public will find acceptable. We can only hope that our most distinguished political leaders will move concern for education to the top of the political agenda. Educators need the backing of politicians if they are to make the bold changes necessary to improve our schools. Politicians must support sound educational innovations where they see them and speak publicly about their visions of effective schooling. Without informed and articulate political support, the next round of educational innovation will be no more successful than the last.

We also need to take the concerns of parents seriously. Do most children develop in positive ways under the schooling conditions we have established, and do their parents value that growth? Do our schools, as we have defined them, meet the diverse needs of the many varied constituencies they serve? Does the local community understand, and strongly support, the curriculum and teaching methods in their schools? If not, we have failed in our task as educators, for schooling, like most things in America, is ultimately a consumer-driven enterprise. As taxpayers, Americans provide the funding, and as parents they are the ultimate judges of the results. Unlike most other countries, Americans have always treated schooling as primarily a local affair. Consequently the opinions of parents exercise a strong influence on educational decision-making, and innovations often falter not because of lack of intrinsic merit but because parents fail to understand them. These parents can be easily swayed by the vigorous lobbying efforts of vocal minorities. It will take responsive and courageous political leadership to sort out these issues in ways that respect the legitimate goals of minorities while protecting the interests of the population as a whole.

In accomplishing this end, both educational leaders and politicians must find a way to communicate effectively with their communities. In the case of MACOS, much of the opposition came from individuals who were driven by motives other than the interests of their own children. Of our most vocal opponents—Onalee McGraw, Phyllis Musselman, Norma Gabler, and John B. Conlan—none ever had a child in the course, and each was driven by personal ambitions that went far beyond the success or failure of MACOS. Their strength, however, came from their ability to stir up the fears of a following that was largely uninformed about the course. They played on age-old suspicions, deeply rooted in the American consciousness, about the dangers of unfamiliar ideas. They aroused the understandable fears of those who are uncomfortable with change and who could be led to believe that our intent was to subvert basic American values. Communities have little defense against these self-appointed textbook watchers, who play on the insecurities of the uninformed by accusing the innovator of attempting to poison the minds of the young. We need bold public leaders who can speak out against the Conlans and Gablers and make a convincing case for constructive educational change.

Legitimate efforts to transform our schools must have the support of an informed public. Given what we have already learned from Head Start and other programs about the relationship between early cognitive stimulation and later educational success, we must invite parents to partake in our reform efforts so that they can understand

and participate in the process of their children's intellectual development. This means that parents must be brought in on educational planning at the earliest stages and that their views about what constitutes proper education for their children must be taken seriously. Parents are entitled to know the rationale underlying how their children are being taught, and they should have the opportunity to take part in the new reform movement. As Barnaby Keeney, the president of Brown University during the tumultuous 1960s, once remarked, "In times of social change we must teach two generations at once." Failure to see this was one of the most serious shortcomings of the *Sputnik* era reformers.

As accounts of the MACOS controversy reveal, once an educational innovation creates a negative impression in a community, that sentiment is very difficult to reverse. To avoid this unfortunate result, promoters of such reforms must learn to take parents into their confidence at the time a new program is first being considered, share the program with them, and listen to their reaction and their ideas. If parental acceptance is the ultimate measure of success, we would do well to involve parents in the decision-making process at the earliest stages. They may often see problems in a program that are not obvious to educators. At the same time, when they understand and support a program, they can be its greatest allies. This is not to suggest that parental resistance can, or should be, eliminated. There will always be parents who reject change in any form or who oppose the introduction of a particular innovation for particular personal reasons, and school systems must learn to respond to these differences by offering appropriate alternatives. With foresight and proper planning, the various needs of parents can often be accommodated, thereby protecting the integrity of an innovation that might otherwise fall victim to the demands of a small but vocal minority. The solution to criticism is not the retreat to conformity or the creation of innocuous, mindless programs that offend no one. The answer is the celebration of diversity. Both educators and parents must work toward that end.

And our politicians must have the courage to support this process. On a recent trip to Washington I had occasion to discuss the MACOS controversy once again with former congressman James Symington. Symington, who now practices law, has been out of Congress for a number of years, but he vividly recalls the congressional debate. As I talked with him he warmed to the memory of the course and his defense of teaching such material in the schools. He spoke about the importance of helping young children understand other cultures so that as adults, they can approach problems with a broader appreciation of humanity than they might get from riding in the carpool or going to the supermarket. He spoke eloquently about how programs like MACOS can help reduce the psychological distance between Americans and people from other cultures:

> I found the whole program both fascinating and quite worthwhile, and I wish my kids had had a chance to see it in their time . . . But it would be good for anybody to see . . . I remember during the Korean War we had the habit of saying, you know, just some Gooks over there. Kill a few Gooks. Well, the Korean people turned out in later times to have a rather wide variety of characteristics, and personality traits, and strengths and weaknesses, that made them almost seem like human beings like we are, . . . not so easily dismissed as Gooks. And I would have thought that, had a generation of Americans, prior to that war, been brought up with a chance to see, not just MACOS but other opportunities to review the cultural differences between peoples worldwide, [they] might not be that easily led into such a characterization. I wasn't opposed to our participation there, . . . but even in war respect for humanity should outlast the killing. And I think a great nation like ours should try in every way to use its power and its influence to share and revere a respect for humanity.[15]

A Final Word

Politicians and parents, school administrators and publishers, scholars and teachers, these are the players who must come together if we are to transform elementary and secondary education in the United States and make our classrooms once again, as in times past, an example for the world. The difficulty with schooling, it seems, is that it is so often anachronistic, based upon a model of learning that was more appropriate to an earlier era. This is the problem John Dewey faced in trying to make schools designed for an agrarian society work for a growing industrial nation. Dewey's genius was in seeing that if children were to be prepared to live effectively in a changing society they needed a new kind of instruction, one that taught them how to deal concretely with the demands of an increasingly scientific and urbanized world. Unfortunately, his proposals were too often trivialized, drained of their conceptual content, and reduced to mindless improvisation, and he died a disillusioned reformer whose vision was never fully achieved.

Today we face Dewey's challenge in a new form: to make schools designed to meet the needs of an industrial society work in a postindustrial age. Our contemporary society needs people who can read and write and follow instructions accurately, but we also need citizens who can speak with fluency, reason clearly, and master a diversity of languages. We need a workforce that is personally resourceful, self-reliant, and even inventive, and we need a citizenry that can live cooperatively and provide moral leadership in a global society of diverse goals, perceptions, and values. To compete in today's world the graduates of our schools must possess a capacity for continuous mental and moral growth. They must know how to learn and respect learning. This is a sizable order. To do the job, our present educational system must be transformed.

In order to accomplish these objectives we must reconsider, I believe, the best of what was learned by the *Sputnik*-inspired reformers. The scholars who led that movement took children's minds seriously. They endeavored to construct a framework for educating the young that cultivated individual intelligence, not to mold students to a single pattern but rather to match instruction in all disciplines to age-specific intellectual needs and individual learning styles. Had this movement been sustained beyond the initial response to the Soviet challenge, I believe we would have discovered new ways of deploying the powerful tools of instruction at our command to benefit a much wider range of students than we are reaching today with our outdated means and methods. The *Sputnik*-inspired reformers, naive as they may have been from a political point of view, were on the right track in attempting to close the gap between intellectual discovery as it occurs on the cutting edge of scholarship and learning as it occurs in a growing young mind. We need therefore to reengage the brightest minds in the academic community in the educational reform problem if we are to bring off the desperately sought transformation of the schools.

Will we be able to fix the schools? The task of educational reform in a complex, troubled society may seem overwhelming when we contemplate the gap between our vision of a well-educated, competent citizenry and the present performance of our educational system. But at one time putting a man on the moon also seemed beyond our grasp. We possess the knowledge, the financial resources, and the technical capability. As citizens we are more aware than ever before of the human cost of our educational weakness. We are shocked by the decline of our industrial strength as skilled occupations are taken over by our foreign competitors. The national concern about the schools transcends even the worries of the *Sputnik* era, for their inadequacy goes beyond the issues of national defense: it threatens to sap the intellectual, economic, and moral strength of our entire society.

But to bring off the desired transformation of our educational system will take more than an expression of national will. It will require the same allocation of money, resources, and talent that made the conquest of space possible. At a time when we are facing mounting deficits at all levels of government and when some claim that money makes no difference in educational matters, the case for spending on educational reform may sound like a voice in the wilderness. Yet it is the future strength of our nation that we are talking about when we discuss the improvement of the educational system. There is no quick fix here. We need a sustained, long-range financial commitment to reform our public schools. Our future is at stake. We must decide to invest in our children.

Notes

Index

Notes

Much of the information for this book is drawn from the very extensive files of Educational Services Incorporated (now Education Development Center). In 1977 all documents relating to the history of Man: A Course of Study were given to the Monroe C. Gutman Library of the Graduate School of Education at Harvard University, where they were to form a permanent archive for scholars of curriculum development and the science curriculum reform movement. Because of limited interest and space limitations, in 1980 Harvard gave the archives to the author, and they now reside in his personal library. Since that time he has added to the collection through contact with individuals associated with the program and through additional personal interviews. It now consists of correspondence, internal memoranda, newspaper and journal articles, classroom reports, formal and informal evaluations, drafts of materials under development, and copies of many of the published materials of the course in various editions. It also includes transcripts of forty-six interviews conducted with individuals associated with the development, implementation, and public reaction to the course. All sources cited in this book, other than generally available published works, are housed in this archive.

1. Historical Perspectives

1. Lawrence Cremin, *The Transformation of the School* (New York: Random House, Vintage Books, 1964), p. 339.
2. Mortimer Smith, *And Madly Teach* (Chicago: Henry Regnery, 1949), pp. 23–24.
3. Bernard Iddings Bell, *Crisis in Education: A Challenge to American Complacency* (New York: McGraw-Hill, 1949), p. 63.
4. Ibid., p. 67.

5. Lynd, a history professor turned businessman and school board member, blamed "half-hearted or uneducated" professional educators for the schools' problems, while Woodring called for a "new road" for education that rejected both the Progressives and other outmoded practices of the past. Bestor's ideas are treated more fully on pp. 16–19.

6. Hollis L. Caswell, "The Great Reappraisal of Public Education," *Teachers College Record* 54 (1952–53): 12–22.

7. I am indebted for this interpretation, and for much of the information presented here, to the late Lawrence Cremin, who develops this argument in his treatment of what he terms "The Crisis in Popular Education" in *The Transformation of the School,* pp. 338–353.

8. John Dewey, *Democracy and Education* (New York: Macmillan, 1916), p. 163.

9. John Dewey, *Experience and Education* (New York: Macmillan, 1938), p. 111.

10. Ibid., p. 109.

11. Ibid., p. 18.

12. As quoted in Arthur Bestor, *Educational Wastelands: The Retreat from Learning in our Public Schools* (Urbana: University of Illinois Press, 1953), p. 83.

13. Bestor, *Educational Wastelands,* p. 86.

14. Ibid., p. 6.

15. Ibid., p. 31.

16. Ibid., p. 21.

17. Ibid., p. 24.

18. Ibid., p. 106.

19. Ibid., p. 189.

20. Max Beberman, *An Emerging Program of Secondary School Mathematics* (Cambridge: Harvard University Press, 1960), p. 44.

21. Ibid., p. 38.

22. Jerrold R. Zacharias, Memorandum to J. R. Killian, Jr., 15 March 1956.

23. Interview with J. R. Killian, 5 January 1975.

24. Paul E. Marsh, "The Physical Science Study Committee: A Case History of Nationwide Curriculum Development, 1956–61" (Ed.D diss., Harvard Graduate School of Education, 1964), pp. 47–48.

25. As quoted in Mortimer J. Adler and Milton Mayer, *The Revolution in Education* (Chicago: University of Chicago Press, 1958), p. 16.

26. "Federal Aid Impasse," *Elementary School Journal* 50 (May 1950): 486.

27. Hyman G. Rickover, *Education and Freedom* (New York: E. P. Dutton, 1959), p. 59.

28. Marsh, "The Physical Science Study Committee," pp. 66–67.

29. Educational Services, Incorporated (ESI) was founded by Jerrold Zacharias in 1956 to develop PSSC and other projects. ESI changed its

name to Education Development Center (EDC) in 1966 when it merged with the Institute for Educational Innovation.

30. "Goals for School Mathematics," as quoted in Jerrold Zacharias et al., *Innovation and Experiment in Education: A Progress Report to the U.S. Commissioner of Education, the Director of the National Science Foundation, and the Special Assistant to the President for Science and Technology* (Washington, D.C.: Government Printing Office, 1964), p. 4.

31. Ibid., p. ix.

32. For a full account of the development of BSCS see Arnold B. Grobman, *The Changing Classroom: The Role of the Biological Sciences Curriculum Study* (New York: Doubleday, 1969).

33. Bentley Glass, *Science and Liberal Education* (Baton Rouge: Louisiana State University Press, 1959), p. 61.

34. Ibid., pp. 68–69.

2. The Origins of MACOS

1. The participants at the Woods Hole Conference were Dr. Carl Allendoerfer, University of Washington (mathematics); Dr. Richard Alpert, Harvard (psychology); Dr. Edward Begle, Yale (mathematics); Dr. John Blum, Yale (history); Dr. Jerome S. Bruner, Harvard (psychology); Dr. C. Ray Carpenter, Pennsylvania State (psychology); Dr. John B. Carroll, Harvard (education); Dr. Henry Chauncey, Educational Testing Service (education); Mr. Donald Cole, Phillips Exeter (history); Dr. Lee Chronbach, University of Illinois (psychology); Mr. Gilbert Finlay, University of Illinois (physics); Dr. John H. Fischer, Teacher's College Columbia (education); Mr. John Flory, Eastman Kodak (cinematography); Dr. Francis L. Friedman, M.I.T. (Physics); Dr. Robert M. Gagne, Princeton (psychology); Dr. Ralph Gerard, University of Michigan (biology); Dr. H. Bentley Glass, Johns Hopkins (biology); Dr. Arnold Grobman, American Institute of Biological Sciences (biology); Dr. Thomas S. Hall, Washington University (biology); Dr. Barbel Inhelder, Institut Rousseau, Geneva (psychology); Dr. John F. Latimer, George Washington University (classics); Dr. George A. Miller, Harvard (psychology); Dr. Robert S. Morison, Rockefeller Foundation (medicine); Dr. David L. Page, University of Illinois (mathematics); Mr. Richard Pieters, Andover (mathematics); Dr. William C. H. Prentice, Swarthmore (psychology); Dr. Paul C. Rosenbloom, University of Minnesota (mathematics); Dr. Kenneth W. Spence, State University of Iowa (psychology); Dr. H. Burr Steinbach, University of Chicago (biology); Dr. Donald Taylor, Yale (psychology); Dr. Herbert E. Vaughan, University of Illinois (mathematics); Dr. Randall M. Whaley, Purdue (physics);

Dr. Don Williams, University of Kansas City (cinematography); Dr. Jerrold Zacharias, M.I.T. (physics).

2. Jerome S. Bruner, *The Process of Education* (Cambridge: Harvard University Press, 1961), p. vii.

3. Ibid., p. 17.

4. Interview with Jerrold Zacharias, 15 November 1974.

5. Jerrold Zacharias, "Woods Hole Revisited" (1965), p. 4.

6. Zacharias interview.

7. James D. Watson, *The Double Helix: A Personal Account of the Discovery of the Structure of DNA*, ed. Gunther S. Stent (New York: W. W. Norton, 1980), p. 194. Watson tells about the moment of discovery: "I quickly cleared away the papers from my desk top so that I would have a large, flat surface on which to form pairs of bases held together by hydrogen bonds. Though I initially went back to my like with like prejudices, I saw all too well that they led nowhere. When Jerry came in, I . . . began shifting the bases in and out of other pairing possibilities. Suddenly I became aware that an adenine-thimine pair held together by two hydrogen bonds was identical in shape to a quanine-cystosine pair held together by at least two hydrogen bonds. All the hydrogen bonds seemed to form naturally; no fudging was required to make the two types of base pairs identical in shape."

8. Bruner, *The Process of Education,* p. 68.

9. George A. Miller, "The Magical Number Seven, Plus or Minus Two: Some Limits on Our Capacity for Processing Information," *Psychological Review* 63 (1956): 81–97.

10. Woods Hole Conference Paper, "Cognitive Factors in Curriculum Design," pp. 8–9.

11. Bruner, *The Process of Education,* p. 33.

12. Ibid., p. 40.

13. Ibid., p. 42.

14. National Academy of Sciences, "The Process of Education," Report of the Conference on Fundamental Processes in Education, Woods Hole, Massachusetts, September 9–18, 1959, pp. 27–28.

15. Wood Hole Conference Paper, "Cognitive Factors in Curriculum Design," p. 22.

16. Bruner, *The Process of Education,* p. 77.

17. Conversation with Lawrence Senesh, 13 June 1975.

18. "Report: Conference of Social Studies and Humanities Curriculum Program held at Endicott House of M.I.T., Dedham, Mass., between June 9 and June 23, 1962," p. 4.

19. Interview with Elting Morison, 11 October 1974.

20. Interview with Edwin Fenton, 15 October 1974.

21. Morison interview.

22. "Brief Report of a Two Week Conference Held at Endicott House, Dedham, Mass., by the American Council of Learned Societies and Educational Services Incorporated to Plan A Program of Curriculum Development in the Humanities and Social Studies," June 9–23, 1962, p. 2.
23. Interview with Jerrold Zacharias, 11 October 1974.
24. "Brief Report," p. 5.
25. "Report: Conference of Social Studies and Humanities Curriculum Program," Appendix VIIa, p. 7.
26. Martin Mayer, *Social Studies in American Schools* (New York: Harper and Row, 1963), pp. 57–58.
27. Interview with Evans Clinchy, 15 October 1974.
28. "Report: Conference of Social Studies and Humanities Curriculum Program," Appendix VIIb, p. 3.
29. Ibid., p. 4.
30. Richard Jones, *Fantasy and Feeling in Education* (New York: New York University Press, 1968), pp. 9–10.
31. Fenton interview.
32. Interview with Wayne Altree, 4 December 1974.
33. Ibid.
34. Other members of the initial committee were Henry Bragdon, Robert Feldmesser, John H. Fisher, Francis Keppel, James Killian, Harry L. Levy, Elting Morison, and Stephen White.
35. Interview with Joseph Featherstone, 29 October 1974.
36. "Basic Generalizations for a Program of Curriculum Development in Social Studies," Educational Services Incorporated, September 1963, p. 6.
37. Ibid., p. 5.
38. Ibid.
39. Ibid., pp. 14–15.
40. Ibid., p. 19.
41. Ibid., p. 18.
42. Ibid., p. 21.
43. Interview with Everett Mendelsohn, 31 January 1975.
44. Interview with George Homans, 31 January 1975.
45. Interview with Asen Balikci, 17–18 October 1974.
46. Ibid.
47. Ibid.
48. Letter from Douglas Oliver to Asen Balikci, 29 August 1963.
49. Interview with Kevin Smith, 17 October 1974.
50. Interview with Quentin Brown, 3 December 1974.
51. Ibid.
52. The Netsilik Film project is described in detail in Quentin Brown and Asen Balikci, *Ethnographic Filming and the Netsilik Eskimos* (Newton, Mass.: Educational Services, Inc., 1966).

53. Interview with Irven DeVore, 20 October 1974.
54. Ibid.
55. Interview with Blythe Clinchy, 13 October 1974.
56. Ibid.
57. Richard M. Jones, "The 'Cities Unit' Summer Conference, 1964: Diagnosis and Prescription," 27 July 1964.
58. Interview with Robert Adams, 13 October 1975.
59. Ibid.

3. The Handmade Cadillac

1. Jerome S. Bruner, "Address to Friends Elementary School, October 12, 1964, at Westtown School," p. 2.
2. Ibid., p. 3.
3. This experiment uses three beakers, two short and fat and one tall and thin. The first beaker is filled half full of water, and the child is asked to fill the second, similar beaker to the same level so that there is the same amount of liquid "to drink." Then the child is asked to pour the contents of one beaker into the tall, thin beaker, and the liquid, of course, rises to a higher level. A five-year-old will typically say that there is now "more to drink," while by the age of seven most children will say that the tall, thin beaker looks fuller but really isn't.
4. Bruner, "Address at Westtown School," p. 9.
5. Ibid., p. 11.
6. Ibid., p. 15.
7. Ibid., p. 17.
8. Information provided here and in the following paragraph is from a tape recording made during the question period. The tape has not been transcribed, but it is included in the MACOS archives.
9. Interview with Catherine Motz Peterson, 13 September 1974.
10. Jerome S. Bruner, "The Emergence of Man: An Elementary Course of Study" (undated working draft), p. 1.
11. The course description set forth here first appeared in print as *Man: A Course of Study,* Occasional Paper No. 3, The Social Studies Curriculum Program (Cambridge: Educational Services Incorporated, 1965).
12. Interview with Anita Gil, 9 February 1976.
13. Bruner, "The Emergence of Man," p. 19.
14. Ibid., p. 21.
15. Ibid., pp. 24–25.
16. Bruner, *Man: A Course of Study,* pp. 13–14.
17. Elizabeth S. Dunkman, "A View of the First Flight" (Language Curriculum Group, 1965), p. 8.
18. Bruner, *Man: A Course of Study,* p. 6.

19. Elli Maranda, *Myth and Art as Teaching Materials,* Occasional Paper No. 5, The Social Studies Curriculum Program (Cambridge: Educational Services Incorporated, 1965), p. 8.

20. Ibid., p. 12.

21. Elli Maranda, "Symbolic Systems of Simple Societies: A Proposal for a Teaching Unit," 15 March 1965, p. 5.

22. Ibid., p. 13.

23. Bruner, "The Emergence of Man," p. 10.

24. Richard M. Jones, "The Summer and Bruner's Theorems . . . ," October 1964, pp. 5–8.

25. Richard Jones, *Fantasy and Feeling in Education* (New York: New York University Press, 1968), p. 125.

26. Bruner, "The Emergence of Man," p. 17.

27. Interview with Kathleen Sylva, 11 November 1974.

28. Ibid.

29. Richard H. Tyre, "Some Observations on Teacher Training: Report from Master Teacher, Yale Master of Arts in Teaching Program," July 1965, p. 2.

30. Although there was no formal evaluation of children's responses to film at Underwood, these informal observations were later confirmed in a nationwide evaluation of the course conducted in 1967–68. See Janet Hanley et al., *Curiosity, Competence, and Community, Man: A Course of Study: An Evaluation* (Cambridge: Education Development Center, 1969), pp. 19–20.

31. Peterson interview, p. 30.

32. Judith Krieger and Howard Gardner, "Sixth Grade Summary Report," 24 August 1965, p. 9.

33. Ibid.

34. Howard Gardner, "On Sequencing," IRG memorandum, 5 August 1965, p. 5.

35. Ibid., p. 6.

36. Ibid.

37. Interview with Anita Gil, 9 February 1976, p. 3.

38. Sylvia Farnham-Diggory, Evaluation Report, Summer Workshop, 1966, Part II, "Formal Observations," p. 1.

39. Ibid., pp. 32–33.

40. Ibid., p. 53.

41. Ibid., p. 40.

42. Farnham-Diggory Evaluation Report, Part III, "Formal Recommendations," p. 3.

43. Ibid., p. 4.

44. *Man: A Course of Study: Perspectives on Man and Animals,* Trial

Teaching Edition (Cambridge: Education Development Center, 1967), pp. 6–7.

45. *Man: A Course of Study: The Netsilik Eskimos at the Inland Camps,* Teacher's Guide Six (Cambridge: Education Development Center, 1969), p. 7.

46. Interview with Michael Sand, 24 March 1976.

47. Jess Reid, "IRG Report on Grade VI," 21 July 1965, p. 2.

48. Jerry Fletcher, "Report of Game Trials during the Summer of 1966," p. 8.

49. Fletcher, "Evaluation of the Crossing-Place Hunting Game," 26 September 1967, p. 19.

50. Gil interview.

51. Barbara Boylan Herzstein, "Notes on Materials Development," p. 2.

52. Ibid., p. 3.

53. Thomas E. Baines and Daniel E. Landis, *Instructional Report on Man: A Course of Study* (Newport News, Va.: Newport News Public Schools, 1970), p. 13.

54. G. Sidney Lester, David J. Bond, and Gary A. Knox, *A Social Studies Curriculum for the Modern World* (Corte Madera, Calif.: Marin Social Studies Project, 30 June 1971), p. 6.

55. Citation presented to Jerome Bruner by the AERA and the AEPI on 9 February 1969.

56. Jerome S. Bruner, *On Knowing: Essays for the Left Hand* (Cambridge: Harvard University Press, 1962), pp. 2, 4.

4. From Widener to Wichita

1. Jerome S. Bruner, *The Process of Education* (Cambridge: Harvard University Press, 1960), p. 90.

2. Evans Clinchy, "The New Curricula," undated essay [spring 1964?], p. 23.

3. Bruner, *Man: A Course of Study* (Cambridge, Mass.: Educational Services Incorporated, 1965), p. 24.

4. Judy Krieger and Howard Gardner, "Notes on Possible Functions of IRG and on Some Important Areas Leading to a Theory of Instruction," 20 July 1965, p. 7.

5. Ibid., p. 8.

6. Richard M. Jones, "Teacher Seminar Report," 16 December 1965, pp. 1–2.

7. Anita Mishler, "First Thoughts—Teacher Training," August 1966, pp. 3–4.

8. The systems were Boston, Massachusetts; Bennington, Vermont; Jefferson County, Colorado; Louisa County, Virginia; Marin County, California (two districts); New York City; Newton, Massachusetts; Niles,

Illinois; Oakland, California; Orange, New Jersey; Philadelphia, Pennsylvania; Washington, D.C.; Webster Groves, Missouri; and West Hartford, Connecticut.

9. Barbara B. Herzstein, Interview with Anita Mishler, 14 March 1970.

10. Informal interview with Anita Mishler, 23 February 1979.

11. Seminars for Teachers (first commercial edition, 1970), p. iii.

12. Anita Mishler, "Notes on Filming," February 1968, p. 1.

13. Carroll Bowen, "Publishing Objectives," undated memorandum, p. 2.

14. Ibid., p. 3.

15. Harper and Row, "Survey of EDC—Man: A Course of Study," 6 January 1969.

16. Dennen Reilley, *Final Report, National Science Foundation Grant GW-4498, 1 June 1969–31 August 1970,* November 1970, p. 6.

17. Ibid., p. 17.

18. Ibid., p. 25.

19. Letter from James Renko of Modern Learning Aids to Peter Dow, 10 April 1969, p. 2.

20. Letter from Wayne Howell to Virgil Howes, 8 January 1969, p. 1.

21. The eleven colleges and universities that submitted proposals were Boston State College, Central Connecticut State College, Syracuse University, George Washington University, Case-Western Reserve University, Northeastern Illinois State College, Florida State University, the University of Minnesota, Temple Buell College, the University of Oregon, and Stanford University. In addition, Ohio State University sought funding to research the dissemination model.

22. Letter from Charles Benton to Peter Dow, 26 November 1969, p. 4.

23. Letter from Jack Gentry to Peter Dow, 28 January 1970, p. 3.

24. Letter from Verne Atwater to Peter Dow, 30 January 1970, pp. 1–2.

25. Letter from Willard Wirtz to Peter Dow, 23 February 1970, p. 5.

26. Ibid., p. 6.

27. See Ronald G. Havelock et al., *Planning for Innovation through Dissemination and Utilization of Knowledge* (Ann Arbor: Center for Research on Utilization of Scientific Knowledge, University of Michigan, 1971).

28. Mishler interview, 14 March 1976.

5. The Perils of Innovation

1. Dorothy Nelkin, *Science Textbook Controversies and the Politics of Equal Time* (Cambridge: Massachusetts Institute of Technology Press, 1977), p. 1.

2. Summary of Lake City Controversy, unsigned and undated, p. 6.

3. *Florida Times Union,* 5 November 1970.

4. *St. Petersburg Times,* 25 November 1970.

5. *Tallahassee Democrat,* 25 November 1970.
6. Quoted in "Community Issues and Man: A Course of Study," EDC-prepared information packet (1972), p. 9.
7. Summary of Lake City Controversy, p. 12.
8. "Community Issues" packet, p. 11.
9. *Human Events,* 14 August 1971.
10. Memorandum from James M. Reusswig to Montgomery County Board of Education, 10 September 1971.
11. *Weekly American News,* 1 September 1971, p. 1.
12. Ibid.
13. Memorandum from M. E. Hatter to Dow Rhoton and Marvin Cornell, 10 September 1971.
14. Statement by Phyllis Musselman, 5 October 1971, p. 1.
15. Letter from W. P. Shofstall to M. E. Hatter, 23 September 1971.
16. Letter from Charlene R. Patty to David Weisendorn, 23 October 1971.
17. Interview with Jerome Bruner, 27 October 1971, pp. 2, 3.
18. Soundtrack of film *Innovation's Perils.*
19. Ibid.
20. Gene Pulliam, *Arizona Republic,* 24 October 1971.
21. Letter from Phyllis Musselman to Peter Dow, 9 January 1972, p. 3.
22. Edward C. Martin, Interview with Dow Rhoton, June 1973, published in *Diversity in the School Community* (Cambridge: Education Development Center, 1973), p. 54.
23. Rosanne G. McCaughey and Mrs. Richard N. O'Hara, "MACOS: Man: A Course of Study," undated memorandum, p. 3.
24. Ibid.
25. Peter Woolfson, "The Fight over MACOS: An Ideological Conflict in Vermont," p. 1.
26. Quoted in Nelkin, *Science Textbook Controversies,* p. 47.
27. Woolfson, "The Fight over MACOS," p. 2.
28. Ibid., p. 3.
29. Ibid.
30. Lorna Lecker, *Burlington Free Press,* 30 November 1973.
31. Nelkin, *Science Textbook Controversies,* p. 105.
32. Ibid., p. 111.
33. U.S. Congress, House Committee on Science and Technology, Transcript of Mark-up Session on National Science Foundation Appropriation H.R. 4723, 94th Congress, 1st session, 6 March 1975, pp. 49–50.
34. Ibid., pp. 51–52.
35. Ibid., p. 54.
36. Ibid., p. 55.
37. Ibid., p. 56.
38. Ibid., p. 58.

39. Letter from H. Guyford Stever to Olin E. Teague, 17 March 1975, p. 1.
40. Quoted from memory.
41. Memorandum from Irving Morrisett to the board and staff of the Social Science Education Consortium, Congressional Hearing on "Man: A Course of Study," 19 March 1975, p. 2.
42. James J. Kilpatrick, "Is Eskimo Sex Life a School Subject?," *Boston Globe,* 2 April 1975.
43. Peter B. Dow, "Open Letter to Friends of Man: A Course of Study," 4 April 1975, pp. 3–4.
44. Letter from John B. Conlan to H. Guyford Stever, 18 April 1975.
45. Letter from Jerome Bruner to Peter Dow, 12 April 1975.
46. Ibid.
47. *Congressional Record,* 9 April 1975, p. H2587.
48. Ibid., p. H2588.
49. Ibid., p. H2589.
50. Ibid.
51. Ibid.
52. Ibid., p. H2590.
53. Ibid.
54. Ibid.
55. Ibid., p. H2591.
56. Ibid., p. H2592.
57. Ibid., p. H2596.
58. Ibid., p. H2601.
59. Quoted in the *Chronicle of Higher Education,* 5 May 1975, p. 7.
60. "Statement of Dr. Onalee McGraw before the Senate Special Subcommittee on the National Science Foundation," 21 April 1975, p. 8.
61. Science Curriculum Review Team, *Pre-College Science Curriculum Activities of the National Science Foundation* (Washington, D.C.: National Science Foundation, May 1975), p. 17.
62. Ibid., p. 18.
63. Ibid., pp. 31–36.
64. As quoted in *Social Education* 39, no. 6 (October 1975): 396.
65. Gerard Piel, "Congress Shall Make No Law . . . ," address to the National Science Teachers' Association, 21 March 1976, pp. 10–11.
66. Science Curriculum Implementation Review Group, "Report to the Chairman, Committee on Science and Technology, U.S. House of Representatives," 1 October 1975, p. 9.
67. "Minority Report of Joanne McAuley, Including Dissenting and Additional Views to Accompany the Report of the Science Curriculum Implementation Review Group to the Chairman, Committee on Science and Technology, 20 October 1975," p. 20.
68. Comptroller General of the United States, *Report to the House Com-*

mittee on Science and Technology: Administration of the Science Education Project—Man: A Course of Study, 14 October 1975, p. 10.

69. GAO *Report,* p. 30.
70. Ibid., p. 28.
71. Ibid., p. 29.
72. This assessment was confirmed by Joseph Stavenhagen, the EDC president, by telephone on 9 March 1979.

6. Aftermath at the Foundation

1. Interview with Harvey Averch, 18 September 1986.
2. Interview with William Wells, 24 October 1986.
3. Langdon T. Crane, *The National Science Foundation and Pre-College Science Education: 1950–1975,* report prepared for the Subcommittee on Science, Research, and Technology of the Committee on Science and Technology, U.S. House of Representatives, by the Science Policy Research Division, Congressional Research Service, Library of Congress (Washington, D.C.: U.S. Government Printing Office, 1975), p. 211.
4. Ibid., p. 203.
5. Ibid., p. 205–206.
6. Averch interview.
7. "NSF's Science Education Programs Discussed before House Subcommittee," NSF PR76-16, 10 February 1976, pp. 1–2.
8. Interview with Richard Atkinson, 6 December 1986.
9. Ibid.
10. *Congressional Record,* 28 July 1976, p. 24256.
11. "National Science Foundation: Criticism for Conlan, GAO," *Science,* 27 February 1976.
12. Telephone interview with George Archibald, 31 December 1986.
13. Comptroller General of the United States, *Curriculum Case Studies Are of Questionable Quality but Helped Precollege Curriculum Activities,* 2 May 1977, p. 33.
14. Averch interview.
15. Ibid.
16. Roberta Ballstad Miller, "Politics and the Social Sciences—Yesterday, Today and Tomorrow," speech to the Consortium of Social Science Associations (COSSA), p. 14.
17. Atkinson interview.
18. Ibid.
19. Interview with James Rutherford, 30 December 1986.
20. Ibid.
21. Charles L. Heatherly, ed., *Mandate for Leadership: Policy Management in a Conservative Administration* (Washington, D.C.: Heritage Foundation, 1981), p. 163.

22. Ibid., p. 187.

23. Ibid., pp. 188–189.

24. Ibid., pp. 192–193.

25. Ibid., p. 197.

26. Letter from William T. Coleman, Jr., and Cecily C. Selby to Dr. Lewis M. Branscomb, Chairman, National Science Board, 12 September 1983.

27. *Educating Americans for the 21st Century: A Plan of Action for Improving Mathematics, Science and Technology Education for All American Elementary and Secondary Students so that Their Achievement Is the Best in the World by 1995* (Washington, D.C.: National Science Board Commission on Precollege Education in Mathematics, Science and Technology, 1983), p. 17.

28. Ibid., p. 21.

29. Marilyn Clayton Felt, *Improving Our Schools: Thirty-Three Studies That Inform Local Action* (Newton, Mass.: Education Development Center, Inc., 1985), p. 214.

30. Task Force on Education for Economic Growth, Education Commission of the States, *Action for Excellence: A Comprehensive Plan to Improve Our Nation's Schools,* June 1983, p. 3.

31. Felt, *Improving Our Schools,* p. 72.

32. Harvey A. Averch, *A Strategic Analysis of Science and Technology Policy* (Baltimore: Johns Hopkins University Press, 1985), p. 97.

33. Wells interview, p. 5.

34. National Science Foundation, "Program Announcement, Materials Development and Research, Directorate for Science and Engineering Education," 1 April 1985, p. 1.

35. Raymond Bye, Jr., "Mr. Fuqua's Recommendation Regarding Precollege Science and Engineering Education," National Science Foundation Internal Memorandum, 4 November 1986, Table 1, p. VI/K-6.

36. Ibid., p. VI/K-7.

37. Resolution introduced by George C. Pimentel, 17 November 1986.

38. Letter from Professor Gerald Holton to Dr. Bassam Z. Shakhashiri, 8 December 1986, p. 1.

39. Telephone interview with Bassam Shakhashiri, 5 November 1990.

40. *Education Week,* 4 February 1987, p. 5.

41. "News & Comment," *Science,* 8 June 1990, p. 1183.

42. *Science & Government Report,* 20, no. 11 (15 June 1990): 2.

7. Reform Reconsidered

1. In a recent science test taken by high school seniors from fourteen countries, the National Science Foundation reported that American students ranked fourteenth (*New York Times,* 7 January 1990, section 4A, p. 18).

2. John Goodlad et al., *Looking behind the Classroom Door* (Worthington,

Ohio: Charles A. Jones, 1974), p. 102. As Goodlad remarks, "The ambitious strategy of bringing scholars and teachers together in the development of new instructional materials and subsequent follow-up in the classroom had some chance of success. But even this promising approach faced formidable obstacles in the structure of schooling."

3. Peter Drucker, *The New Realities* (New York: Harper and Row, 1989), p. 249.

4. A conversation with Elting Morison, reprinted in *Curriculum Improvement and Innovation: A Partnership of Students, School Teachers, and Research Scholars,* ed. W. T. Martin and Dan C. Pinck (Cambridge, Mass.: Robert Bentley, 1966), p. 114.

5. Ibid., p. 116.

6. Craig Lambert, "The Electronic Tutor," *Harvard Alumni Bulletin* 93, no. 2 (November–December 1990): 42–51.

7. Lynda Carl Falkenstein, "Man: A Course of Study—A Case Study of Diffusion in Oregon" (Ph.D. diss., Stanford University, 1977), p. 222.

8. *Education Week,* 17 May 1989.

9. *Education Week,* 1 August 1990.

10. *Education Week,* 7 March 1990.

11. Phyllis Schlafly in *Child Abuse in the Classroom,* quoted in the *Nation,* 8 June 1985; *Buffalo News,* 25 October 1986, pp. A 2, 4.

12. *Education Week,* 11 March 1987, p. 19.

13. *New York Times Magazine,* 19 July 1987, p. 34.

14. Ibid.

15. Interview with James W. Symington, 31 December 1986.

Index